BIBLICAL CHARACTERS WE ONLY THOUGHT WE KNEW:

A PHARAOH, A GODDESS, A NAKED YOUNG MAN, EVEN MOSES & JESUS

Phillip Truckenbrod

A Holly Grove Book

Cover Photo: Coronation of the Virgin, façade of Orvieto Cathedral, Italy

"The first century of our era, particularly as it relates to the story of Jesus
and the origins of early Christianity in the midst of the complex social and
religious context of the Mediterranean world, is one of the least
documented eras of history, relying essentially only on the biblical accounts
for any historical evidence. This book is a fascinating venture into the
imaginative speculation that has sought to fill in these gaps in the biblical
narrative with proposals about the origin and development of early
Christianity—characters and events, including the question of the historical
Jesus. Purporting to be not about faith, but "reportage," still it is more, as
the concluding chapter with its compelling 'riff on contemporary religion"
and the prospects for the future of religion makes eminently clear.
Although the author admits that many of the proposals in this book are not
'new,' he has presented the arguments in a compelling way, including at
times with a touch of irony or humor." –Dr. James L. Boyce, Emeritus
Professor of New Testament and Greek, Luther Seminary, St. Paul MN;
graduate degrees from Luther Theological Seminary and the University of
North Carolina

Also by this author

"Winterset in Time: Growing up Gay in Small Town Iowa"

and

**"Organists and Me:
Half a Century as an Agent for Musicians"**

Both available from Amazon.com

Contents

Preface: The Prelude is even longer than the Postlude

To discover something previously unknown about a familiar figure can be much more than a surprise. It may be welcome and liberating. Or it may be disillusioning and sobering. Either way, though, it alters one's worldview, however slightly. The next day we are working from a slightly different perspective.

Most of us have long since taken for granted the characters from the Bible we met as children. We think we know them so well that they have probably lost our interest to a great extent. However, we almost certainly know a lot less about them than we assume we do. Many of them have been hiding secrets from us.

Christianity has been around for a long time, and most ordinary adults who would consider reading a book on the subject at this point probably assume they already know as much about it as could possibly be interesting. What surprises could be left?

Well, Christian origins, for example. Everyone knows Christianity was started around two thousand years ago by a man from Nazareth named Jesus.

However, there are at least two potential surprises lurking in that sentence right off the bat. Jesus is probably the wrong candidate to see as founder of the religion, and the first strains of what we know as Christianity reach many more millennia back into human history than just two. On top of that, scholars are not sure what Nazareth has to do with anything in this context, although it might have something non-geographical to contribute—that 'Jesus of Nazareth' may be a corruption of Jesus the Nazarite, and just one of many little details in the Good Book which may still have the potential to stir fresh interest.

Bible stories may be a lot more interesting, and complicated, than we remember from Sunday School. And the characters who populate the Bible still have a few surprises left in them. Even the biggest headliners: Jesus of the New Testament, and Moses of the Old Testament. The Bible is populated with characters who are difficult to interpret and about whom we're simply not sure whether we're being told historical truths, memories which may have gone off track over long periods of time, or even just fantasies which were retold so often they acquired a community respectability.

i

Preface

Recent scholarship has raised questions about familiar names. Was Moses really Jewish (a Hebrew)? Did the Exodus really happen like it is depicted in the movies? Was Jesus actually a mushroom? For that matter, was Jesus even a Christian? Or an actual historical figure? Is there an Egyptian pharaoh prominently featured in the Bible but hidden so that almost no one knows he's there? Was Lazarus Jesus' long-time boyfriend? Was God originally female? Was the Virgin Mary the first 'Queen of Heaven'? Did Jesus die in France after retiring there?

Well, okay, the mushroom idea was universally dismissed despite not being quite as off-the-wall as it sounds at first blush, and that scholar has been discredited despite earlier solid contributions. But the 'who was Moses?' question has not been completely answered, and may never be. And lots of other familiar Biblical figures are being seen in a new light.

The Jesus story is far more complex and extensive than most people today would assume. It involves not only thirty or so years of a man's life at the beginning of the age of Pisces. It also involves two millennia of interpretation and swings of perspective after his lifetime, as most of us appreciate even if our grasp on all the details is a little vague.

But there's a lot more than that involved. There are even more millennia before his birth which are a necessary part of the story, and that may be more of a surprise. The prelude, as it turns out, is even longer than the two thousand year postlude. There are characters in the Bible we may be only beginning to see with some clarity despite the familiarity of their names.

Most of this book is not itself a work of original scholarship. It could be more accurately described as a work of synthesis and reportage. I have tried to outline some of the more recent ideas and questions raised by actual scholars; ideas and questions which might be interesting to a wide range of people in the general Judeo-Christian tradition.

There are a number of ways to look at, or study, a phenomenon like Christianity. One can approach it as a theological system, full of intricate interlocking ideas and possible inconsistent loose ends. It can be seen as a great competition between various ideas and worldviews—the gradual triumph of something called "orthodoxy" over competing ideas that came to be labeled "heresy." One can study it as a long historical development, gradually organizing itself by myriad ways and in myriad places and affecting the politics and lives of many people along the way, whether those people considered themselves to be Christians or not. It can be understood and studied as a grand social movement with far-flung implications for human social development and interaction. It can be seen as a mirror to the human psyche, or an exhibition of the great unconscious mind, as can any religion. And of course it can be seen on the level of faith—of personal piety and belief. None of these are the intended approach of this book, although all of them have something to say which will be needed occasionally for perspective or illustration.

Christianity can also be looked at simply as a religion; one among many which lay hold to the imaginations of large groups of humans. It's on that level which this book will approach Christianity. The mechanism will be taking a revised look at several characters from the Bible who may be more complicated than the average contemporary Christian remembers or suspects.

Some good Christian souls may find it uncomfortable to look at the purely religious aspects of Christianity. They may rankle at the idea that Christianity shares themes, ideas, symbols, practices, and concepts with groups, both historical and contemporary, which they regard as "pagan" or un-Christian. This book was not written with the intention to either reassure or off-put such people, although they are invited along for the ride if their curiosity is stronger than their reflexive piety.

The purpose here is definitely not devotional. But I hope it is not iconoclastic either. We will be looking at Christianity as religion, not as faith. I'm not trying to uphold or demean issues of faith, but just to tell a story of Biblical characters as they appear today in the thinking of some scholars in the field—the story of Biblical characters you probably don't know as well as you thought you did. In case you get caught up in some of these ideas or questions and want to pursue them beyond this little book, there are eighteen-plus dozen important books listed in the back which will flesh out the themes touched on in these pages. ⌘

1.

An Hallucination which Changed the World?

In the course of mankind's general religious experience the number of people who felt that God, or a god, spoke directly to them and gave them specific instructions or information must be legion.

Sometimes these people have had followers who believed their stories—sometimes a whole new religion even grew out of the episode. Sometimes the person having the vision was just written off as an eccentric, or a madman, or a charlatan. In any case, we need to consider Christianity from this angle too, because a key figure in its early history claimed to have had one (or some) of these personal visits from God, and he was far from quiet about it. In fact, he ultimately shouted down anyone who disagreed with him—including both the brother of Jesus and the first Pope.

There's a prior question at this point which can aid our understanding: Were 'Christians' always Christian? For that matter, was Jesus himself a Christian? Quick answer: No. They used to be Jews. The first people labeled 'Christians' were Jews, and it's almost certain that they never thought of themselves as anything other than Jews, even though we now may put a "Saint" in front of their names and label our church buildings in honor of them.

And Jesus was not the first Christian (he was never one at all), or even the founder of Christianity. Almost every reputable scholar today gives those honors to St. Paul, a.k.a. Saul of Tarsus.

Jesus didn't even get a religion named after him. Christ is a Greek word (Christos) meaning "anointed one" which Paul slathered throughout his writings. (The 'Christ' word was also used in place of 'Messiah' when the Hebrew scriptures were translated into Greek, so it can get a tad confusing. Anyway, "Christ" is not Jesus' surname, but when Jesus and Christ are placed next to each other, Christ is being used as a title or descriptive. Technically it would be more accurate to say or write 'Jesus *the* Christ,' but the shortened version seems to be firmly ensconced by this point.)

1

Biblical Characters

Jesus was the leader of a small Jewish sect who was then executed for basically political reasons by the Roman-appointed authorities who occupied his country. He left behind a small group of followers headed by his brother, James, who was also later executed. This group, often called the "Jesus movement" operated within Judaism, and became what in a way seeded Christianity. Sometimes its adherents are referred to as the "first Christians" or the "early Christians."

Jesus' brother, James, is often termed "the Just" because of his resolute and determined adherence to the Mosaic law of Judaism. He was definitely no rebel straining to propound a new religion. If anything, he represented the most zealous practice of the inherited Mosaic/Jewish religion. And scholars tend to ferret out the real Jesus by looking at his brother, James the Just. As devoted a Jew as was James, they believe was Jesus also. We can safely assume that the idea of starting a new religion never crossed Jesus' mind, and that he would have been aghast at the suggestion.

We are told in Acts 12:26 that the first use of the word Christian to describe members of the Jesus movement group came in Antioch while at least some of the original apostles were still alive and preaching. Some contemporary writers use the term 'Christians' to describe certain people before the Antioch incident, which can get confusing, so we'll limit the term to people after the lifetime of Jesus.

In any case the new religion (if it really deserves that designation before Paul) was then taken over lock, stock, and barrel by Paul. At first it looked and behaved like an offshoot of Judaism, being still a small Jewish sect. But only a few years down the road it was essentially disciples of this Paul who wrote what we now call the New Testament, along with Paul himself. The management had shifted from James the Just in Jerusalem to an interloper named Paul, and with it the story and concept of who Jesus was, what he stood for, and whether he was human or a god, or some combination of the two. Changed forever too was the character of the Jesus movement, now drifting away from Judaism toward a stew of ancient religious concepts propounded by the cosmopolitan, fully Hellenized, and Roman citizen Paul.

A great many historians and scholars of religion now say flatly that Paul invented Christianity. And it was essentially Paul who gave Jesus his promotion up from a human who had some facility with religious magic with the assistance of God, to being himself God. (That is not to say that Paul was necessarily the first person to associate Jesus with a divine status, but that he was the pioneer in turning that concept into a religious system.)

Jesus' group of followers saw him as special, indeed, but only as a man. They knew him as a magician, a healer, a wisdom teacher, a companion, a brother. Some of them argued about whether he could be the expected Messiah (with its mix of political and religious images). But they didn't think

2

he was God—that would have been blasphemy. Despite some potentially confusing statements reported in the New Testament, Jesus probably didn't think he was God, or a god, either. Instead he coached his followers in how to pray to God.

It was Paul who decided Jesus was God (although it seems Jesus' disciples as well may also have begun to flirt with the idea shortly after his death). It was Paul, a Hellenized Jew, who brokered the divorce of early Christianity (the 'Jesus Movement') from Judaism, and then negotiated its marriage back into the world of ancient general religious myth and formula. The Jews had gradually whittled their gods down to just one, at least for the most part. Their offspring religion, Christianity, after Paul was finished with it, invented a new religious version of arithmetic containing three gods while still claiming to be monotheistic.

Now they could sneak in a couple more gods, yielding a 'Trinity' of gods: three persons but officially really just one god. Then these Christians kept adding minor ones, essentially mini-gods—minting a continuous flow of "saints" who had some of the powers of the gods (healing, the capacity to cause small miracles, the ability to receive and answer prayers, etc.) and who had the ear of the major gods.

The Christians even prayed to these mini-gods although officially they were supposed to restrict themselves to asking the mini-gods to plead for favors from the three main Gods. Nevertheless, these Christians continued to claim to be monotheists, but that was just a faint echo of the new religion's Jewish parentage. In actuality they had left monotheism in the dust and rejoined the ancient world of religion with its vision of multiple gods—although most of their religious descendants will deny it to this day. A little case of religious schizophrenia has come down to us through the centuries, and is deeply embedded in what we know as Christianity today.

Anyway it's certain that Paul introduced a Greek perspective into the Jesus movement which essentially replaced any real Jewish orientation (despite the retention of the "Old Testament" as part of the Christian scriptures), and that he presided over the transition of the membership of this new religion from Jewish to Gentile.

Eventually this split took on very dark overtones and Christians started to see Jews, who were essentially their religious parents, as enemies (Hitler's Nazis being only the most extreme example).

● CHRISTIANITY'S ODD COUPLE

None of this happened instantly. Paul engaged himself in a long and increasingly bitter battle with his ideological opponents (the left-over disciples of Jesus back in Jerusalem) for the rest of his adult life. His letters in the New Testament read like diatribes against those with whom he disagreed, and he was not at all shy about expressing his frustration that his

3

own ideas were encountering opposition. He claimed, after all, to be an apostle on an equal footing with those apostles in Jerusalem who had been actual students of Jesus, and it's not a stretch to get the impression he really thought he knew more than they did about this Jesus.

The church in Jerusalem (what was left of Jesus' followers after the Romans offed him) had to start sending out mop-up crews to try to correct errors they felt Paul had planted in various cities where he had started new congregations among diaspora Jews. Paul's big enemies list grew to be a who's who of the Jerusalem "church." Not only did it include James the Just, Jesus' brother, but even the redoubtable St. Peter himself was seen by Paul as an enemy.

Paul evidently believed that he was not only an apostle on equal footing with Peter and the rest of the twelve, but that he was actually a truer and more important version of apostleship despite his never having met Jesus in the flesh. He even accused the Jerusalem group of "disguising themselves as apostles of Christ" (2 Corinthians 11:13). In other words, Peter and company were just faking it, whereas Paul was the real deal. In fact, Paul went so far as to call down damnation on Peter and the others for attempting to correct his message: "If any one is preaching to you a gospel contrary to that which you received [from me], let him be accursed" (Galatians 1:8-9). Even an angel sent directly from Heaven was not to be accepted as a trustworthy authority if his message differed at all from Paul's teachings.

And Peter was evidently writing equally flattering things about Paul (or at least whomever may have written the letter from Peter which is in the so-called Pseudo-Clementines, perhaps an educated disciple of Peter able to write on his behalf). The letter refers to "the man who is my enemy," who elsewhere is identified as Paul without any beating around the bush.

If you're a Bible reader you may immediately contrast this with Peter's second letter that actually made it into the New Testament, which refers to Paul as "our beloved brother." However, this epistle also contains a hefty dose of 'between-the-lines' implications. It refers to "false prophets" and "false teachers among you." And the apparent pat on the back for Paul is immediately qualified when he says that Paul wrote to you "according to the wisdom given him," (in other words he wasn't fully in the Apostolic know and was dependent on those questionable 'visions') and that some of what he wrote is "hard to understand." He warns his readers in the very next sentence not "to be carried away with the error of lawless men." Maybe the tip of the hat to Paul was merely a public relations device to gain the good will of the recipients of the letter, and thus open them to considering Peter's rebuttal.

4

Somehow both Peter and Paul ended up in Rome, the Imperial capital, as the story goes (Peter on a preaching mission and Paul as a prisoner), and both were martyred there (probably—there may be something of a question about Paul in this regard some think). But of the two, it was Peter who got the highest accolades—it was decided later that he had been the first Christian Bishop of Rome, and therefore the first Pope. It's Peter's name that now graces the magnificent Vatican basilica of Michelangelo. Paul, however, had completely shaped the new religion to his own liking.

It's difficult to say who the biggest winner or loser was of these two. Paul essentially created a new religion; Peter was credited with being the most important living man in administering that religion. So now they're treated as the dynamic duo of Christianity: Peter and Paul, bitter enemies now stirred together in the porridge that we know today as Christianity.

Ironically, Christianity continues to remember and honor them as a couple on June 29, the feast day of Sts. Peter and Paul. And they are, together yet again, joint patrons of the city of Rome. No one (except scholars and historians) seems to notice or care that they were at loggerheads with each other during their late adult years, or that they represented significantly different, actually probably radically different, views of Jesus and emerging Christianity. In the popular view they are two stalwarts upholding the same religious ethos, equally responsible for the spread of the Christian message into the Roman Empire, and thence into the world at large. In the popular view they must have been allies.

● A DO IT YOURSELF APOSTLE?

Paul appointed himself an "apostle" on an equal footing with Jesus' original twelve. (And there were only supposed to be twelve—the zodiac, from which the number was drawn, did not allow for thirteen.) Paul had never met Jesus, so we can understand why this had to be a do-it-yourself project for him. Well, actually Paul didn't look at it that way. He thought Jesus, post crucifixion, had come seeking him out and had personally given him religious authority—had ordained him, if you will.

Paul by his own description had been an implacable enemy of this nascent Christianity, this Jewish Jesus cult. He was even a ring leader in the stoning death of St. Stephen, considered to be the first Christian martyr.

One day Saul (Paul) was traveling to Damascus when, by St. Luke's account, Jesus appeared to him in a blinding revelation and asked why he (Saul) was persecuting him (Jesus). Saul's traveling companions reportedly heard the voice (although perhaps did not understand what it said—Luke does not tell us) but could not see this intervention.

Should we call this a 'vision'? Some have suggested it could have been an epileptic seizure. Others have compared it to what today we call a 'near death experience.' Sunstroke has been floated as an explanation.

5

Hallucination; hysterical or psychotic reaction? A guilty conscience could easily have been involved.

Anyway, for Paul this 'vision' was the real thing. Jesus, whose followers Paul had been persecuting, took the personal time and trouble to reach out to Paul, he was convinced. And he was convinced that this gave him authority inside any Jesus-oriented group. It left him temporally blind and in need of an extended recovery, but we don't have many more details. Of course, Luke was writing about a legend he had only heard about, and he was writing perhaps some eighty years after it took place. Details are a little difficult under those circumstances.

Saul/Paul felt that great divine secrets and understanding had been imparted to him in this so-called conversion vision. He recounted to his congregation in Corinth that he "heard things that cannot be told, which man may not utter." One is reminded of the reactions of many who had undergone initiation into the mysteries in ancient Egypt, who later spoke of "things too holy for utterance" or "things too holy for them to be expressed." (We will consider these initiations in Chapter 2.)

Paul experienced subsequent such divine interventions (again, at least according to Luke the evangelist) and believed he had been given access to an understanding which surpassed that of any of the close associates of Jesus during Jesus' lifetime, i.e. the twelve 'original' apostles. They had only known Jesus when he was a mere man. Paul had heard directly from the Jesus who had risen up from death and was now sitting 'at the right hand of God;' the Jesus who was himself now a reigning god. So Paul was not only sure that he was an apostle, he was sure that he was the most favored, the most in touch with Jesus of all the apostles—he had no doubt of that.

Thus Saul became Paul. He was converted, but now there's the question of converted from what, to what. Some scholars of religion call it not a conversion *to* the Jesus movement alive in Jerusalem at the time, but rather a shift *from* Judaism under the strict Mosaic law, over to Hellenic Christology. They also point out that many of the idioms and phraseology of the Mystery cult ceremonials and literature can be found in Paul's New Testament epistles. They note that when Paul speaks of the "Lord Jesus Christ" as he does constantly in his letters, he obviously refers to the Christos principle of Greek spirituality.

Since the earliest and most basic parts of the New Testament were written either by Paul or by followers (disciples) of Paul, our understanding of Christianity is unavoidably Pauline. The sermons I heard growing up were all lectures on or about Paul—what he said or wrote, what he meant by writing it—sometimes also what the preacher just thought he meant, or wished he had written, but in any case it was "all Paul all the time." If you wanted to get to Jesus, you did it through Paul. And there was never a question in the minds of those clergy that Paul spoke directly *for* Jesus. For most Christians that's probably still true. And for anyone who calls himself Christian even today, the route to Jesus has been through Paul; there was no alternative. Paul and followers of Paul wrote the story; they are, most likely, the only reason we would ever have even heard about Jesus in the first place this far down the road.

Some information on the early Jesus movement can be gleaned from the New Testament directly as well, but it's a more difficult job because it is usually filtered through Paul's new take on Christianity. As a scholarly writer phrases it, Paul's 'heresy' became the basis for what became Christian orthodoxy, and the 'legitimate' church, i.e. Jerusalem's Jesus movement, was outlawed as heretical. Early on in the life of Christianity, the first known attempt at recording the history of the movement, the book of Acts, morphed into a sort of reverential biography of Paul. Paul and his followers were already in control of the story at this early stage.

The original Jerusalem apostles were not members of the St. Paul Fan Club, however. For them, having been close to Jesus during his lifetime was an essential qualification for authority in the new cult. When the betrayer Judas was replaced in the group of twelve with a new apostle named Matthias (the number needed to remain twelve, remember, no more, no less), a requirement was that the successful candidate had to have been with the group from the beginning—during the Jesus years. Clearly Paul would not have qualified, having not been with Jesus for even ten minutes (unless one counts his probable hallucinations, although we have no idea how long they may have lasted). And Peter, leader of the twelve, even suggested that Paul's visions could have been the work of a demonic spirit. No, the only safe route was to pay attention to those who had known and followed Jesus in the flesh (those who had most likely been initiated into the mysteries directly by him, as we will see). Nonetheless, Paul continued to claim that he had "seen Jesus our Lord."

What was evolving into "Christianity" was a series of departures from what Jesus taught—some say that Jesus was altogether lost to history in the process. From the perspective of the 'Secret Mark' discussion in the next chapter, Paul not only did not know Jesus personally, but was never given the wisdom of Jesus through Jesus' version of initiation into the mysteries, whereas the Jerusalem disciples presumably had received that initiation and certainly that teaching.

So Paul never met Jesus, at least not in the flesh, but of course the reverse is also true. We don't know whether Paul's Hellenistic concepts and terminology would have rung any bells at all with Jesus of Nazareth. Could Jesus even have imagined what it would mean to be considered the 'cosmic Christ'? Scholarly opinions about Jesus' education vary widely. The only

7

educational sources we can be sure of are a Jewish heritage (religious teaching) and time in Egypt (where he probably underwent initiation into the mysteries). He might have fancied himself to be the Messiah (as did a number of other men in and around his era). But it's very doubtful he would have translated either the word or the concept into Greek (his own language was Aramaic), so he would most likely not recognize himself as the "Christ." And he couldn't have called himself a Christian because such a category didn't exist during his lifetime.

Judging from what we consider Christianity today, it is not far-fetched or disrespectful to say that the great St. Peter himself, the first Pope, was never a 'Christian' either. Christianity was what Paul eventually made it to be. Peter was a Jew, like Jesus himself. And he opposed what Paul was teaching vociferously.

● DRINKING GOD'S BLOOD: DID PAUL INVENT THE EUCHARIST TOO?

Many of the characteristics of Christianity which are so familiar to us originated with Paul, at least as opposed to originating with the Jerusalem 'Jesus Movement' group. For example, the quintessentially Christian notion of sin and guilt—both necessary because otherwise we would not have need of the salvation and atonement offered by Paul's cosmic Christ. The Christian definition of exactly what man must be saved *from* has always been rather vague. Paul made the death (sacrifice) of Jesus *theologically* necessary, regardless of its historical cause (which was apparently mostly political). Remember that Paul's genuine letters are the oldest material in the New Testament, so the gospel accounts also rest on, or at least were strongly influenced by, his thinking.

This, in turn, ties in with (or perhaps caused) Paul's orientation to death as the means of atonement. There were parts (sects, as it were) of the Jesus movement and its offshoots which were more oriented to life and were more upbeat, but in due course they succumbed to Paul's emphasis on Jesus' death as the key to the whole Christian mystery. And thus another of the great gifts Paul has bequeathed to us: Guilt. Christians usually carry a nagging sense of guilt even though they may not be quite sure just what it is that they're guilty of.

As a matter of even greater consequence, it is possible that one of Paul's "inventions" has completely dominated and defined Christian worship from perhaps near the beginning of the religion. The Eucharist (Mass, Holy Communion, the Lord's Supper) is the central act of Christian worship. It rests on the accounts of Jesus' last supper with his closest disciples "on the night in which he was betrayed."

An Hallucination which Changed the World?

These accounts come to us only in Paul's New Testament writings (notably the first letter to the Corinthians) and the synoptic gospels (Matthew, Mark, and Luke), which are widely thought to have been written by Paul's disciples or to depend on sources which ultimately came from Paul or his disciples. We can't find the same story in other places where it would seem to belong, such as the gospel according to John. The Eucharist certainly is discussed in John, often in cleverly encoded ways, but the story of its inception at "the Last Supper" is missing. Some have suggested it was omitted in John in order to protect the sacred formula.

But why should the 'formula' matter this much unless John felt that its mere recitation was somehow consequential even on the lips of an unbeliever, i.e. that it was magical or quasi-magical and had inherent power even in just the repetition of its formulaic words? Many scholars believe the formula actually originated with Paul, in which case Paul essentially dictated the form and content of Christian worship for all time after the original Jewish Jesus movement, the first generation who can be called 'Christians.' But this group did not practice such a magical sacred meal (although as Jews they *would* have conducted Seder rituals).

This is not necessarily to say that there are no Eucharistic references in John's gospel, as I've said, but just that the last supper story of the synoptic gospels, containing the 'words of institution' formula, is missing. John does offer a long section (6:48-59) in which Jesus dwells on the eating of his flesh and the drinking of his blood. The influence and overtones of the magical traditions of Egypt are unmistakable here. It is noteworthy too that participation in this magical rite is presented as mandatory if one hopes for 'eternal life.' So here Paul and his disciple gospel writers tap into the great ancient mythology of the god feeding his flock with his own body and blood—not at all a *new* idea in religion, but certainly *not* an idea which came out of Judaism.

John is inventive in how he tells the Eucharistic story and yet keeps it heavily veiled and secretive at the same time. One of his Eucharistic references, for example, is the story of the feeding of the multitude with just five loaves and two small fish. But the synoptic gospels can be pretty non-direct as well. One of the key Eucharistic references in Luke, for example, is the Emmaus story where the resurrected Jesus is revealed at the breaking of bread. John's gospel also has an interesting section (6:53-56) which is not only a direct and unmistakable Eucharistic reference, but also an unabashed throwback to the general religion of pagan mythology.

If the Last Supper story actually did originate with Paul, who was not an eye witness to it in any case, it would be nearly impossible to overstate the consequences for the shaping of the Christian religion. Mass, Eucharist, Holy Communion, whatever it's called, is the backbone ritual of

9

Christianity. For most Christian groups it is conducted ("celebrated") whenever members come together. Roman Catholic priests are supposed to "say" Mass daily, even if they are alone (with just one server) which plays a little havoc with the sacred communal meal concept, but does underline the centrality of the rite.

Paul himself gives us a clue in first Corinthians that he was the first to tell the story of the Last Supper and these 'words of institution' ("my body; my blood") when he introduces that story by saying "I received [it] from the Lord." Not 'I received it from Peter' or 'from the Jerusalem apostles' who would have actually been present at the event if it occurred. Remember that Paul was not present for this supper, if it happened, so he was dependent on some outside source—or, possibly just his vivid imagination inspired by his probably reasonably extensive knowledge of the general religious history of mankind.

The Eucharist is an "unmistakably magical rite" states Morton Smith. He calls it a typical piece of the intercultural magic of the time, and says its origins are Egyptian.

From Smith's perspective the 'words of institution' theoretically *could have* come directly from Jesus because they were used so broadly in magic, and the Biblical Jesus appears to be so steeped in these magical traditions. If so, however, it is odd that the Jerusalem Jesus movement did not practice any sort of Eucharist along these lines. But the commonality of the magical formula would have made it very possible that the earliest New Testament writers (Paul and his disciples) could have added it to the Jesus story from their own knowledge of the wider religious world—another instance of painting Jesus with the colors of other known 'gods' in order to bolster his being seen as a god himself.

When Paul says he received his Last Supper story "from the Lord," is he referring to one of the times he claims Jesus appeared to him in a vision and gave him instruction not given to others? If so, there was a period of time when he was the only living human to know that story of the 'last supper.'

Paul then would have passed the story on to his own disciples and congregations, and the tradition would have been born—and Christian worship would have been fundamentally altered from that of the Jewish Jesus movement, as indeed it came so dramatically to be.

The raw religious idea, however, certainly preceded both Jesus and Paul. Religious people for ages had been eating the body and drinking the blood of their gods. In Christian parlance then, the whole concept is thus "pagan."

The basis of this concept and the resulting ritual was agricultural; it was intended to insure a good crop and a plentiful harvest. The means involved the sacrifice (or later the ritual sacrifice) of the king or his substitute and the ritual feeding of the people with his body and blood. In due course, historians speculate, the original agricultural basis of these rites was forgotten even though the rituals themselves persisted. This could then lead to a re-invention of the underpinning stories, opening the way for a new interpretation based on theology (sin, atonement, etc.) rather than the insurance of a good harvest.

And even the Bible hints that this central Christian rite of worship may have roots which go back many generations before either Jesus or Paul when it tells us about Melchizedek, King of Salem, who presented Abraham with bread and wine in welcome. Many, including some serious scholars, think this may be the first Biblical mention of a ritual act which became enveloped into the later Communion ceremony. However it should be noted that not all scholars accept such a connection between Melchizedek's bread and wine and those of the Eucharist.

Some consider the bread and wine of Melchizedek to be merely the elements of common hospitality at the time. Part of the trouble with Melchizedek's place in this discussion (aside from our not really knowing who he was—another Biblical mystery man) is that the phrase 'bread and wine' has little place in our language anymore beyond the Christian Eucharist, so its mention in the Bible rings that bell first for us. When our intent today is to discuss hospitality, we would most likely use a phrase such as 'wine and cheese' which would carry no religious implications of any sort. So the Biblical Melchizedek question, in a sense, revolves around whether he was greeting Abraham with 'bread and wine' as a forerunner of the Christian sacrament, or with 'wine and cheese' in the sense of simple hospitality.

It is not at all difficult to find serious scholars who have concluded that Paul himself was the inventor and creator of the Eucharist. And once one takes that step, they will point out, the next realization is that if one believes Paul was the creator of "the central sacrament and mystery of Christianity" one has also concluded that Paul, rather than Jesus, was the founder of Christianity. Further, scholars largely conclude that Paul came up with these words of institution supposedly spoken by Jesus by "direct revelation", rather than by any information received from the Jerusalem Apostles. This would explain why the Eucharist was not observed by the Jerusalem Church during New Testament times, but only by those congregations Paul had founded or that had come under the influence of Paul.

Many scholars agree that it is unlikely that Jesus instituted the Christian Eucharist, and that the Eucharist strongly evokes the mystery cults of the Mediterranean and has little to nothing in common with Judaism. Paul emphasized the death of Jesus (as the Christ), and built the Eucharist around that death (sacrifice). So now Jesus, like Mithras, God of the

Morning, can be drunk from an uplifted cup of blood, one of them writes. Paul had succeeded in grafting onto his new Christianity a rite reeking of paganism and suggesting cannibalism.

It is claimed that Paul's expression 'the Lord's Supper' was so reminiscent of mystery religion that the early Church fathers were embarrassed by it, and for that reason they substituted for it the name 'Eucharist'. But whatever title was applied the rite continued to have magical associations, because it was (and by many still is) believed that a miracle occurred every time it was celebrated—the bread and wine miraculously became the actual flesh and blood of Jesus (eventually giving rise to the adoration of a Eucharistic host; a piece of bread in a monstrance). And then the magic continued in Paul's emphasis on the consequences of unworthy reception of the sacrament.

There are some scholars who feel that there may have been Jewish shared sacred meals which somehow evolved into Paul's "Lord's Supper." Evidently the Essenes did routinely share a meal of bread and wine. However this area of speculation is more characterized by what we don't, and can't, know than by known history. Meanwhile the Eucharistic associations with magic, theophagy (the ritual eating of a god), and the religious mysteries stretching down from ancient Egypt are too strong to ignore.

The real question here is can we safely trust Paul's visions. Scholars have pointed out that such visions were much trusted and routinely experienced in Jesus' and Paul's time, but that today we are actually prejudiced against accepting them as sources of truth.

Our times are different, and we understand 'visions' much differently, and we have different perspectives on what is "real." In this matter, and probably also in the general interpretation of Christianity, one has to decide whether the visions of Paul can stand as source material (as the 'Word of God'). Or, if they should be viewed with the same hesitation with which we would interpret the hallucinations of a man today (albeit an educated and literate man such as Paul) who was caught up in ecstasy. It can be noted that possible hallucinations such as Paul's on the road to Damascus have played sometimes pivotal roles in the development of Christianity through the ages. Legend has Luther throwing a pot of ink at the devil while translating scripture at Wartburg Castle, and evidently the stain on the wall is still visible. And of course there are countless ecstatic visions contributed to our Christian mythology by religious [monks and nuns] figures.

For Paul it was a point of pride that he got his 'truth' not from the Jerusalem apostles, but from the 'Lord' himself individually and directly through visions which imparted all he needed to know. While we don't personally know exactly what transpired at Paul's 'conversion,' we are 21st century people and therefore we must look for explanations in areas which make sense to 21st century humans. It needs to make sense in the world we live in, just as has been true for people of all ages. To at least some extent, that almost automatically undermines the value of Paul's visions for us today. When we think of someone having a 'vision' today, we probably assume the person is 'high' on some chemical (of course, the role of chemical inducements to religious visions has a history stretching back long before Paul's time, so we can't automatically assume they had no role to play in his visions either).

These Eucharistic words (approximately "eat, this is my body; drink, this is my blood") surely spotlight the intrusion of magic (eating the flesh of the gods) into the heart of Christianity at its very beginning. Is it any wonder then that the Christian Eucharist has so long been seen from outside the church as a magical rite of cannibalism or quasi-cannibalism, giving rise to the culture-wide magical incantation "Hocus Pocus" (corrupted from the priest's Latin words of consecration "Hoc est enim Corpus Meum")?

The Eucharist is simply a magical rite not rooted in Judaism as a parent of Christianity, but rooted in ancient Egypt and in the general religious mythology of mankind, which are also parents of Christianity along with Judaism.

The source of Paul's material is Paul's visions (plus perhaps to some extent his Hellenized education). Regardless of what pre-Pauline Eucharistic formulae may or may not have been in use, Paul based his story on whatever 'the Lord' had communicated to him privately during at least one of his visions. That indeed makes Paul essentially the origin of the formula of the Eucharist, as well as the source of the insertion into Christianity of the concept of theophagy, or eating God. With Paul's Eucharist, Christianity shifted ground from Judaism and the original gospel, into the general religious history of the human race, and into the religious mythology of the ancients.

The notion of drinking blood and eating flesh, contained in the "words of institution" of the Eucharist, supposedly originating with Jesus, would have been abhorrent to Jews (and thus to the Jerusalem 'Christians' under James the Just, Jesus' brother, not to mention Jesus himself). Indeed, Jews were strictly forbidden to drink or eat even the blood of their sacrificial animals, although they could eat the meat. It is hardly surprising that we find no record of any ceremony celebrated by James' 'church' in Jerusalem which utilized the formula in which Jesus supposedly said "This is my body; This is my blood." Scholars say that such an idea simply could not have come from Jesus, because he was a Jew, and probably a rabbi to boot.

What evidence scholars can find of communal meal rituals among the earliest Christians contain no reference to the death of Jesus, whereas the

13

post-Pauline Eucharist rests on his death. Paul therefore must have been the one to add that element. Likewise they point out that neither the Didache (document from the primitive church setting out ecclesiastical order) nor the Dead Sea Scrolls description of the sacred Messianic meal mention wine representing blood, more evidence that the Eucharist did not originate with Jesus. They also remind us that human sacrifice is "anathema" to Judaism.

The general verdict from scholars, then, is that it was Paul who grafted pagan concepts of atonement into Christianity by giving us a ritual in which the blood of a god needed to be ingested to achieve salvation. He didn't leave us with much explicit insight into what this salvation consisted of, but he did irrevocably tie Christianity into the ages old practice, and concept, of humans connecting with their gods by eating them.

● A MAGICAL CURSE?

When Paul gives his story of the origin of the Eucharist in his first letter to the Corinthians, he doesn't stop at what would seem to be a logical place, but goes on in a somewhat circular way to talk about some negative possible consequences of participating in this rite. It can lead to illness and even death, he indicates, for "anyone who eats and drinks without discerning the body."

Whatever Paul meant by this, it is laid over the story like a magical curse, further emphasizing the magical aspects surrounding the whole phenomenon of Eucharistic origins. Is Paul saying that this sacred meal belongs only to the (fully?) initiated, and thus that those without such enlightenment from initiation should beware and stay away lest illness or death magically retaliate? This seems a likely, if unsettling, interpretation.

But maybe Paul has simply returned to his trademark concept of 'faith'—if you *believe* it is the body of Christ you benefit from the ritual, but if you *don't* believe you risk death. Even if so, he seems to be overlaying the sacrament with (black?) magic.

One historian writes of primitive religions in which there are instances on record of men and women who died of fright upon learning they had unwittingly eaten the remains of a chief's meal, which was strictly taboo. Another reminds us that "A curse can kill—if the victim believes in it". Even now, for many Christians the thought of the peril of unworthy communion is a terrifying reality, writes a European bishop. (This death-delivering magic can be glimpsed also in other reports from the New Testament, such as Acts 5:1-10.)

The Koran also seems to echo this warning/curse over the Eucharist. It is in a story from the fifth chapter wherein the disciples ask Jesus to request from God that he send down a table loaded with food in order for them to have a feast. The consensus is that this is a reference to the Christian

14

An Hallucination which Changed the World?

Eucharist as practiced by Ethiopian Christians during the time of the birth of Islam.

"Jesus son of Mary [as he is styled in the Koran] said, 'God, our Lord, send down a table to us out of heaven to be a feast for us'....God said, 'I will send it down to you but if anyone among you is an unbeliever after that, I will punish him with a punishment the like of which I will not inflict on anyone else in all the worlds.'"

So again, why this emphasis on great danger from participating in the Eucharist with an unbelieving heart? Plenty of other miracles in the New Testament have no such warning attached to them. God's warning in the Koran parallels Paul's warning closely and suggests that there is something unique about the Eucharist which we've lost track of—namely its basis in magic.

Paul twice speaks of those "guilty of the body and blood of the Lord" and called it "eating and drinking unworthily" and "not seeing through to the body of the Lord." One scholar says that the implication of these two maledictions is that Paul is actually "calling down the blood-libel accusation of being 'guilty of the blood' of Christ on his opponents."

We may have one case history of this curse laid out for us in the Bible. Judas, of lamentable fame, was probably the first person to be administered the sacrament of the Eucharist by a priest—and it did not end well for him. The Bible pictures Jesus in his priestly role giving the two Eucharistic elements to Judas (Jesus dipped the bread into the wine and gave it to Judas to eat, an administering custom, or mechanism, called 'intinction' which is still used today in some church circles.)

This got wrapped into the betrayal angle of the ongoing plot, but it is nonetheless a clear Eucharistic reference and it was an immediate prelude to Judas' exceptionally messy suicide. To see this vignette as an illustration of Paul's curse on unworthy reception of the sacrament is not farfetched—the whole point of the story fragment is that Judas was unworthy because he was about to betray Jesus for money. This gospel account was written after Paul's epistles, so Paul's concerns about 'unworthy' reception of the Eucharist, and his warnings about the consequences, were well known to the writer.

A more prosaic explanation, perhaps, is where Paul's mental time placed him in history. For him the end times were soon to be manifest—perhaps this is also why he urged his converts not to marry; the end of human history was at hand so there was little time to deal with such mundane concerns as marriage. But people were frequently dealing with illness and death regardless of whether the end of time was near, so why would Paul feel this was even noteworthy, let alone a sign of God's particular displeasure with their attitude about the Eucharist? Could it be because Paul expected death and illness should be 'on Hold' until God played his final hand, which was sure to be soon? This eschatological orientation could explain why he issued the warning about unworthy reception of the sacrament—because Paul felt that it upset God to the extent that He was letting these people die even now when the end was so near anyway.

Thanks to John M. Allegro who wrote the notorious book which equated Jesus with the *Amanita muscaria* mushroom, we can add one more possible interpretation of Paul's 'curse.' The magic mushroom is, of course, poisonous and an overdose could indeed lead to violent sickness or even death. For Allegro the sacrament (the Eucharist) meant eating the magic mushroom, i.e. eating the body of god (Jesus) and/or drinking the god's blood (an infusion of the mushroom). Allegro suggests that when Paul writes that failure "to discern the body" equals big trouble, he means just that—watch what you're doing with those mushrooms!

The scholarly community ultimately did not go along with Allegro's elaborate interpretation of Biblical names and terms which led him to conclude that Jesus was actually code for a hallucinogenic mushroom. However, it's no secret that hallucinogens played a significant role in the religious rites of the era, so the idea that mushrooms could have been involved in the liturgical life of some groups of early "Christians" is a lot less far-fetched than Allegro's basic conclusion. Therefore, it's possible that Paul's warning to "discern the body" in this hallucinogenic context was still a piece of good advice.

● ON A DIFFERENT WAVELENGTH FROM JERUSALEM

So, is Paul the actual source of the foundation of Christian worship? If so, this goes a very long way toward confirming Paul as the inventor of Christianity as we know it. History, it's said, is written by the victors. Right or wrong, Paul won his argument with the Jesus movement. It was Paul, not the original apostles and not Peter their leader, who shaped Christian civilization.

Paul did not even think and conceptualize like the Jerusalem disciples. He lived in a different mental world entirely. He was in all aspects Hellenized. He and the Jerusalem disciples were simply talking *past* each other as much as disagreeing. And it seems Paul was quite adept at being a hot-head as well as a major ego. It's probably little wonder he and the Jerusalem group soon came to loggerheads. I'm not even totally convinced that Paul ever intended to, or thought he was, writing about an historical Jesus of Nazareth in his epistles to the congregations he founded.

Unlike the Jerusalem apostles, Paul had not rubbed shoulders with this man called Jesus. To Paul, Jesus was just the name of someone else's companion and teacher. Paul met a universal, cosmic Christ in his visions, and that was as close to "Jesus" as he ever got in his lifetime. He usually referred to this Christ as "Lord" or "Christ" in his writings; if "Jesus" was used it was in combination: "Jesus [the] Christ." To Paul, Jesus was not 'Jesus of Nazareth,' but whatever apparition it was who had appeared to him in mystical visions.

Paul wrote about Christ, the voice in his visions, without concern for a man of history who was named "Jesus." The Jesus Paul was actually writing about had already become God in his view.

The Jerusalem apostles talked (and wrote, when, or if, they did write; authorship identification for New Testament material often being iffy) about Jesus, the brother of their current leader, and a man who had walked among them. It's quite plausible that Paul was not even trying to write or teach about this man called Jesus—and certainly not about Jesus unless he was transformed into "the Christ." Paul's link to the Jesus movement of Jerusalem was possibly more a matter of guilt than theology—and for theology Paul did not really need a historical Jesus because he had his cosmic Christ.

One way of looking at it is that Paul gave Jesus a big promotion.

Some scholars speak of Paul as moving from the religion *of* Jesus to a religion *about* Jesus. Is it possible that Paul's religion was not even *about* Jesus of Nazareth? Paul's religion instead seems strictly about the Christ figure he knew from his visions.

It seems Paul really intended to articulate a completely different religion, more than to re-shape the fledgling Jesus movement of Jerusalem—and indeed he did so. And it seems that it was mostly Luke who tried to tie the two strains of perception up into a single package with his stories of visionary Jesus appearances to Paul and with the sometimes dubious history he painted in Acts.

Even if Jesus of Nazareth had played no part in this story at all, it is possible (probable?) that Paul's religion could have surfaced then and there anyway—great pieces of it were already extant in earlier thinking, myth, and religious legend. In short, although it is tempting to see Paul as somehow the villain in the early disorientation of a young Christianity, it is probably more sound to see him as the creator of a great world religion with minimal reference to the Jesus movement.

While piety shrinks from admitting it, the Jesus movement fizzled (and not really *because* of Paul; it probably would have in any case), while the Paul movement clearly triumphed, at least for a couple of millennia.

If one chooses to look at Christianity as a Jesus religion (or as a should-be Jesus religion), then Paul becomes not only the first schismatic, but the first major heretic. How odd that a religion which continues to try to wrap

17

Jesus and Paul up in the same package has even made it this far in history. If we take Jesus of Nazareth out of the picture, and just leave Paul's Christ in his place, Christianity suddenly loses much of its inner tension and begins to make sense—maybe not rational sense, but sense as a religious system.

For especially the Protestant portion of western Christianity Paul is the key, but the unifying story is really a vacuum or a question—we know we're saved (we've been told that often enough in any case), but what is it that we're saved from? Paul's Christianity can be perceived almost as a solution without a problem in need of solution. Paul, however, was quick to provide an answer about *why* we needed to be saved, which unfortunately gave us an even stronger community theme: Guilt. Paul's answer was that we are rank sinners, and have been so from Eve and Eden forward. So the Protestant great Bible story may be Eden and a snake and an apple (?) tree, plus a woman who was a little too curious for her (and our, as her descendants) own good.

It may be interesting to note that all three of what might be called the major Judeo-Christian themes or stories: the Jewish (Exodus), the Catholic (longing for the "Queen of Heaven"), and the Protestant (guilt); have their foundations in ancient Egypt. The Jews felt the need to escape Egypt, the Catholics were searching for their own version of the great goddess Isis, and the Protestants were mired in Original Sin, which the ancient Egyptians had invented long before Paul got around to it.

If there is a single story for all of western Christianity, it is probably that of one man sacrificing his life for the many—an innocent man paying the ultimate price for the guilt of others. Paul led the way here, too, by tying salvation and atonement to the death of Jesus rather than to something which did not focus exclusively on his death, such as the Incarnation. Why this death-oriented approach should have been needed to accomplish the task is never really explained. Again, though, the idea first surfaced in ancient Egypt.

● ANSWERS?

So, did Paul invent Christianity?

"Invent" is probably the wrong word, even though several very competent scholars use it in this context.

Most of the elements of Paul's approach existed already in ancient Greek and Egyptian religious thought, philosophy, and mythology. What he did was overlay this mythology onto the 'Jesus movement' of Jerusalem, thereby altering the movement fundamentally, and essentially replacing Jesus the Jew with Jesus the Greek Christos. After Paul, 'Christianity' meant something entirely different than it would have meant had this Jesus movement gone on to develop naturally from its Jewish roots.

An Hallucination which Changed the World?

Paul didn't so much invent Christianity like pulling a new rabbit out of an old hat. What he did was essentially to rewrite the Jesus movement into an ancient Sun God religion. In any case, he left an indelible outline which has defined the religion ever since, while largely stripping it of its original religious focus and flavor.

And, did Paul invent the Eucharist?

Again, "invent" is the probably wrong word, although again reputable scholars use it in this context. He certainly did not pull this one out of a hat either. The concept of the hero (god, king, high priest, shaman) feeding his people with his own body and blood is one of the oldest religious ideas that can be traced back into the mists of time, with its most visible roots seen in ancient Egypt. Again, what Paul did was to overlay this ancient mythology onto the Jesus movement of Jerusalem.

He did introduce theophagy (eating God) into Christianity, but he certainly did not *invent* the concept of theophagy. However, he probably did invent the foundational story that goes along with it in Christianity—the story of a 'Last Supper' at which Jesus gave the 'words of institution' for what became the main sacrament of Christianity.

So we could say Paul invented the cover story but not the religious concept. He invented a way of plugging an ancient mythological religious idea into a religious sect with Jewish roots which otherwise would never have conceived of such a thing. If Paul thought he had originated the idea of theophagy it would belie the lofty intelligence and education he is usually credited with by scholars. One scholar has also suggested that Paul, a Roman citizen, may have been trying to thread a needle between his citizenship and his membership in an ethnic group (the Jews) which was always stubbornly uncooperative with its occupying Roman force. Be that as it may, he did move the Jesus movement from Judaism to someplace wildly different.

And with the Eucharist Paul and his followers gave us a great Biblical conundrum, not to say outright contradiction. The very mixed message was that you *must* participate because it's your only hope (for example, John 6:53-58) but on the other hand it may very well kill you (I Corinthians 11:29-30). So good luck, you could well be a goner either way.

Several contemporary writers have allowed themselves use of the word "invent" in attempting to answer either or both of these questions, as we've noted. There is such a sharp contrast between Pauline Christianity (especially as it has developed through the centuries) and the Hebrew religion Jesus would have known in his lifetime, that the word has seemed not only useful but almost warranted. It carries a mild shock value which may help make the point. I'm a bit shy about its use in this context, however, because the antecedents of both the overall shape of Christianity

19

and the specifics of the Eucharist were so established early-on in mankind's religious experience. They were both there well before Paul. He surprised everyone, as it were, by overlaying them on nascent Christianity, but "invention" in this context just seems not to be the right word.

Paul could be seen as a sort of a railroad traffic controller for Christianity. The train was beginning to pick up steam down a track leading from Jerusalem to a place yet to be named. Paul pulled the junction switch and diverted the train onto a different track. It gradually did pick up a lot of steam hurdling down the centuries, but now its original station was less clear. Was it Jerusalem? Was it Athens? Was it Heliopolis or Amarna? We do know that its most important early station stop was Alexandria in Egypt.

Or maybe to update the allegory, and also to bring it more into line theologically, we could compare Paul to a modern terrorist. The flight takes off on schedule headed to its intended destination. Then the flight (the Jesus movement) is hijacked by Paul, and the pilot is ordered to fly to a different destination. The flight that started as a sect of Judaism now has become "Christianity," constructed more on ancient Greek and Egyptian religious traditions and concepts than on Jewish ones.

It seems reasonable to say that the birth of Christianity happened on the road to Damascus, scene of perhaps the most consequential hallucination in the human experience so far. Paul has been the center of gravity in Christianity ever since, even before the first gospel writer set pen to parchment.

This chapter has suggested that Paul may be the most prominent character in the New Testament. Jesus got the marquee title, but Paul wrote the script and did the public relations. In that last bit Paul did have a monumental near equal whom we've neglected—the emperor Constantine. The reason for stopping with Paul is not only that Constantine is a not a Biblical character, but that his role, enormously consequential as it was, came in the historical and political realms rather than the religious. The goal of this book, however, was only to look at Christianity from the point of view of religion, and to do so through Biblical characters.

Without Constantine (and later the Emperor Theodosius who outlawed every religion except Christianity), however, Paul's work of making Christianity into a major world religion would probably ultimately have fallen short. Christianity as we know it is the product of history and politics every bit as much as it is the product of religion. It is interesting to note too that Constantine's conversion involved a heavenly vision just as did Paul's. Without either vision (hallucination?) the world would probably be a profoundly different place today.

● NOTE ON ANOTHER STRANGE BIBLICAL CHARACTER:

Judas, mentioned earlier as a probable recipient of Paul's Eucharistic curse, is in and of himself one of the Bible's least understood figures. He easily draws our condemnation and disdain, and indeed his name has entered our language as a potent symbol for betrayal and duplicity. But lurking in the background is also the sense that he was almost a victim of circumstances beyond his own control. Was he a villain or a victim? A sense of irony swirls around him.

First off, he was personally selected by Jesus to be one of the elite disciples—a member of the august twelve, set apart from the many rank and file followers of Jesus. Then he was treasurer of that apostolic team, a move Jesus must at least have approved of. Was Jesus such a bad judge of character? Or was Jesus setting up a fall-guy for the inevitable betrayal. Was it Judas' destiny all along to play the bad-guy role in a pre-determined drama over which Judas himself had no real control?

Then we are told how badly Judas regretted his betrayal of Jesus, and how he rushed to kill himself in shame and despair. So what does this mean? Did Judas really love Jesus as he had seemed to do before the betrayal? Was he scripted to take a brief hiatus from his nice guy persona in order to fulfill a nasty bit of business which had to be done by someone. Was he just unlucky enough to be tapped for the role of the betrayer and then left alone to face the agony of his actions? The entire scene leading to the crucifixion is treated in the Bible as an inevitable unfolding of God's plan for the salvation of mankind—even Jesus himself is painted as wishing the plot could be avoided, but then faithfully submitting to the divine plan. Where did that leave poor Judas? Was he an unwilling and unwitting actor in an unavoidable drama orchestrated by God?

It seems that no matter which Biblical character is under discussion, some scholar or historian is always ready to pop up and cast doubt on the character's existence or on an angle of his story. Judas does not have much of a role in the New Testament aside from this betrayal of Jesus sub-plot. Jesus' existence is challenged, Moses' existence is challenged, so we almost expect someone to claim Judas never existed either. Well, he has been challenged, but not his existence, just his story—his 'star turn,' if that phrase can be tolerated in this context, in the story of Jesus.

The proposal is that the whole betrayal episode was invented. By the time of the crucifixion Jesus had been abandoned by his followers, including by the twelve. To cover such an embarrassment, and to exonerate those who should have supported Jesus in his time of greatest need, it has been proposed that Mark simply invented the Judas part of the story. The general mythological tradition in describing great heroes was just such an

21

invention of a false friend who betrays the hero (King Arthur, Siegfried, etc.). If this theory is true, then it indeed is the case that Judas was falsely accused. In either case, he maintains his position as a probable victim of circumstances beyond his control—a tragic figure of Shakespearean dimension.

● NOTE ON THE PEJORATION OF TRADITIONAL CHRISTIAN TERMINOLOGY

"Am I not an apostle?" Paul asks the Corinthian Christians rhetorically. Well, no, you aren't, if for no other reason than that Biblically it's a technical term (meaning one of the twelve chosen *directly* by Jesus *during his lifetime* to meet Zodiacal specifications, or one chosen later by remnants of the original apostles to maintain the number at twelve) and you don't meet the qualifications on either front.

But Paul's attempt to become the thirteenth member of a club limited to twelve may have set in long-term motion an attitude of willingness, in wide evidence today, to trivialize traditional Christian leadership titles. In Paul's day he was the only 'do-it-yourself' apostle we know of (although Simon Magus gave it his best shot but failed)—today, however, the woods seem to be full of them. Do you want to be a bishop, or better yet perhaps an archbishop? No problem at all. Just set up a storefront church in the city or build a mega-auditorium in the suburbs, and declare that you are an archbishop—and while you're at it, you may as well label the building a "cathedral." It's a lot more impressive that way.

When I was growing up as a Lutheran last century our church (denominational) overseers disdained use of the title 'bishop,' even though that was the universally accepted and understood term for the role they played—even as laid-back a group as the Methodists used it. European Lutherans had bishops all over the place, but in this country the word evidently was not democratic sounding enough (or maybe, just *maybe*, it was *too Catholic* sounding).

Anyway we still had overseers and they still needed to be distinguished from the ordinary run of clergy. So shortly after one of them was newly elected, one of the colleges supported by our denomination would rush to give the man (it was always a man back then) an honorary doctorate. 'Dr. Smith' sounded a lot more important than merely 'President of Synod Smith' evidently. This system of honorary 'Doctors of Divinity' came to be derided behind the scenes as "Donated Dignity."

Today's system is even more streamlined. One simply 'donates' the 'dignity' to oneself. There are "bishops" all over the place, including bishops of single small congregations which belong to no larger denomination. So now Paul has a fair amount of company as a d.i.y.

"apostle" and nobody has to worry about stopping the count at twelve, or even thirteen.

● NOTE ON INTERPRETING THE BIBLE

An interpretation of any Biblical passage is seldom, if ever, going to be unanimous. At various points in this book I've tried to call attention to the fact that there will almost always be another opinion on what was meant by the Biblical writer, and sometimes a great many opinions running in a surprising variety of directions.

In the Eucharistic section of this chapter I mentioned in passing that the feeding of the five thousand story in John's gospel was code for the Eucharistic 'miracle.' Most observers who go anywhere beyond seeing this story as merely a literal retelling are probably on the same track of interpreting it as a coded discussion of the Eucharist—that is the generally accepted 'feet-on-the-ground' interpretation. But as usual, there are also some exotic counter proposals.

One interpretation which illustrates the point is that the whole story is about the reported numbers involved. Each number mentioned supposedly relates to the next number mentioned, it is said, in such a way that we end up with a geometrical construct of twelve arcs in a flower design which translates mathematically into 888 which was supposedly the number of Jesus. This, according to one author, was "intended both to entertain and edify" and was "designed to bring enjoyment even to children." This approach sees the New Testament as composed of allegories based on "geometric ratios" which are part of the "harmony of the cosmos."

With that expanse of range in play, you can see why it is unlikely that anything the Bible has to say will ever find a universal consensus no matter how brilliant are the scholars who labor sincerely to uncover its meaning. We are dealing with texts which are many centuries old, and which were influenced by even older texts, concepts, and the authors' own interpretations of those older sources. We are dealing with texts which are somehow expected to be mysterious and to carry a wealth of hidden and esoteric meaning available only to those with special insight. And we (the vast majority of us at least) are dealing with them in translation—and in many cases in translations of still older translations. The understandable desire of so many to have a book which gives a clear and simple division of truth from untruth is enormously frustrated by these circumstances, at least among those who are willing to acknowledge human reality.

Then on top of those scholars who labor honestly to sort out probable meaning, despite their many different conclusions, there are those who *intentionally* indulge in the temptation to search for hidden meanings, esoteric and even bizarre fringe ideas buried in the Bible's pages. Is it any wonder that the institutions (church groups) claiming the Bible as their religious text by now vary so wildly from each other, and sometimes will barely even talk to each other or even acknowledge each other as fellow Christians? Even those who claim to take the Bible literally are fooling themselves because they, too, have applied an interpretation to what they read—applying an interpretation is inevitable when humans try to understand writings which fall outside their own direct experiences.

One of the interesting things about religion is that despite the huge role it plays in human affairs, its message can't be proven or demonstrated to be true. It can only be 'believed.'' Religion is not a matter of science, history, fact, or even rationality. It is a matter of faith. Therefore it is never a matter of right or wrong—it simply defies both categories. It is, perhaps at best, always a matter of 'maybe'. ⌘

2.

The Bible's Naked Young Man

It's a reasonably safe bet that many people raised as Christians have at one time or another been puzzled by a Biblical reference to a young man naked in public. Some may have even been offended by the insertion of a reference to nudity in what we were told was the "Word of God." At the same time it's also a fairly safe bet that many other Christians may never have even noticed the presence of this naked young man—his star-turn lasts only two verses (Mark 14:51-52) and just twenty-nine words in the Revised Standard Version Bible (RSV).

The reference seems strange—actually at first glance it's weird, maybe even deserving of the word 'bizarre'. And it comes out of nowhere, with no prelude and no follow-up, just plopped in from left field and sitting there with no explanation of any kind. The naked young man is a walk-on. He makes a cameo appearance with no speaking lines, and is gone (apparently) almost as quickly as he appeared.

Nor does he seem to fit the context. In fact, he may seem to almost insult or demean the context.

The nude guy makes his appearance during one of the heaviest scenes in the New Testament. Jesus is praying in the garden called Gethsemane begging God for a reprieve. Then he is betrayed by one of his close followers and arrested by the local Roman-backed authorities. Christianity tells us this is very serious stuff; in fact, that it's the first step leading to our salvation. Jesus is going to die—and what's more, that's because we are sinners, the clergy told us.

So this scene in the garden is not a walk in the park. And if we didn't read the episode for ourselves, we were hearing it read to us at a service during Lent, that big downer stretch where we were supposed to deny ourselves something we otherwise enjoyed in order to somehow share just a little in the suffering. This naked reference was decidedly not the sort of stuff we usually heard about in church. In my day, being in church meant showing as little skin as possible. Some women even still wore veils.

Nor was any serious attempt made by the clergy to explain this odd sounding reference. They dutifully read the passage (it was in the Bible, after all, so it must be salient whether we can understand why it's there or not) and then preached as if it hadn't been there—ignored because not even the clergy could divine what it was all about.

So, why *was* a naked young man needed in this solemn scene? Was it a bit of comic relief? Was it a mistake, maybe inserted by accident (or as a prank) later when a monk was copying scripture? Was St. Mark daydreaming about childhood skinny dipping when he wrote his gospel? Had Jesus stumbled into a nudist colony when he went to pray in the garden? Was someone trying to distract the attention of the arresting officers?

Among the many attempts to make sense of this short and strange Biblical passage was the suggestion by one prominent author that the naked guy was a boy prostitute. He pointed out that such prostitution was legal and even institutionalized in the Roman Empire. While not exactly impossible, that interpretation seems both improbable and simplistic. Instead of answering the question, it actually deepens the mystery of why the young man was included by Mark.

It's extremely difficult to imagine why Mark would have wanted to plant the inference that Jesus might have been negotiating, or in the process of, a business arrangement with a male prostitute. If that description of the young man in the sheet were accurate, it is exactly the sort of incident that the evangelist would have wanted to omit so as not to sully Jesus' reputation. So I think we can safely ignore that solution to the question, precisely because Mark *did* include the incident.

No, the first key to some understanding of this mystery is that the naked man was NOT needed to advance the plot in this scene, and yet he was there *anyway*. It's that combination which becomes a first clue.

Well, if he was not needed, why on earth did he show up, especially at such a fraught juncture? Most Biblical scholars believe that he was included in the passage basically because he *was* actually there. When Jesus was betrayed, there actually *was* a young man watching the proceedings and with only a wrap of linen covering his otherwise naked body. The sheet was grabbed and to avoid capture, the young man ran from the scene stark naked, leaving the sheet behind.

Okay, so there was a naked weirdo standing around. That doesn't explain why Mark would include such a seemingly irrelevant detail. It doesn't seem to add anything worthy to such a serious story line. In fact, it almost seems to detract from the story. It is a jarring element in the midst of a somber and sad retelling—a diversion which distracts us from the story rather than contributing to it; or so it seems at first glance.

The Bible's Naked Young Man

But scholarship can lead to wonderful insights. It's the job of Biblical scholars to ponder just such odd details and to figure out all the 'whys' involved. And indeed Biblical scholars have come up with a theory to answer at least part of our question. Not only this particular question, but also any other similar questions about stories in the Bible which carry a surprising element which seems out of place.

The theory, stated very simply, is that the incongruous incident was known to so many people of the writer's time that it could not be ignored safely. Lots of people knew about the naked man, or others like him, to the extent that his mention in Mark's gospel was no surprise at all. And these people had passed it down as an integral part of the plot that reached Mark's ears before he wrote out his account some decades after the fact.

It's even possible that Mark himself didn't completely understand the role of the naked man, but he knew it was relevant because that's the way the story came down to him. It would be my guess that Mark intentionally included this character because he knew exactly why he was present, but in theory, fifty or so years down the road it could have been just an odd scrap of detail that reached Mark through oral history. In any case all of the eye witnesses knew about the naked man and, presumably, most or all of them included a reference to him when they retold the story which eventually reached the writer of the earliest gospel.

Okay, so let's agree that the naked man was not an accidental or fictitious insertion into the story. He was actually there. But his presence still needs an explanation. Why wasn't he wearing proper clothing? And even more to the point, why was he so physically close to Jesus as to risk getting arrested himself. Did Jesus normally hang around with people covered only by sheets? (a question we'll look at later). Was he reduced to a mere bed sheet because he was too poor to afford conventional clothing? Could he have been an exhibitionist out looking for a crowd to shock? Not likely.

As you'd expect because we're talking about the Bible, the most likely explanation has to do with religion. And it turns out that the story of the naked young man who fled into the night is not really about him at all—it turns out to be a story about Jesus—a story we definitely did not learn in Sunday School.

Religion back then utilized initiation rites in a big way. Christianity still does, of course, if you stop to realize that Baptism is an initiation ritual. Think John the Baptist. He was roaming around out in the wilderness and attracting curious crowds and serious followers by baptizing people with river water. One of the followers he attracted along the way was a guy named Jesus. Then for a while, Jesus took over the franchise himself, it appears.

Even today to enter many churches one must pass a Baptistry, or a Baptismal font. This layout follows long tradition, and is a reminder that one becomes a Christian (enters the church) through Baptism; through an initiation rite.

It turns out that the young man who ran off naked when Jesus was arrested *did* add to the story. In fact, his presence probably explains why Jesus was actually in the garden that evening in the first place, and it probably tells us a great deal about Jesus and his ministry we might otherwise not know.

The most likely explanation is that the young man was himself a candidate for initiation by Jesus, and that the ritual was essentially interrupted by the chaos of the evening.

● SHROUDS FOR THE LIVING

Initiates by age-old tradition, stretching back to the Egyptian origins of Christianity and even beyond that, were naked. Linen coverings were a fixed part of the routine. Symbolically they were shrouds signaling ritual death—that the candidate's previous life was yielding to a new birth into a completely *new* life. Ritual death would clear away ignorance and yield insight at the point of ritual re-birth.

By the time Christianity brought this long, long tradition down to our day the ritual death part in Baptism had pretty much been forgotten and replaced with a mere "washing" away of sin—the sin part being essentially a religious invention which Christianity inherited from its ancient Egyptian origins.

The original goal of religious initiation was centered on enlightenment, not so much on purification. And it was participatory.

But by the time it reached us in (usually) infant baptism, the goal had been eroded down essentially to sanctification. And the active participation of the initiate had pretty much disappeared. We can't blame ourselves if all of this seems mysterious, because we were never given accurate instruction. In fact, we can't even blame those who should have instructed us because they walked in the same fog of communal memory loss.

Another clue which ties the naked man to a pending initiation and a legitimate place in the story, is that Mark says that the young man was following Jesus, i.e. he was a follower of Jesus. His presence would not have been surprising in context. He may not even have been the only such young man on the scene that evening, which makes for an interesting aside.

Some scholars have suggested that the "young man" in Marks' gospel who was encountered at Jesus' tomb on Easter morning was our very same naked young man from the garden. They say that he, or possibly a small group of young men who were scheduled to be initiated by Jesus on the night he was betrayed, had stayed past the crucifixion in order to shield

Jesus' body from theft. They theorize that it was this group who moved the body to a safer, or in their view a more appropriate, place than the initial temporary tomb—hence the "empty" tomb discovered by the Easter women.

This theme of the body having been moved, maybe even multiple times, is a frequently proposed idea, probably because the earliest account of Easter we have, in Mark's Gospel, ends abruptly with an empty tomb and no mention of "resurrection" (other than perhaps the dubious quote from the 'young man'). That idea, or solution to the dilemma (i.e. resurrection), had to wait for later evangelists who wrote after the new faith had evolved a little more. The original Easter reaction was simply 'who moved the body and where has it been taken?'

Back to our naked man story, however. People who remembered the scene and passed it down remembered the young man stripped of his sheet precisely because he belonged there. He was not an extraneous by-stander. He was a participant. He was the very reason Jesus was in the garden that night.

Mark doesn't tell us much about Jesus initiating young men—just this passage, at least in the text which has come down to us and has been deemed canonical. Although there may be hints, sometimes vague or coded, elsewhere in his and the other canonical gospels.

It's possible that the reason is because everyone back in those earliest of Christian times routinely knew of this aspect of Jesus' ministry. Why spell something out which everybody knows? It's also possible, of course, that the gospel writers would have been happy to skip over some of Jesus' activities because the evangelists were trying to protect Jesus' reputation and image. The idea of Jesus initiating naked young men on a one-by-one basis at night may have been as uncomfortable an idea to the gospel writers as it is to many contemporary Christians who come upon it for the first time.

And then there's the obvious problem that none of the evangelists had witnessed Jesus or his activities in person. They were completely dependent on what lore was passed down to them, and elements of the story easily could have disappeared along the way (or could have been added, for that matter).

On the other hand, maybe St. Mark *did* spell it out.

We don't have all of the gospel he wrote. Your Bible likely has a number of footnotes at the end of Mark's gospel. They point out variations on the text in different ancient manuscripts and they may add bits of material which show up in versions which didn't make it into the official canon. These notes may even give you an alternate ending. On top of that, we now know that the version of Mark's gospel which was accepted into the Biblical canon was not the only extant version.

29

Mark's gospel was the first written and thus the closest to the events it describes. That probably gives it extra credibility, at least if one is looking at the Bible as an historical account (which was not its primary purpose and therefore its writers were relieved of the responsibility of being accurate historians, at least by their own standards).

But human communication was as tricky and difficult back then as it has been at any stage of the human experience. Especially with written documents, which had to be copied to be passed down in hand written manuscripts. Errors could creep in easily during all of the copying. Copyists could omit or add material by accident or even by intention. Sometimes copying scribes disagreed with the author and took it upon themselves to "correct" the text. And Mark's gospel being the oldest just gives it an increased exposure to such risks.

● 'SECRET MARK'
But there's a story which illustrates all of this and also probably takes us back to the naked man in the garden. It's the story of one of the most fascinating discoveries in recent Biblical scholarship—a real blockbuster; an actual game changer. Nothing about the Jesus of the New Testament looks quite the same as it did before, after we learn of this discovery.

One of the brightest bulbs in Christian historical scholarship last century was an American: Morton Smith, a professor of history at Columbia University in New York. In 1958 while Smith was doing research at the library of the Orthodox monastery of Mar Saba near Jerusalem he discovered a previously unknown fragment of a letter by Bishop Clement of Alexandria. This material is generally now referred to as "Secret Mark" because it is not part of the canonical gospel of Mark and is known only from Prof. Smith's discovery.

This letter, copied in excerpt on the end paper of another document, presumably by a long gone monk, was written by Clement to answer questions he had received from a certain Theodore, who is thus the recipient of Clement's reply. Theodore's questions were about a provocative story concerning Jesus and a young man who enters wearing only a linen sheet but otherwise was naked. The sheet was symbolically a shroud, as would have been expected for a candidate for Baptism.

Clement quotes from a version of Mark used in Alexandria which contained this story. He says this version was "read only to those who are being initiated into the great mysteries". But then he also refutes some aspects of the questions from Theodore which he says are additions to Mark's story by an extremist Christian sect, the Carpocrations. One of these sentences which Theodore asked about refers to Jesus and the initiate and contains the phrase "naked man on naked man."

This Carpocrations group was accused of enslaving an Alexandrian priest in order to get from him a copy of the 'Secret Gospel' version of Mark. The Carpocrations were also accused of consecrating female priests (at that time not sanctioned by orthodox Christian groups, of course).

Summarized quickly, the passage Theodore asked about and which Clement confirms, is that a woman whose brother had just died asked Jesus for mercy, or in effect to raise her brother back to life. Jesus went to the tomb and rolled away the stone covering its door. Jesus entered and stretched out his hand and raised the youth, who in turn "looking upon him [Jesus], loved him and began to beseech him that he might be with him." Jesus stayed on in the household and after six days he instructed the youth, who then in the evening came to Jesus wearing a linen cloth over his naked body, and "remained with him that night." Jesus "taught him the mystery of the kingdom of God."

Sounds oddly familiar, doesn't it?

Many, probably most, scholars feel this is related to the Lazarus story which *did* make it into the canonical New Testament. But it's not merely a retelling of the same Lazarus story in the canonical gospels, nor is it exactly a new Lazarus story. Many, by now probably most, scholars believe the entire Lazarus story in the gospels is basically a community memory of the ritual passage through death to new life contained in these ancient initiations. So the 'Secret Mark' version would represent another such incidence of ritual initiation, suggesting that Jesus initiated young men routinely as a standard part of his ministry.

In other words, the Lazarus story in the Bible is thought by experts to be a coded reference to ritual initiation rather than an actual, literal, story of a miracle. The 'death' referred to was a *ritual* death rather than a clinical death, and the 'resurrection' referred to was a calling forth to new life and enlightenment at the end of the initiation ritual.

You can imagine the scandal this discovery of 'Secret Mark' caused for many Christians in the mid-20th century. Scholars were dumbfounded because nothing of this nature had ever been associated with the New Testament gospels before, aside from the Lazarus story itself which was not then well understood. Never had there been the suggestion of such an elaborate initiation ritual associated with Jesus. And never had it been suggested before that Jesus had taken any personal or tactile interest in candidates for initiation (Baptism). And never had a respected and top ranked scholar suggested that Jesus might have spent a night naked in bed with another naked man.

The few good souls from the pews who might have stumbled onto news of the discovery had their firm mental images of Jesus shattered. Jesus spending the night with a naked young man! If that idea wasn't heresy (or at least totally offensive), what could possibly be?

Some of the news media reporting the discovery even suggested right out loud, in black and white, that Jesus was being portrayed by the 'Secret Mark' material as homosexual. (A suggestion which can be counted on to provoke rage among the 'faithful.' A few years ago a Netflix movie depicting Jesus as a gay man was produced in Brazil. The production company's reward was to have Molotov cocktails lobbed into its headquarters on Christmas Eve.)

Well, Morton Smith was homosexual. So that must explain it, some thought. Smith must have wanted to paint Jesus as a gay man to make himself look better, or maybe even just for the sport of it. In any case, the pious knew with certainty that Jesus could not have been gay. Some of them still doubted that he even had a penis. (Have you heard about the teacher nun who sent a student to the principal's office for asking if Jesus ever had to "use the bathroom"? Naughty child!)

If Jesus ever slept naked with another naked man, obviously it must have been an accident. It can't imply he was 'gay' because that would be a sin. We know Jesus was not a sinner, so.... Oh, let's stop before we get a headache.

It is maybe interesting to note that some gay writers welcomed the 'Secret Mark' discovery as evidence, when added to the Biblical Lazarus material, that Jesus had a life-long love affair with a younger man. In fairness, the Bible *does* say Jesus "loved" Lazarus.

The problem, though, is that among serious scholars of the Bible there aren't many who believe anymore that Lazarus was a real, i.e. specific, person. Rather, he seems to be a name applied to a class or group of people: young men who were initiated by Jesus.

The consensus is that the whole Lazarus thing is code for initiation rites, as we've noted, which pulled candidates into ritual death in order for them to be brought back to life in an improved (enlightened) state. In other words, the idea that Jesus initiated young men in this way was sitting right there in the canonical Bible all along. We just couldn't recognize it because we'd been assured that Jesus could raise actual dead people for so long that we mistook code to be history—we took written allusions to initiation rituals to be, instead, stories about actual specific 'miracles.' And maybe the Lazarus story *per se* is not the only Biblical account which is encoded in this way. The account in Luke 7:11-17 and the phrase, "Young man, I say to you, arise." seem to fit the same mold; it sounds formulaic and rings the 'initiation' bell fairly loudly.

So in that sense Jesus was indeed involved long-term with "Lazarus," because he evidently conducted such initiation rites routinely. But the chance of physical love being involved, if it was, would not have centered on just one particular young man. There would have been a string of men over a long period of time. So if Jesus had a love life, we can safely conclude that it was *not* centered on a lad named Lazarus. (A string of *men* being initiated because women at that time and in that place were not considered worthy of such concern, or of enlightenment. There's plenty in the New Testament about that too, especially if you look between the lines.)

Scholars have by now detected all kinds of Biblical material which suggests that Jesus conducted long and involved initiation ceremonies for those of special importance to him, such as his leading disciples. These were not the garden variety Baptisms which crowds of people seem to have received in groups from John the Baptizer, and probably from Jesus himself. These individual initiations required a full night to be devoted to each candidate evidently, and hence they had to be limited to a hierarchical strata of individuals in ascending importance. We don't know with any certainty whether hallucinogenic drugs ('magic' mushrooms) or hypnosis and trances may have been utilized, but judging from the history of other ancient initiation rites it's not a bad guess that they were.

One recent scholar became convinced, or convinced himself, that to achieve the mystical experience or to induce visions, the Jesus initiations must have involved hallucinogens in a big way. That was the key. Again, it's hardly a wild guess, except that this guy, who published his book on the subject in 1970, went a trifle too far with the idea. He decided that Jesus never even existed as a human, but that Biblical references to him were actually references to a hallucinogenic mushroom (*Amanita muscaria*) shared at sacred meals. Possibly close, but no cigar.

Actually the 'mushroom guy' was a hitherto respected scholar and one of the translators of the Dead Sea Scrolls. Given the paucity of solid information we have about Jesus as a historical figure, and given the preceding millennia of religious use of hallucinogens to achieve ecstasy and enlightenment, the sacred mushroom theory had its points of plausibility. And among the several scholars who have ultimately arrived at the conclusion that Jesus was not an actual man, this treatment of the idea was by far the most imaginative and bold. Most have just rather sheepishly said, well, there's not enough evidence available to consider Jesus a real historical figure, and then went on to another subject before the resulting storm broke.

Even though the author was a highly educated academic, his fellow scholars didn't bite, and the publisher dropped the book amidst the furor it caused. All of this is a sort of entertaining insertion into the discussion about Jesus and initiation into the mysteries—entertaining because at first glance it seems so off-the-wall—but it doesn't answer the question about hallucinogens. A lot of very sober scholars think magic mushrooms could, indeed, have been part of the initiations Jesus conducted.

The ancients believed that once the body was asleep (induced by hallucinogenic drugs) the soul could roam at will. Initiates under the influence could thereby experience for themselves the supposed immortality of the soul. It was believed that knowledge acquired while 'high' on hallucinogenic drugs was more trustworthy than knowledge acquired while sober. Then the soul could return, or be prompted to return, to its body with no physical harm done, but a lot of wisdom and enlightenment gained. These concepts stretch back to ancient Egypt at very least. They are the essence of the rationale for ancient religious initiations into 'the mysteries.'

When the New Testament refers to the "kingdom of Heaven" or the "kingdom of God," as it does frequently in discussing Jesus' teachings, you're right in the middle of this whole discussion.

Such 'kingdoms,' of Heaven or God are earthly statuses. They don't refer to some sort of after-life experiences awaiting the righteous dead, as a lot of popular Christianity might infer or even proclaim. They are the place, the status of enlightenment, Jesus wanted for his top disciples *during their lives*. They are the end result of the initiations he evidently conducted. Morton Smith describes those who entered this kingdom as having escaped Mosaic Law, another fairly open New Testament concern attributed to Jesus. (Oddly, while Jesus was concerned about the quality of his followers' lives in the here and now, a few years later Paul, in Jesus' name, would shift the action to heaven and an afterlife—initiation (Baptism) was no longer for enlightenment while alive on this earth according to Paul's teaching, but instead became an admission ticket to a life hereafter.)

Some of the disciples probably learned the initiation formula, the tricks of the trade as it were, and carried on such initiations after Jesus was pulled from the scene by the Romans. We are certainly told by the Bible that the twelve main disciples conducted miracles after Jesus was gone, and they are described in similar language as had been those of Jesus. Since we now understand that descriptions of Jesus' miracles were at least in some instances code, it is not a big jump to assume that may be true also for later 'miracles' described by Luke in 'Acts of the Apostles' (i.e. that the apostles carried on the tradition of initiations Jesus had utilized).

Anyway, back to reactions to the discovery of 'Secret Mark.' The scholars to a large extent initially expressed deep doubt (or fell into deep jealousy). Smith had all the tools he would have needed to fabricate the document he said he "discovered." He was literate in the ancient languages involved and he was without question a major authority on the historical era involved.

So, bingo. It must be a hoax. Smith himself must have written the text on the endpaper and then tried to pass it off as legitimate. Problem solved.

A number of people got really huffy about Prof. Smith's discovery and set about to discredit it by writing whole books of rebuttal on the matter. Some of these folks (most of those I've read at least) could claim no personal knowledge or scholarship whatsoever relating to the various disciplines and fields of study involved. Their main qualification, apparently, was just that they didn't *like* the idea. That, or they wanted to go on record as being pious sorts who were willing to stand up and defend poor Jesus against a perceived besmirchment.

In the end the most solid idea they could come up with was a sin against logic—that because Smith *could have* faked the document (he had the requisite skills and knowledge), therefore he *must have* faked it. (And as if that wasn't stunning enough, one of these clowns tried to base his refutation on the fact that Prof. Smith was bald! One could just as easily maintain that Jesus was effeminate because the Western artistic tradition usually portrays him with shoulder length hair.)

But that was then. There have been ensuing decades for study and further discovery, and for that matter for jealousy to cool. Over these decades 'Secret Mark' has begun to provide the answers to lots of questions in Biblical scholarship—far more questions are now *answered* by "Secret Mark' than were originally *posed* by its discovery. It has become a valuable scholarly tool for unravelling other mysteries of Biblical Christianity. By this point *almost* every serious Biblical scholar believes it was a genuine discovery of an ancient lost segment of the gospel of St. Mark. Our image of Jesus and his ministry has now expanded into previously unforeseen turf.

Jesus' sexuality is still debated, of course. And folks who don't want Jesus to be gay point out that our concept of such things is significantly different from that of the ancients. These days we tend to think that if a man is sexually involved with another man, that's it. He's gay. We've got him pegged. He has a label which describes him for life.

But as scholars, and some would-be defenders of Jesus, point out, in times past sexual activity was seen in terms of the occasion. A man who went to bed with a male today might go to bed with a female next month—sexual orientation was not necessarily a lifetime commitment. The ancients saw humans as pretty much like their gods. The gods flirted with a girl here, a boy there. And they took their pleasure the same way—here a boy, there a girl.

I'm certainly not able to sort out Jesus' sexuality, so you'll have to ponder that for yourself. In order to move on it is probably sufficient to note that most observers by now take the implications of 'Secret Mark' pretty much at face value. A popular writer on Christian subjects has noted, simply, that Morton Smith's discovery showed that Jesus "engaged in sex with the men he baptized." Enough said.

The debate over the authenticity of Prof. Smith's discovery was further fueled because the document was ultimately lost. However, it should be pointed out that other scholars did see it and study it following Smith, so we're not working with the word of only one scholar. After discovery the manuscript was subsequently taken to Jerusalem for safe keeping, further study, and tests on the paper and ink.

But no one can find it now. Perhaps it was misfiled and is still at the Institute. I suppose it's not impossible that a zealous Christian, or even a zealous Jew for that matter, could have hidden it away on purpose. Or maybe even destroyed it as an act of religious homage. Anyway, we have only photos of the document now.

Although 'Secret Mark' is without question extraordinarily intriguing, it is not at all inconsistent with a lot of other knowledge we have of the religions of the early Christian period and the Gnostics of that general era.

Nor is the method by which this story reaches us as unusual as it may seem at first glance. There are many other important writings which have come down to us only because they are quoted by other writers (who often disagree with them), the originals having been lost, just as in the case of Clement quoting this lost passage from Mark.

In fact, Clement's successor as bishop in Alexandria, Origen, also preserved for the future an attack on Christianity by a philosopher named Celsus. He did this by writing a rebuttal which quoted Celsus sufficiently that scholars can study the views of Celsus even though none of his own manuscripts survive.

Nor is the idea of a foreigner discovering unknown but Biblically related material in an ancient monastery library unusual. About a century previous to Morton Smith's discovery the Englishman Robert Curzon had discovered a non-canonical document, the "Acts of Peter and Paul," written in Syriac, in a Syrian Monastery in Egypt. This opened the eyes of scholars to the whole phenomenon of religious texts which had not been included in the canon but were still awaiting discovery and study—and which could add useful perspective to the existing canon.

Another aspect of early Christian life we learn about with this 'Secret Mark' story is that initiation seems to have involved more than one level, as opposed to the Baptism we know today which is pretty much one-size-fits-all, with the only significant difference being sprinkling or immersion. Scholars now speak of "progressive grades" of early Christian Baptism, working up to the one taught by Jesus to those he considered "worthy of the mysteries." Remember, Jesus was likely a deputy to John the Baptist before he set up his own shop, so he was deeply into the idea of initiation rituals.

A bit of internal evidence in the Clement letter fragment seems to bolster the authenticity of Clement's admission that Alexandrian Christians used the "secret" version of Mark he described. Clement was overtly anti-homosexual (today we'd probably call him 'homophobic'). It was Clement who introduced into Christianity the somewhat platonic notion that "pleasure sought for its own sake, even within the marriage bonds, is a sin and contrary both to law and to reason" (although actually it was *not* contrary to law in Clement's Alexandria at that time).

In practical terms, Clement held that the intent to produce offspring is the only acceptable justification for sexual activity, so obviously this ruled out homosexual activity altogether. For this reason (to avoid attraction between men) Clement held that beards were required because nature so dictated. Beardlessness was a dangerous symptom of effeminacy in men, and was unnatural, Clement felt. That's likely why Egyptian Christian clergy (in the Coptic church) are always bearded, and why the same is true for clergy in all of the Orthodox (Eastern) churches.

And yet Clement clearly debunked the most potentially scandalous part ("naked man on naked man") of the quotation his recipient had asked about. Clement said that part, that phrase, had been added by the Capocratians, a libertine Christian sect of the time. One can guess, then, that Clement could not be very happy with the suggestiveness of the part of the 'secret' text that he actually did authenticate because of its suggestion, nonetheless, of erotic activity between Jesus and the initiate (i.e. spending the night with a naked stripling). So this would appear to add weight to Clement's admission that this version of Mark did exist and was indeed used in Christian rites in Alexandria at the time, whether Clement was personally happy about it or not.

If we had first heard about the 'Secret Mark' rite from a source who said it was performed by Zoroaster or Buddha, or some other non-Christian name-brand religious figure, would we even have paused long enough to be surprised? Most of our negative reaction to this story is not even religious in the broad sense—rather, instead, it springs from our residual piety and from our naïve conviction that we already know all that needs to be known about Jesus.

However, if 'Secret Mark' demonstrates anything conclusively it's that we really didn't know as much about Jesus as we thought we did. And most of what we think we know about him are later ideas and piety being read back into his story after many elapsed centuries. We need to remember, too, that like John the Baptist, Jesus himself was never a "Christian." We can't sum him up by applying to him a concept which developed after his lifetime.

The truth is that this initiation material is supremely religious territory, getting to the very essence of ancient religious practice. Any discomfort we may feel is likely owed to a naïve assumption that Christianity should be completely different from ancient religion *per se*, not sharing in its essential assumptions and rituals as it actually does to such a large extent.

● AFTER 'SECRET MARK'

In any case, after 'Secret Mark,' the story of the Bible's naked young *man* becomes the story of Jesus' naked young *men*. Singular becomes plural. There were a string of initiates, not just one. It was an ongoing ministry.

For starters, it is a fairly obvious assumption that Jesus must have initiated his close followers into the "kingdom of God." They, in turn, would presumably have initiated a wider circle as part of their inherited ministry, perhaps along with Jesus for a time, but certainly after his death.

Eusebius, the early church historian and Bishop of Caesarea in the early fourth century, wrote that Jesus had imparted "the higher knowledge" (enlightenment) to James the Just, John and Peter, and then that they entrusted this higher knowledge to the other apostles and in turn to a still larger group. That this is a reference to the enlightenment of initiation into the mysteries can hardly be avoided as a conclusion, especially after our learning of 'Secret Mark.'

This would seem to be fairly uncomplicated evidence that the Jesus initiations continued after his time, carried forward by those he had initiated. Eusebius dated this succession as "after his resurrection," but it is likely that this phrase is a mixture of true and false memory rolled into one, after four hundred long years. Jesus would have initiated these men during his lifetime, obviously, and they, in turn, probably carried on with their ministries of initiation after Jesus was no longer with them as a way of extending the ministry of their master as well as honoring his memory.

● JESUS AND NUDITY

On a more particular scale, what Jesus may have thought about nudity, or taught about it, or practiced of it, is pretty much beyond knowing, except that he was very familiar (and for his sake hopefully also comfortable) with it from his involvement with religious initiation rituals. There are some strange supposed quotations of his on the subject left behind, however. The Gospel of Thomas found at Nag Hammadi in Egypt, which hadn't made it into the official Bible, quotes Jesus as saying, "When you strip naked without being ashamed and take your clothes and place them under your feet like little children and stamp on them...."

Is this some kind of statement about having innocent hearts? Or could it be, as many scholars think, somehow about initiation rites? They suggest that the passage has to do with early Christian Baptismal practices, i.e. initiation, wherein nudity would have been a routine aspect because of immersion in water, as well as the symbolic need to take off old clothing and put on new clothing, a traditional feature of religious initiation stretching back well into ancient Egypt or longer. Egyptian initiates finished the ritual not by just putting their clothes back on again, but by donning a totally new garment which had never before been worn.

Another saying from the Gospel of Thomas is equally perplexing. In answer to a question, Jesus says his disciples "are like little children who have installed themselves in a field which is not theirs. When the owners of the field come, they will say 'Release to us our field.' They [the disciples] will take off their clothes before them to release [the field] to them…" It certainly seems that there must be some meaning to the reference to clothing (or the lack thereof) here, but you're doing a lot better than I am if you can figure out what that meaning is. Is it again possible that this seemingly gratuitous reference to nudity could have some link to initiation rituals such as Baptism where nudity or partial nudity would have been a routine part of the ritual? Probably. At least so think the experts.

In any case, we know nudity was part of religious initiation, and we know (from the canonical New Testament as well as from 'Secret Mark') that Jesus was a practitioner of such initiation. So there's no doubt that Jesus saw a lot of naked or extremely scantily clad people in his day. And realizing that, it's not such a big surprise to imagine that he was naked, or nearly so, together with others with some frequency given his line of work. What we can't tell at this distance is how he might have been erotically affected by such exposure, if he was at all. Our only significant hint is 'Secret Mark.'

All of this religious (or mystical) initiation stuff, which can appear so eccentric and exotic to our 21st century eyes, had been going on eons before Jesus, and it's kept going on after him too. It continued in organized Christianity even though we don't hear a whole lot about it from official sources. By the time the later evangelists put their words down on parchment or papyrus, the Christian community had lost its eye witnesses to Jesus completely and was beginning to edit its communal memories (probably already by Mark's time, but certainly by the time of the three who followed him as evangelists). Theology was taking hold, and with it a variety of takes on who Jesus was. The later New Testament record had already begun to be influenced in various directions by one or another of these interpretations.

There were also secret traditions which were closely held by the elite of the church, but thought not suitable for the plebeian masses; for what I like to call the guys in the pew. Bishop Clement, our man in Alexandria, is quoted as saying, "Not everything that is true needs necessarily to be divulged to all men."

Not much later his successor, Origen, refers to a semen anointing ritual that evidently went on in church circles there. The leading participant, called "Father," applied the chrism, or "seal," to one described as the "son" or "youth." The recipient then avowed: "I have been anointed with the white chrism from the 'Tree of Life.'" This rather outlandish sounding ceremony has been linked by scholars, not very surprisingly, to the 'Secret Mark' initiation. (Alexandria in those days must have been a rather interesting place to come of age for a male Christian!)

Through the ages since, Christian initiation has tamed down quite a bit. For probably the majority of the Christian world Baptism has shifted to infants, which it would seem has taken the sex out of it, but not always the nudity. And definitely not the magic. If anything, infant Baptism has become even more of a magical rite. A splash of water, a few words, and presto—the baby, who has not the faintest notion what is going on, has been "saved" and is now eligible to spend eternity with the good guy, not with the red guy with horns and a pointy tail. (Maybe because of the sheer irrationality of "initiating" infants into the mysteries of religion, many today call these Baptisms 'Christenings,' and focus on the aspect of officially naming the baby. This at least makes some sense, although it pretty much decimates the ages-long tradition of religious initiation.)

As recently as last century Christian missionaries would sneak into African huts when the parents were out hunting, and would baptize the infants. No follow up was necessary because the babies were now saved; they were now "Christians." Magic. Much earlier a Marian shrine in Bern, Switzerland, was famous for the miraculous revivals of stillborn babies, but revived just long enough for them to be Baptized. Once again, the dead babies were saved. Magic again? Or just really disappointingly crass religious superstition? Either way initiation into Christianity is now reduced to a formula which confers a magical benefit, but discards the resulting enlightenment which for previous eons had been the treasured prize and primary point of the exercise..

Infant Baptism in effect broke Christian initiation into two parts. Instruction had always been a major part of the rite. This impartation of wisdom was an integral part of the ritual, maybe even its whole point. But infants are not very accomplished at digesting wisdom on the spot. So the church tore out the instruction part and moved it a few years down the road from the actual Baptism. It was then labeled "Confirmation" and in a large part of the Christian world it has become a sacrament, on a nearly equal footing with Baptism itself.

Still, the whole process has been diluted with time. The "wisdom" imparted with Confirmation is hardly the life-changing mystical vision of ancient initiation. It's now basically just being instructed about church doctrines and being made to memorize some stuff which the teenager is likely to quickly forget, to his probable relief. Christian initiation has become a tepid echo of what it was in its heyday.

It has, however, kept a certain resonance in modern life. Secret societies still preserve secret initiations which involve nudity (at least 'ritual' nudity, as in the case of the Masons); enact ritual death, ritual burial, and ritual resurrection; physical manipulation; and a hoped for transformation of the initiate—from Masons around the world to the secret societies at Yale. Even the Boy Scouts get in on the act with their Order of the Arrow inductions. And many a guy has experienced a fraternity initiation at university which in all likelihood involved some nudity, often accompanied with tactile involvement as well. Whether wisdom is actually imparted in any of this is a totally different question. In any case, rites of passage in general are probably an echo of early religious initiation, minus most of the enlightenment.

The Europeans who first came to the 'new world' discovered indigenous people who used mushrooms which they called "flesh of god." Religious initiation and rituals of mystical discoveries had preceded the European Christians, reminding us that as deeply invested in religious initiation as Christianity is, the concept is hardly exclusive to our current religion. Its roots stretch far back into the practice of the general religious instincts of mankind and the general mythology of religion all men share.

● BEFORE 'SECRET MARK'

St. Mark, by popular Christian tradition, has been seen as the first bishop and founder of Christianity in Alexandria, and if so this would lend even more weight to the idea of many bits of his complete writings circulating in the city long after his time there, even though perhaps they were not known to Christian circles in other areas. Some scholars disparage the tradition of Mark having been the first bishop of Alexandria but, on this and many similar historical questions, popular traditions handed down over generations are the best, if maybe the only, evidence we have.

For my purposes in telling you this story, however, St. Mark and 'Secret Mark' being tied to Egypt provides a good segue—because Egypt is an indispensable key to understanding Jesus and Christianity, and even more specifically, to understanding the initiations described in 'Secret Mark.'

Morton Smith argued that the story of Lazarus began as a memory of a ritual, but then ended up being treated in the Bible as history. In Baptism

41

the candidate is symbolically drowned (the 'old man'), buried (the linen shroud), and then arises from death (as a 'new man,' now enlightened). But such rituals certainly didn't begin with Christians, or even with figures like John the Baptist (who of course was never a Christian at all despite many churches being named for him).

The roots of such rituals, and maybe the seed of the Biblical Lazarus story itself, are deeply embedded in ancient Egyptian religion—beginning with the myth of the resurrection of Osiris by Horus.

Ah, ancient Egypt! Those ego-mad Pharaohs who built themselves monumental tombs we call pyramids, and did so on the backs of the Jews enslaved in Egypt. Our story continues there.

If we wanted to detour, our scholarly friends might have more surprises in store for us. Many of them believe the pyramids are not what we thought, and that the Jews may not even have been there in significant numbers to provide useful labor as they were being built. Some even suggest that it was the Jews who were the slave masters and not the enslaved. It seems that much scholarship today points to the purpose of the pyramids as not being tombs at all, at least those at Giza. They seem to have had functionality as astrological observatories, water system pumps, and perhaps all manner of other technological and practical engineering purposes, these newer theories say. There are still those who believe they were merely tombs, of course.

However interesting all of this may be, our story does not center in sociology, the history of Judaism *per se*, or ancient archeology. So let's not get sidetracked. But we do have to consider those pyramids in any case; at least the 'Great' pyramid of Giza, not all that far away from Alexandria where 'Secret Mark' held sway.

To get right to the point, a number of serious scholars believe that the whole and sole purpose of the Giza pyramids may actually have been to serve as places to conduct the initiation of young men into the great mysteries. Certainly they have served that function for centuries past and were well known for that role. Even Napoleon Bonaparte, knowing of this tradition, spent a night in the great pyramid of Khufu after his army conquered Egypt, and emerged the next morning quite shaken. He is said never to have uttered a later word about the experience. (For a fascinating description of spending a night in the Khufu pyramid see Paul Brunton's "A Search in Secret Egypt" republished 2015.)

Among the Giza pyramids, Khufu's (the largest, or "great" pyramid) contains roughly at its center (so far as explorers have been able to discern and measure) a large granite box which for all the world looks like a sarcophagus and for a long time was thought to be one.

42

But more recent Egyptologists have been puzzled by at least two strange aspects—the "sarcophagus" has apparently never been used for a burial, and it has no lid. A lid would have been necessary if it was intended for the king's burial. And any idea that the lid had been stolen by tomb robbers has been discarded because no one can figure out how an object that large and heavy could have been removed through steeply inclined passage ways so small that explorers have to nearly crawl through them on their bellies— almost no adult could navigate some of the passages completely upright.

Some scholars think the stone boxes, or at least the one in the Khufu pyramid, were indeed built as sarcophagi, but just not to hold the king's body, or even anyone's body after death. At least after actual death. Instead, they were built and installed in the pyramids to facilitate ritual death during initiations into the mysteries, the theory goes. A rather elaborate cousin to the shrouds over naked bodies we've been considering.

And even if the main function of the Giza pyramids was not to serve merely as the setting for individual initiations, scholars have pointed out that they can and do serve an initiatory purpose just by being. By subsuming within themselves all of the relevant statistical (mathematical) ratios needed to have a clear picture of the earth from a northern hemisphere perspective, the pyramids could "initiate people far ahead in the future" (Graham Hancock) by causing them to ask the right questions. This process was termed "initiating yourself," or initiating oneself.

This long after the building of the great pyramid it is pretty unlikely we'll ever know the true intention which motivated the enormous expense and effort needed for its construction. Its connection with the initiations into the mysteries is not necessarily lost no matter what that intention was, however. Even if it was built as a tomb for the king, it could have, and evidently was, also used for initiations in due course. In other words, if, as first thought, it was built to house the actual dead and facilitate their transition to the after-life, it could also have been used for substantial periods of time to initiate the ritually dead and facilitate their ritual resurrection.

Life and death, or at least the effort to understand life and death, may be the most easy to trace common concern of most of mankind's religions. It may be manifested as trying to placate the gods, or trying to get right with God, but the common denominator is still trying to have as good a life as possible in the here and now, while trying to avoid any evils that death might bring, such as eternal punishment.

But it was more than that at the same time. It was about understanding the mysteries of life and death while still living. It was about experiencing first-hand the freedom of the soul so the fear of death would not dominate life. It was about deciphering mysteries through initiation.

Religious initiation's origins fade into the mists of time. But their footprints are everywhere, even among native peoples of the "new world." It is those of ancient Egypt which are more germane to our Biblical naked man and to Jesus, however, because Christianity in such a large measure itself came out of Egypt (a theme we'll explore throughout this book from a variety of perspectives).

We know that the initiations into the mysteries in ancient Egypt centered on the experience of death (in a trance which mimicked death) and then resurrection. The 'death' and the 'resurrection' covered a three day period (ring a bell?). Linen sheets were utilized. The subjects were striplings. Scholars have discovered other similarities with the Bible's Lazarus stories, such as the use of some specific words and gestures which came from the Egyptians and ended up in the Bible.

Many scholars think Jesus learned his magic in Egypt, and even the much edited New Testament material admits a link between Jesus and Egypt—a link which early Christians, who kept the Jesus story alive and ultimately wrote the New Testament, might have preferred to downplay or erase, yet felt obligated to at least acknowledge quickly in passing. So the Egypt admission in the New Testament, though perhaps sort of begrudging, is a powerful one indeed. In the long run, the separation between the ancient initiations into the mysteries in Egypt and the Jesus of 'Secret Mark' is a very tiny separation, if it is a separation at all.

The initiated stripling was supposed to experience the freedom of his soul from his body. The soul could then wander at will and see its true status unencumbered by the body. Christians are still singing that song all these centuries later, only now they say it happens only after real death, not after ritual death during an initiation. The image of the soul rising up from a body is still used in religious circles—never mind that it doesn't represent what Biblical Christianity actually teaches. That image, nonetheless, is a good visualization of what was believed to happen during ancient initiations—the soul left the body and then returned at the initiate's awakening, in the meantime having experienced deep mysteries which words alone would have been inadequate to convey. Some writers have described these Egyptian (and Greek) initiations into the mysteries as controlled, or chemically induced, NDEs (the accidental near death experiences talked about so much in our time).

As I've indicated, a number of writers understand this 'secret Mark' story as a more detailed version of the story of the raising of Lazarus found in John's Gospel. They call it a "mystery school" initiation, but encoded when mentioned in the Bible. Among the clues are the usual three days of death, and the words "Lazarus, come forth," the same words used in ancient Egypt (just change the name of the initiate each time). Such

44

initiation was to give the recipient personal experience that the soul can live outside the body, and that the awakened initiate would emerge enlightened. Many scholars point out that cycles of ritual death and rebirth used in the mystery cults are common patterns and themes in mythology throughout the world and that they reach back as far as we can know anything about our ancestors.

Experience is the best teacher. Our civilization understands that—so did the ancient Egyptians. They looked at religious ceremonies as drama from which people could learn, could absorb the lessons, by participation, by direct experience. That was the basis of initiation into the mysteries. Wise men could lecture young men until they went blue in the face telling how the soul could rove unencumbered outside the body, and how it would leave the body at death, and thus why fear of death should not dominate life, and/or whatever other religious message they wanted to relate. But how much would the young men actually absorb? The best way for these lessons to be learned, for this enlightenment to occur, was for the young man to actually experience them. Well, you don't kill off the younger generation for the sake of a religious lesson, so you do it ritually. Initiation was a ritual experience of death yielding back to new life.

Initiation was participatory religious drama. The lesson was experienced rather than conceptualized. Jesus had learned the technique too, apparently. The enlightenment he gave to his initiates was achieved by an experience, not a lecture (or a sermon). The Bible suggests that he was an accomplished preacher, but thanks to Morton Smith, we now know that he may have had other, more exotic and more potent, ways to convey religious enlightenment.

● NOTE ON INITIATION

As we've discussed it here, religious initiation seems to be an esoteric and complicated affair—and not that many centuries ago it was indeed. It's worth keeping in mind, however, that at its heart initiation is a fairly simple and straight-forward human custom. It is merely, at heart, the ritualization of a significant transition. It can take on elaborate form and formula, but it doesn't need to.

The individual being initiated is about to leave something of significance behind, such as childhood, and then to enter a new reality. In the ancient initiations into the religious mysteries, the individual left behind a status of ignorance and naivety and entered the new reality of enlightenment. Initiation takes place when the individual embraces a new status, being helped and prompted to do so by individuals who themselves have previously made the same transition. In our time a religious initiation can be as relatively simple as a bar mitzvah, or a bat mitzvah, or a confirmation ceremony. In our secular lives it can be as simple as a birthday party at a key age, or as elaborate as a high school graduation party. It is the acknowledgement of the individual taking the first steps into a new situation or condition or status.

As we look back to Biblical times or even earlier, the basic difference between then and now is that initiation then was not only the mark and acknowledgement of a transition, but an attempt to force and shape that transition and the status to be entered. It was thought that the transition happened, at least to some extent, because the initiation event took place. The initiation was seen as an active cause of the transition. That could still be said about Baptism, technically and theologically.

Nowadays we're rather more casual about these things however, and our initiations are basically just celebrations of transitions which have already taken place or will take place regardless of whatever ritual we attach to them. We've definitely eased up on the enlightenment aspect, probably unfortunately. And we rarely think of the initiation as the cause of the transition; just as a mark (acknowledgement) or celebration of it. In that sense, the religion aspect has in large measure dropped out of our understanding of initiations.

One aspect that may have survived the passage of time, at least to a minor extent, is the use of chemical enhancements in shaping the experience. Most of us have left 'magic mushrooms' in the distant past but not necessarily their modern equivalents, especially if one sees alcohol as one of the potential hallucinogens. But any chemicals used during contemporary initiations are most likely regarded as part of the celebration rather than part of the initiation itself. Their function is no longer to open the eyes of the initiate to new reality.

● NOTE ON THE NAKED YOUNG MAN

It nearly goes without saying that not everyone professionally steeped in the New Testament will agree with the understanding of the naked young man I've put forward here. For starters, not all Biblical historians, and especially not all theologians, have yet come to accept Morton Smith's discovery as genuine. They may not accuse him of an outright hoax, but they nevertheless don't accept at face value what the discovered text says (so maybe I should not say they don't accept Morton Smith; maybe they refuse to accept the church father Clement of Alexandria, or for that matter the evangelist St. Mark). Accepting 'Secret Mark' at face value is, after all, a gigantic leap for a traditional Christian—it fundamentally changes one's assessment of Jesus and his ministry.

Without that acceptance, they are free to (actually probably forced to) lean on older and sometimes rather esoteric sounding explanations for this challenging Biblical passage about the young man who fled from the scene naked. One of these is that there simply never was a naked young man in

46

the garden when Jesus was arrested, despite Mark having written an apparently uncomplicated declarative sentence claiming that there was such a person at the scene. Mark's intention, some feel, was only to make a literary allusion, but that he did so by inventing and inserting a minor character.

This approach sees the explanation in Mark's use of language. Nakedness is taken to represent poverty. It's an involved construction, and rather than attempting to describe it I think it's more honest if I just admit that I have some trouble following it, and also to the extent I do understand it that I don't really buy it. The context also seems to argue against this interpretation. One can come up with reasons for a young man in a sheet to be part of the scene at the arrest of Jesus, even if it's a challenge to do so. But that scene seems on the surface to be a very odd place for Mark to want to insert a coded discussion about poverty.

What is especially interesting to me here is that those who espouse interpretations like this are opting to declare a piece of the New Testament as a fiction even though it is stated as what would appear to be a piece of history. In most other areas these same people may argue that aspects of the New Testament others view as allegory should really be accepted as history (such as the resurrection itself). Ultimately it's the same pick-and-choose method of Biblical interpretation which has tempted so many, generation after generation, including even people of great scholarly achievement.

Young men exist and they did during Jesus' day as well. They can be naked or they can be covered. They can show up in unexpected places and circumstances. So far there is nothing offered by Mark in this passage which unduly strains credulity. The only questions are why Mark called attention to the young man and why did he fit into the story Mark was telling. So there's no reason to assume that Mark did not mean what he wrote—no reason to say that he was really just making a rarified literary allusion instead. 'Secret Mark' provides the easiest way to understand and interpret the young man in a sheet.

Resurrection of the dead is a different story, however. Credulity is mightily strained for the sober observer at its very mention because both human experience and science tell us that it doesn't happen in the world of cold, hard reality. Mark may have believed it happened to Jesus, as increasingly did his religious community. But that's a matter of faith and witness rather than history.

Now we have learned but pious observers looking at Mark's gospel and telling us that Mark's simple and apparently straight forward reference to a young man is not what Mark was actually saying. The young man didn't really exist because...why? Because he was inconvenient to the way they want to see the whole of the Jesus story? Yet at the same time they expect that the Biblical reader should readily accept the incredible claim that Jesus rose from the dead.

If Mark presented two ideas—the perfectly credible, if confusing, one that there was a young man in only a sheet at Gethsemane, and the infinitely less credible one that Jesus rose from the dead—why aim one's disapproval at the more credible of the two? The only answer I can see is that these good folks want the resurrection to be true (as we all would prefer), but for some reason find the naked young man somehow threatening (to Jesus' image?) or at least mightily inconvenient. So the incredible becomes more palatable than the credible.

My point is that religious faith is not needed to accept the young man's presence at Gethsemane as history, but religious faith is necessary to accept Jesus' resurrection as history. It would seem to turn things upside-down to insist that the young man was merely a piece of allegory while the resurrection was straight-forward history. Based on humanity's long experience, resurrection is implausible, not to say impossible (from a historical viewpoint). Finding a scantily clad young man in any number of settings is at least plausible, even when it seems a bit exotic or inappropriate.

In any case, I add this footnote only in an attempt to be prudent, balanced, and respectful of some very learned and intelligent professionals who would disagree with the picture I've painted. Throughout this book you can safely assume that my conclusions or suggestions do not sum up the whole of scholarly opinion, although usually they point to the majority slice of scholarship, I think. Scholarship itself, even at its most erudite, always has its dissenters. And when the topic is religion, there are probably an equal number of opinions as there are people paying attention. Christianity in its peculiar way is a very democratic religion—full of dogma and doctrine, yet in the long run its adherents pretty much believe what they want to believe and reject what they don't care to believe. ⌘

3.

Just doing what Gods are supposed to do: Virgin Birth

Time magazine during my student days ran a column labeled "Religion." One of my seminary professors found that to be upsetting because they used the same space to report on Christianity as well as news from any other religion which merited reporting. His beef was that Christianity should not be lumped in with any other religion because, I guess, Christianity was the truth whereas other religions were mere collections of superstitions and myth (Christians worship God, while others worship the gods, plus a few nit-picks about the nature of religion). He felt Christianity should not even be categorized as a religion—it had risen above mere religion. I was always a little mystified as to the distinction he was making. I've come across a writer or two who try to make the same point—that Christianity is somehow a different category than mere "religion"—but I'm not convinced that making the distinction is much at all beyond piety and religious loyalty to Christianity.

I could not in seminary, and still can't today, put my finger on any aspect of Christianity which is not religion in the traditional sense the word implies. Christianity's chief character was born, yes. But his mother supposedly never had sex with a man, and his father was not a human being. Then this guy without a human father taught, according to the Bible, that the road to salvation was open only to people who ate his flesh and drank his blood.

That doesn't sound like Ozzie and Harriet. It sounds like religion to me, whether you want to label it Christianity or not. There simply *is no* distinction between Christianity and religion in general. Christianity is religion, with all of the participation in mythology and superstition thereby implied. Ultimately Christianity gets around to dredging up, in one way or another, every feature of mankind's general universal religion, admirable or lamentable, reasonable or fantastical.

Christians naturally think of Jesus as unique. Who else had a virgin for a mother? Who else rose from being dead to being alive again? If you're talking about humans, very few if any, we can say with some confidence.

But if you're talking about gods, Jesus is suddenly just a face in the crowd. Lots of them had virgin mothers. Few were adversely affected by death. As a god, Jesus has lots of company. He set about doing what a god does routinely. His birthday wasn't even unique—gods back then seemed to have a propensity to be born on 25 December.

In other words, the religious woods were full of figures born of a virgin, figures who could cause 'miracles,' figures who were at least partially god (if perhaps just one parent was divine), figures who fed their people with their own flesh and blood, figures who could fend off permanent death, etc. And these figures appear everywhere, in all areas of the world and in lore with roots as far back in time as we can trace. Jesus is unique only in our particular religious folklore, not in that of the world at large. He is just one entry in a long list of Hero-Gods (and the early Christians worked hard to gain him a spot on that list, claiming to all who would listen that their Jesus was just as much of a god as those already recognized as such).

● VIRGIN BIRTH(S)

The idea of the hero's mother being a virgin is part of a larger set of ideas and themes which appear everywhere we can find evidence of ancient religious and cultural mythology. We could think of this as a kind of universal religious format or template. It also includes resurrection of the hero figure, a place where the dead go to continue some sort of existence (for Christians, think Heaven), and usually a great flood affecting all of humanity (think Noah and his ark—the one in the Bible, not the one in Kentucky).

These ideas could be given the gloss description of "pagan" because they precede Christianity, which is where the linguistic and chronological line is usually drawn in our use of the word (although academics might draw the line later because of linguistic and historical factors). Just as in the Judeo-Christian tradition, these mythological elements found expression in song (hymns and psalms) and dance, gave work and status to a priestly class who celebrated and taught them in liturgical formulae, and attracted theologian-type thinkers to ponder and interpret them.

These themes first show up in "modern" times in the ancient Greek mystery dramas and the equally old mystery religious practices and ritual of ancient Egypt. From there they eventually filtered into Christianity.

In other words, Jesus was by no means the first of these 'heroes' and Christianity did not invent most of the ideas we associate with him, including that of being born of a virgin. Christianity did not even begin with all of these universal themes, but came to them as part of its development, having been pushed irrevocably in that direction by Paul in his shift away from Judaism. Both the virgin birth and the resurrection are Jesus themes which took some time to be fully incorporated into the Christian story, so Christianity began to be plugged into the great universal religious mythology several decades down the road from the supposed time of Jesus. It was a gradual process rather than a sudden revelation.

At first Jesus was evidently seen mostly as a wisdom teacher or a magician (those frequent miracles). It took Christianity a few centuries to settle on a uniform way of viewing and speaking of the Incarnation (the idea that Jesus was actually God who took on a human body and existence, and then entered into his own creation). A lot of the ideas and concepts we associate today with Christianity seem like they must have been part of the package from the very beginning because we are so familiar with them, but in actuality most of them developed through a process of thought and debate over some time, whether just a few years or in some cases several centuries.

Even the declaration of Jesus as the Messiah does not seem to give him unique status. There were plenty of men in that general era who decided they were likely the long awaited Messiah, or who were seen in that role by others. Jesus was probably one of them, although much of the Biblical language pointing in that direction may have been added later so it gets a bit murky, as is the case with so many of our images of Jesus.

The Dead Sea Scrolls discovered at Qumran suggested to scholars that many of the themes and teachings believed earlier to be specific to Jesus were actually in circulation long before his time. This is why a famous *New Yorker* article on the Dead Sea Scrolls said the monastery of Qumran "is perhaps, more than Bethlehem...the cradle of Christianity."

Even inside the New Testament the idea of the Incarnation of God as a man is not treated as unique to Jesus—the Biblical character Simon Magus was thought to be an incarnation of God, and when Paul and Barnabas preached in Lycaonia they were recognized by the crowd as Zeus and Hermes, and the priest of Zeus began preparation for a sacrifice to them. Acts 8:9-24.

Simon Magus, or Simon the Magician, did bequeath to us an interesting word, "simony," by trying to purchase apostolic power in the early Christian church (he wanted to be able to produce miraculous healings and other apparently magical feats he observed the real apostles accomplish). When that didn't work (because the apostles thought he was trying to buy his way into their club), he gave us a foretaste of much later behavior by many disgruntled Protestants—he is said to have just gone off and started his own church. Some scholars think, by the way, that Simon Magus was just offering "thank you" money, according to his understanding of Greek custom, rather than offering an actual bribe. Nevertheless he was turned down in his quest to become an apostle with miraculous powers, and he became just another minor Biblical character who was little more than a quick blip on the book's radar. His self-promoted apostolic candidacy, however, puts him in big-time company in the person of Paul—although Paul, of course, was never accused of trying to purchase the apostolic title, which he simply appropriated for himself instead.

Almost everyone who studies Christianity agrees that the concept of the Virgin Birth of Jesus was borrowed from widespread and ancient mythology. It was used not because early Christians wanted to make a biological point about Jesus, but it *was needed* to *make* a point in any case— that point was to assert that Jesus was divine, as supposedly were those born of virgins before him. Jesus was being portrayed as divine because he stood in the company of other 'gods' who were also born of virgins.

The concept was a symbol used to make a theological point. The discussion was about religion, not about biology as it might seem to have been at first glance. It wasn't even so much a description of a particular 'miracle,' as it was an attempt to plug Jesus into a list of gods so that he was also seen as a god. It has also been suggested that the same process was applied by ancient story tellers to the other of the Bible's towering figures, Moses. The baby-in-the-bulrushes story has many folkloric counterparts throughout the world, scholars say, and was used in the Bible as a device to set Moses apart from mere mortals.

In the long run, the whole 'virgin birth' mythology which began as a way of demonstrating that Jesus was a god like other gods who were born of virgins, evolved from belonging exclusively to the Jesus cult to belonging more to the cult of Mary the mother than of Jesus. For many Christians today, 'virgin birth' evokes the mother, not the son.

Some even think it was Mary herself who had the virgin birth, confusing it with the doctrine of the "immaculate conception" which does apply to Mary. Immaculate conception belongs to the sex-negative area of Christian thinking.

Routine conception was thought to pass along 'original sin.' Normal conception therefore was not pure enough for a woman destined to give birth to God the Son. So God the Father had to give a pass to the particular sex act which produced her—a waiver from the deed which under normal circumstances would have passed on 'original sin' to the next generation. Mary did have a human father, unlike Jesus, the church says, but unlike everyone else, unlike the rest of us, she was not contaminated by the act which made her mother pregnant. (The Virgin birth theme might seem to belong to the sex-negative Christian attitude as well, but in actuality it is not a commentary on sex at all, but on the transmission of divinity.)

As one moves from north to south in Europe, Jesus seems to move from the center of the Christian story into almost a bit part. Mary takes over center stage. On the magnificent mosaic façade of Orvieto (Italy) cathedral it is the coronation of the Virgin which holds the primary space and focus, as it does also in the apse mosaic inside the great church of Santa Maria Maggiore in Rome. Mary by this point was considered, at least in popular piety, as nearly part of God herself, as if the Trinity had gained a fourth member. (The concept of the coronation of the virgin mother of the hero is a theme which can be found in the most ancient of religious mythology, and thus is not a Christian invention at all, but a 'pagan' one.)

As if this tendency to place Mary on an equal footing with God (or the three Trinitarian gods of Christianity), were not surprising (or idolatrous) enough, an even more extreme devotion was flirted with by some for a time—that Mary was not only mother of Jesus, and hence "mother of God," but that she was mother of the *entire* Trinity, i.e. mother of God writ as large as the idea could possibly grow in Christian terms. Iconographic images started to appear by the fourteenth century in which the whole Trinity was pictured in Mary's womb. While this trend remained a fringe devotion of a minority of Christians and later faded away, it found later echoes in the (also eventually dismissed) theological concept that Mary should be regarded as "Co-Redemptrix" (co-redeemer) along with her son.

By the time a European traveler moving southward reaches Rome, the pilgrim is enveloped in an area deeply enthralled with Mary to this day. The iconography for Jesus has also shifted, now relying heavily on the sunburst, one of the clearest examples being the elaborate golden sunburst with a simple IHS in the center at the church of Andrew and Bartolomeo in Orvieto. Mary has begun to take on quasi-divine status and her son has become a Sun God. It begins to feel as though the border with Egypt should be just a few miles down the road, but in fact, the *religious* border with Egypt has already been crossed.

Rome may have officially adopted Christianity, but it was Christianity that was changed in the bargain, not so much Rome. The Romans were not about to abandon their goddesses or religious virgins, so Christianity had to replace the ones she had stolen from the Romans. It took a little time, but relatively soon things were back to normal and the Romans were again besotted with their goddess, this time flying under the name "Mary," or better yet, "Virgin Mary."

● MOTHERS OF GODS

The Koran also speaks of Jesus as born of a virgin. It has been observed that, ironically, this may mean there are more Muslims who take the concept seriously today than there are even Christians who do so.

Important as the 'virgin birth' doctrine is in some parts of Christianity (because of cultic devotion to the virgin mother) it is interesting to note that the whole concept of the virgin birth of Jesus may be the result of a translation error. Isaiah 7:14 "Therefore the Lord himself will give you a sign. Behold, a young woman shall conceive and bear a son, and shall call his name Immanuel." In Matthew 1:23 this became "Behold, a virgin shall conceive..." Evidently the best translation would be simply "young woman of marriageable age." In trying to write the story of Jesus, Matthew and Luke seem to have relied on the Septuagint version of Isaiah (the Greek translation from Hebrew) over the Hebrew version, because they add a word which is specific in describing a young woman who is still a virgin.

Lest we assume that Mary fixation is only a mark of Roman Catholicism, we're told that some Protestants burned early copies of the RSV translation of the Bible in the mid-20th century because it translated the "young woman" word correctly rather than as the "virgin" these protestors were sure was the actual 'word of God.' Of course, such a protest was also a commentary on Biblical literalism—the excised 'virgin' could not have been a mistake because it had been right there in the Bible in black and white!

Nothing in our education as Christians has prepared us to look at these markers as anything less than unique to Jesus. So to find out that concepts such as these were fairly commonplace religious notions of the early Christian period and earlier, and that many other "gods" were said to have been born of virgins and to have been resurrected after death, can come as a relatively big shock to some. However, virgin birth (or sometimes merely birth seeded by a god without the involvement of semen from a human male—not quite the same thing as a virgin giving birth) has been attributed to many prominent religious figures. Even some Roman emperors were given the virgin birth treatment because they were seen as super-human figures. To be born of a virgin was to be an exceptional human—not a run-of-the-mill guy on the street, but extraordinary in one or more ways.

The Egyptologist E.A. Wallis Budge says that the early Christians were bestowing some of the attributes of Isis upon the Virgin Mary by describing her in ways which they had regarded as peculiar to Isis. Indeed, the link between the great Egyptian goddess and the exalted mother of Jesus shows up in a lot of writing about Mary.

This is the track another Egyptologist, Ahmed Osman, finds himself on when pointing out that the virgin mother concept in Christianity likely grew out of ancient Egypt. Isis, it was said, conceived her son Horus by re-creating and using the phallus of Osiris, her brother and husband, after his death and dismemberment when the phallus was lost. But later, he points out, development of the legend rid it of its physical connotations and related the pregnancy of Isis to a cosmic force. In Egypt the cosmic force was the sun, the chief god, while in Christianity the force was also the chief god who was iconographically and metaphorically linked to the sun.

These and many other Egyptologists point out that the numerous pictures and sculptures of Isis suckling her child Horus formed the foundation for the figures and ubiquitous paintings of the Madonna and Child in Christian culture. They also suggest that stories of the wanderings of the Virgin with the Child in Egypt, recorded in the Apocryphal Gospels, reflect scenes from the life of Isis.

One of them asserts that Christianity grew so rapidly in Egypt (the Copts) because it closely resembled the worship of Isis. Now, the 'mother of the god' was Mary, the new Isis. The framework for understanding religion had not really changed very much.

Historians are quick to point out that much of the Biblical Christmas story doesn't hold up as history. Such aspects as the mother being impregnated by a god, the trip back to Bethlehem, the manger birth, the shepherds, the Magi ('wise men,' actually magicians; probably Zoroastrian priests), the slaughter of the innocents—they are not historical facts but metaphors used by early Christian writers to enhance the significance of Jesus. The flight to Egypt is also probably not history in the way it is portrayed in the Christmas story (unless, as has been suggested by some historians, Jesus was actually born in Egypt), but it is very likely actual history if placed elsewhere in the Jesus saga (probably during Jesus' 'lost' or 'silent' years). In other words, early Christian writers often strengthened the case for Jesus being a god by ascribing to him the same attributes associated with other humans who came to be regarded as gods.

After reading Chapter 1, you may wonder what happened to the venerable James the Just, considered the first bishop of Jerusalem, and the other siblings of Jesus, one of whom may have (it could actually have been a cousin of Jesus and James) succeeded James after James' martyrdom. Why did they fade so completely out of our Biblical account except for a small role for James in Acts?

The reason, most likely, is that they were gradually edited out because their existence conflicted with the growing cult of the Virgin—Jesus could have no siblings if Mary were "ever virgin." That's also likely the reason that Mary of Magdala seems so buried in Biblical accounts—any woman who could be seen as a rival to the Virgin, even just for attention, needed to be pushed into the background, even though the Magdalene's piercing light still shines through occasional cracks in the story. (If one's concept of Christianity ended with a face value reading of the four gospels, one could come away thinking Mary Magdalene was a character of major importance in the story but that Mary the mother played only a minor, albeit utilitarian, role—the Magdalene is mentioned twice as many times as the mother.)

So Jesus' "virgin birth" was not unique to him. One prominent Christian thinker has suggested it was not even intended to be believed literally, and that indeed it may not have been believed literally by most early Christians. He points out that it took almost one hundred years for the virgin birth part of the story to really take hold.

The Christian 'cult' of the Virgin, which developed gradually, seems to owe its existence and imagery mostly to Egypt, and especially to the early Christian monasteries in Egypt. Egypt already had the "Mother of God" concept and symbolism in the goddess Isis, which seems to have opened the way for Mary to be eventually also considered, and loved, as Theotokos [Greek: "bearer of god"], essentially becoming, for Christians, a replacement for Isis.

Throughout this book my approach to Mary the Virgin Mother is that for Christians she became the embodiment of the great mother goddess figure of general universal religion, and thus at least an echo of Isis, the Egyptian Queen of Heaven. In the first chapter I suggested that the signature story of Roman Catholicism was the search for a Christian version of that mother goddess.

There are scholars who love to start splitting hairs at this point. One can find discussions of some religious virgins who had lots of sex and yet could claim virginity because their hymens were still intact. These are then contrasted with Mary whose hymen was supposedly still intact despite her having given birth (to Jesus). That focus twists the story into evaluating various types of virgins and arguing about whether they play the same function religiously, etc. Does it really matter that some 'virgins' with religious roles to play might have differed from Mary on technical, or theoretical, grounds? And for that matter, the word 'virgin' was used at times to designate a married woman who had renounced sexual activity at a certain later point in her life, so the technicalities of what constituted a religious virgin were already a bit amorphous.

My point is just that Christianity wanted and needed a goddess and spent a lot of effort and adoration (and time) coming up with one. She didn't necessarily have to be a virgin. Isis, another mother of God, was not portrayed as a virgin. The great mother goddess of general religious mythology was not associated with virginity. That Christianity ended up installing a goddess who was reputed to be a virgin is almost an accident, or at least incidental in that "virgin" and "goddess" are not mutually dependent. We certainly don't need to fret about the physical technicalities of her virginity.

The real point is that general universal human religion demands a goddess, and Christianity eventually came up with one which satisfied that need within its own emotional and mythological system. Sophia might have done the job, or maybe even Isis. But it ended up being Mary the mother of Jesus, and she also already carried the label of "virgin."

Mary was first seen as a virgin because Jesus needed to be born of a virgin in order to be seen as a god—gods in those days tended to be born of virgins. So at first it could be said that Mary's virginity had more to do with her son than with her. Mary needed to be a virgin for Jesus' sake, not for her own sake.

Then as Christianity evolved, she began to take up the role of mother goddess. But she had already been tagged a 'virgin' for other reasons. The goddess role did not depend on her being a virgin, just as the virgin designation at the birth of Jesus did not require her to be (yet) a goddess.

Therefore it seems to me that it helps clarify our understanding if we look at the doctrine of the Virgin Birth this way: At first it was about Jesus (he needed a mother who was a virgin because he needed to be seen as a god). Then, gradually, the focus of the concept shifted to Mary herself (she was religiously potent because God had chosen her to give birth to his son with God himself being the father). As Christian thought and practice evolved, virginity became increasingly regarded as a marker of 'holiness.' This resulted from, and at the same time further fed, the general Christian attitude that sex and sexuality belonged to our lower natures. But it did leave Mary as the great, or perhaps the greatest, exemplar of being holy.

You may notice that (consistent with this book's overall orientation) my approach to attempting to understand the cult of the Virgin Mary is from the perspective of religion and how religion manifests itself over the great arc of human existence. Many approach it from a psychological orientation instead. To give their explanation a much too-quick summary, they tell us that sons of weak or "inadequate" fathers (sometimes discussed as "father-ineffective" families) tend to inwardly lust after their mothers and therefore need a motherly female figure as a god. The steep rise of Marian devotion in Christianity appears to have begun by the late fourth and early fifth centuries, at which point the 'young' religion was incorporating large numbers of poor and rural people into what theretofore had been largely an urban phenomenon. The theory, at least of some, is that with poor agriculture-oriented people came a sudden flood of inadequate (poor) fathers whose sons gave a platform for the need for, and rise of, a mother goddess in Christianity.

I have no doubt that there is a psychological aspect to the cult of the Virgin in Christianity—there is a psychological aspect to religion on almost every level. But to concentrate on the emotional relationship between mothers and sons seems to me far too narrow, and far too Freudian, an explanation for the cult of the Virgin in Christianity. It could better serve to describe why men became priests in significant numbers, which admittedly in turn speaks to the growth of the Marian cult. But it doesn't explain the role of women in the growth of the cult. From my vantage (limited to parts of the 20th and 21st centuries—a very significant limitation) the cult of the Virgin is fueled much more by women than men, at least if one is talking about lay people and one leaves aside the Catholic clergy.

Those whose theory is that Marian devotion arises in men because they have repressed desire for their mothers, simply turn it upside-down for women—females, they tell us, have repressed desire for their fathers and hence become devotees of Mary the Virgin. For my taste this seems a little too circular, too simple and neat to be entirely credible, although it is certainly true that sexuality does play a role in religious devotion.

One aspect of the Marian cult today which I am perfectly willing to consign to the psychological realm is that of the many apparitions claimed for the Virgin. Even so, these hallucinations or illusions do fit into the general religion experience as well, quite obviously—Paul as discussed in Chapter 1 being a vivid example.

● WAS JESUS AN HISTORICAL FIGURE?

When we begin to look at the Virgin Mary as a manifestation of the great Mother Goddess of ancient mythology, or as a manifestation of the Egyptian Isis mythology specifically, we begin also to see the ties between the characterization of her son and such allegories as Isis' son, the Sun God Horus.

These strong roots back into the religion of ancient Egypt, and beyond that into universal human religious myths, have caused some scholarly observers to question whether 'Jesus of Nazareth' was a real human or just a collection of mythic concepts and allegories. In other words, was he a flesh and blood man of history, or just a story? Of the two, we know with certainty that he was (or became) a story. That's not in debate. What might be debatable, to the probable consternation of many pious souls, is whether the story was built around a flesh and blood man or around religious ideas and mythology already in existence during the time period we ascribe to Jesus.

Scholars who try to sort out the history of Christianity are quick to tell us that finding any mention of Jesus by secular historians of the time we assume he lived is an extremely tall order. There are some short passages in Josephus, Suetonius, and Pliny which are dismissed by many scholarly schools as probably having been added later by Jesus apologists, but otherwise the field of history doesn't turn up any real evidence as to the existence of Jesus during his day.

Furthermore, the life of Jesus as it does come to us in our scriptures seems modeled on the ancient Sun Gods. Historians point out that there is nothing much new in the Biblical descriptions of Jesus. All of the terms and allusions written of him in the New Testament had been used previously and ascribed to other so-called gods and messianic figures. And we need to remember again that even the guys who wrote the gospels had never met Jesus—his story was set, or his life was spent (take your pick), some decades earlier than the time of the evangelists. It is not at all difficult to come across scholars who feel Jesus was not an actual historical man.

The great Christian apologist St. Augustine, held that "True Christianity, the religion of the Christos, is far older than the Christian church", and he is also quoted as saying, "The Two, the human being, Jesus, and the metaphysical personage, Christ, were blended into one."

The church father Origen, bishop of Alexandria after Clement, is quoted as writing, "The Christian religion contains nothing but what Christians hold in common with the heathen; nothing new." And he, in turn, quotes Augustine, "That which is called the Christian religion existed among the ancients and never did not exist."

We are being told that the Jesus story, in effect, has been told and rehearsed in liturgical and ceremonial ways for many centuries, or much longer, well before our calendar turned from BC (BCE) to AD (CE). Jesus, in other words, is another in the long line of heroes (kings) who fed their people with themselves, usually through dying (planting) and rising (as food). His story, or the story which grew up around him, comes from the general religious story of mankind.

The Christian passion narrative may rely on the myth of Dionysus, which has many motifs of wine and fertility by a dying and rising divine figure. Among this and similar mythologies it is the agricultural cycle which is the theme of resurrection stories. The hero overcomes death through self-sacrificial suffering which leads to food, wine, and joy for his people after the hero's awakening from three days of death, triggered perhaps by the spring rains. It expresses itself in the Jesus mythology in feeding through the Eucharist, as well as perhaps more subtle themes.

Images from ancient Egypt depict ears of grain, watered by a priest, growing from the supine body of Osiris. A human form was evidently molded out of earth and grain seeds on a bier. The sprouting of the grain signifies the resurrection of the god. Could it then be maintained that photo-synthesis is the never ending act of creation which both gives life to the gods and life (food) to the people? Again, it is the sun at center stage; the main god.

Scholars remind us that the Gospels of the New Testament are our only significant source of information about this Jesus, but that their purpose was not historical or biographical—their purpose was religious. They were written to glorify him and to associate him with great gods and heroes.

Furthermore, they quote him in Greek which, if their stories about him are historically true, would not have been the language in which he spoke.

The only reason Jesus was written about at all was because some people had come to think he was a god. No one we know of wrote about Jesus because they thought he was an important human who deserved to have a biography on record (disappointing as that may be to historians).

One Egyptologist, Ahmed Osman, believes that the Jesus story is much older than we are led to believe, and goes so far as to say that all of the main characters in both the Old and New Testaments were actually historical Egyptian figures. He equates Jesus with Joshua of the Old Testament (as also do others) and says that was once part of the teaching of the early church fathers.

These ideas surrounding Jesus, that the story is an old one being retold in a new setting, can be rather confusing. And they add confusion on another level as well—when to begin using the term "Christians." Some scholars speak of Christians well before the time we assume Jesus of Nazareth walked the earth, and of course even the time of Jesus was before anything we would recognize today as Christianity. So one can run into a fair amount of writing about "early Christians" which would seem to us really should be termed "pre-Christians" or maybe "proto-Christians." What these writers are saying, in essence, is that the story of our Jesus character had been told in many ways over vast amounts of time, and/or that the Jesus story may be based on, or highly influenced by, much earlier figures—and thus that the outline of Christianity existed well before +/- 30 CE. As I mentioned earlier, the Bible (Acts 12:26) says the term "Christians" was first used in Antioch while at least some of the apostles were still alive and active.

My solution is to keep it as simple as possible. To my mind Christianity began with the 'apostle' Paul and then took ultimate shape over the next few centuries of theological development and historical-political pressure. So to avoid being confusing, and to avoid confusing myself for that matter, my definition for Christianity is pretty much what we have under that designation today. That approach leaves "early Christianity" and "early Christians" back in the area of a few years after the crucifixion. By this (probably) over-simplified measure there were no Christians before Paul, and that would include the current reigning 'Queen of Heaven.'

While it is true, somewhat frustratingly, that the Bible doesn't give us much by way of standard biographical detail for Jesus (marital, paternal details, for example), it does give us hints about his personality—many of them rather surprising, and not at all in the "Jesus Loves Me" Sunday School mold. Yes, he is pictured as often being empathetic to an individual's needs (usually in the lead-up to his performing a healing miracle), but he is also portrayed as frequently hard tongued, a bit sassy, and maybe possessed of a short temper.

The curse of the fig tree, for example, on its surface paints a Jesus who had a petulant, almost irrational, side. Why curse and destroy a tree just because it had no available fruit when Jesus happened to want some? Even the Bible seems to side with the tree, pointing out (Mark 11:13) that it was not even the right season for the tree to be bearing fruit.

And throwing out the money changers from the Temple seems to paint a Jesus who was capable of violence, in contrast to the meek and mild Jesus (the 'Prince of Peace') we thought we knew. There are a number of images of Jesus in the gospels which can strike us as not in character and make us rush on, seeking a more sweet personality. (Some scholars see the Temple money-changers episode as evidence that Jesus was a Nazarite [Nazirite], which could also explain why Nazareth was attached to him as his identifying town of origin when there is no particular evidence that he ever lived there.)

But who knows if these personality hints are on target? The gospel writers had never seen Jesus in action, so there could have been other reasons for their including these rough edges. For example, the curse of the fig tree could be seen as a lesson about good works. Live up to your duty by yielding the fruit of godly behavior or you will be cut off. The tree was not living up to its mandate of producing figs, so it was of no use in the kingdom of god. This was Jesus' usual way of teaching, the gospels tell us, frustrating as it may be as we try to decipher the record left to us by the evangelists.

So what does the Bible actually tell us about Jesus? There's no way of knowing with certainty. Maybe some of these anecdotes and descriptions were true. Maybe they were all made up to make some kind of point. Ironically, religion itself has become a barrier to our knowing the man Jesus. So it is that the true believer who "knows" Jesus as his "personal" savior has accomplished more than some of the brightest minds of our race—the scholars who are still trying to figure out just who this Jesus character was.

The Jesus-wasn't-a-real-man or Jesus-didn't-exist lines of thought can be a little confusing because those who espouse them are not always exactly on the same page with each other. Some of them are making a simple statement—there never was a man known as Jesus of Nazareth; just stories about such a man. Hence, he was only a story, not flesh and blood. This is mostly, or at least to a large extent, a complaint about the relative obscurity of Jesus—he just doesn't show up in records from the era where historians think he should. So it's to a degree a conclusion of historical analysis. Jesus is a Paul Bunyan type figure, real only in the retelling of his story.

But others are not necessarily denying that there could have been a human Jesus of Nazareth. Their problem is with the story built around him. The story tellers, they contend, used him as a framework upon which to hang an impossible assembly of ancient religious ideas, titles, hopes, allegories, and fantasies. Such an assembly never existed in one human being in the past and could not exist in Jesus as a human man either. Hence the Jesus who is being described never existed even if there was a real man named Jesus who sparked the discussion among his surviving followers. From this angle it isn't obscurity that's a problem, but too much hype.

And there's even a third strand in this "did Jesus exist?" question. So much of the religious overlay applied to Jesus consisted of very old themes, stories, and allegories that it became difficult to know if the evolving story about the man Jesus was a new one, or an old one which had already been told to many past generations. If the story was an old one, maybe the subject of the story had lived a long time ago rather than at the general time the story was being freshly told. If the Jesus being talked about now was said to do everything an ancient character (from the Old Testament, from mythology, from another religion such as that of ancient Egypt) did many generations ago, maybe the 'now' Jesus was just a memory or a composite.

How this all gets sorted out by anyone who cares to ponder the issue is going to be quite individual. There is no way to know when or if we arrive at the ultimate truth (except in the minds of those whose criteria revolve only around faith and dogma, and who are willing to ignore historical accuracy if it gets in the way of their beliefs). My own working hypothesis is that there was indeed a human Jesus figure and that the gospels were at least in part attempts to tell his story (and most serious observers of Christianity seem to agree with this assessment pretty much).

But the men who wrote the story were motivated by religion rather than history. They were already at a significant distance from Jesus in time, and they were dependent on a group memory (oral history) to give them anything resembling biographical details. Their motivation for writing was to help codify a young religion into which they probably had been born, and to provide evangelistic tools for those trying to spread the young religion. So they did the best they could in telling us about the man Jesus; but what they were able to do was so restricted that it's not very helpful on the biographical front. The Jesus passed down to them was already a divine figure—on his way to being God if not quite completely there already.

That's why I find the New Testament miracle stories of Jesus so interesting. They are likely to be a tangle of factual memory, religious overlay, and coded references all at the same time. Jesus, as Morton Smith concludes, probably was primarily known in his own time as a magician—a worker of miracles. These were probably based on the magic of the time as well as somethings Jesus learned in Egypt or from Egyptian sources. They were probably very close to what today we call "faith healing." The recipient was a partner in the healing and had to be judged receptive to healing before his plea was accepted. This sort of healing is described in Acts 14:9 where Paul decided to accept a healing client because Paul saw in advance that "he had faith to be made well." Despite the necessary faith, the healing at the time was seen as magic; as a miracle. Jesus' healing as described in the gospels seems to follow this 'faith healing' pattern with its need for participation by the one about to be healed as well as the healer (Matthew 9:28-29; Mark 5:34, etc.). Viewed from that angle, Jesus' 'miracles' in the New Testament can be seen as participatory, with two actors rather than just one.

Then, on top of these possibly true bits of actual biographical story there were added grander, more impressive miracles as the perception of Jesus grew closer and closer to his being a divine figure (first seen by a few as Messiah, and then by growing numbers as God, or a god)—miracles that came from the pious imaginations of the followers of the late Jesus rather than from memories of actual events. These followers now were in the business of claiming and seeking to demonstrate that Jesus was a god. Raising the dead a miracle at a time became part of this enhanced theme, no longer limited to healing the lame and blind who had enough faith to cooperate. And stories of raising the dead got tangled up with memories of Jesus conducting Egyptian-like initiations of striplings wherein they died ritually and were then ritually brought back to life.

So the New Testament miracles tell us a lot about Jesus. The problem is that we can't tell at a quick glance whether we are being told about an event in the life of the man Jesus, or about the writer's determined faith that Jesus was a god. When others decided a man was really a god, whether it was Jesus, Apollonius, or someone else, the judgement was always made looking backward at signs which during the man's lifetime might have been taken routinely at first but gradually grew to define the man. By the time the guy died, an image of such stature had been built up around him that people were left to find an explanation. The explanation usually became "he was a god," although the development of that explanation may have taken some time to settle in.

As to whether Jesus thought of himself as a god, it's possible he was totally innocent on the subject. Indications in the New Testament that he may have flirted with the idea were likely added down the road by writers already committed to the concept and trying to shore it up with evidence. He was, after all, a sort of coat rack upon which following generations hung all of their religious ideas, hopes, and hang-ups. Whether he might have

63

thought he was the long-awaited Messiah is a somewhat different question, however. He might have thought that. Echoes of that sort in the gospels have a better chance of having actual roots in history.

However we decide to approach Jesus, the question that still dangles in front of us is: Was he a man, or was he merely the description of a Hero from the realm of the general religious mythology of mankind? Ending up with a few unanswered questions is not much of a surprise when one begins by trying to understand a man whose very existence is questioned by some apparently sober academics. But the effort is worthwhile in my opinion, and may be its own reward.

The subject of this chapter, Mary the mother, despite her attendant baggage of religious lore, is in a sense one of the most solid and trust-worthy figures in the life of Jesus and therefore one of most solid figures in the New Testament. While we know precious little about this Jesus which is beyond question or speculation, we do know that if he was a human man he had a human mother. That, at least, is one thing about Jesus which is not in dispute and not open to revision. Perhaps that is part of the reason Mary became such a focal point for Christianity—we know she was there and we know something about her because we have all had intimate experience as, or with, mothers. Maybe it is no surprise that she became such an anchor to the Christian experience. She may be the only New Testament character to reach beyond mere plausibility, and enter solid reality.

● NOTE FOR CLARITY

In case all of this hoopla about virgins may have given anyone the wrong impression, it needs to be stated that it was *not* the virginity of the mother which conferred divinity on the offspring. The baby was a 'son of god' only because its father was a god before it. The baby was not a son of god because his mother was still a virgin.

The virginity of the mother was not the source or cause of the miracle at hand. But the virginity of the mother did serve as both a guarantee and a sign that the child's father was not a human male, but rather was a god. The religious significance was not that a virgin could give birth to a baby, miracle though that would have been, but that she had been impregnated by a god rather than a man.

The reason virginity was needed was as a vehicle to insure that the new god (the 'son of god') was not actually sired by a mere man. If mamma was a virgin, then daddy could not have been a man. The ancients were well aware of the physical aspects and problems posed by such born-of-a-virgin stories, to the extent that at least one school of thought described both the impregnation and the birth as happening through virgin's ear so that the hymen could remain undisturbed.

Just doing what Gods are supposed to do: Virgin Birth

Oddly, perhaps, we still use virginity in a vaguely similar way today, at least in rarified quarters. Many of us can remember the sad story of Charles, Prince of Wales, and Diana, Princess of Wales. At the time of the courtship it was widely known and reported that Charles was in love with another woman. She was eventually divorced, but despite the earlier saga of Edward VIII divorce *per se* was not the main problem by then—the problem was that she had been married at all; having been married meant she was not a virgin. As heir to the British throne, it was the duty of Charles to produce his own heir. There could not be any risk that Charles' heir might not actually be his offspring, so he was under pressure to marry a virgin. The function of the bride's virginity was to guarantee that Charles' firstborn would be a legitimate heir to the British throne, i.e. of the royal bloodline.

So it was not the virginity of the royal bride which conferred a place in the succession to Charles' firstborn. The virginity was just a vehicle to (hopefully) guarantee that the royal succession would not wander off into genetically murky waters.

Jesus and his companion sons of gods did not need virgins as mothers because of anything inherent in female virginity. They needed virgins as mothers in order for their credentials as gods to be recognized and not disputed. Of course, the 'miracle' aura surrounding a virgin giving birth was an added bonus which some may have thought pointed in the same direction, but it was never the point of the story.

As it happened, Christianity's chief virgin became, over time, an extremely big deal in her own right. However, it could fairly be said that she started her career as a figure whose importance derived from the need of another (her son, who needed the religious marker of a virgin mother so that he could be seen as one of the gods). Religion has to an extent used the character of Satan, or the Devil, in a similar way—as embodying a factor which was needed to explain others. Hitler and his ilk may be described as "spawn of the Devil," or when I fail to live up to my best standards I may try to excuse myself because "the Devil made me do it." Mary the Virgin has ascended in religious importance while it seems Satan may have slipped a bit in the other direction as Christianity marched into the scientific age. But even the Devil is still useful in characterizing people, events, and circumstances beyond himself—a concept kept alive partially, at least, because he was needed by others.

As we've discussed, the Virgin Birth doctrine or concept is mostly about Jesus even though it might first appear to be about Mary the mother. The Immaculate Conception doctrine or concept, on the other hand, is more directly about Mary herself in that otherwise she would have passed on to her off spring mankind's original sin—the solution therefore being to erase original sin in her before she became a mother, and in the process to elevate Mary theologically above all other women past, present, or future.

There are those who point out, however, that the Immaculate Conception is also ultimately about Jesus, and this needs to be acknowledged because, of course, it's true. The only reason Mary needed the purgation of an Immaculate Conception was that she was slated to be the mother of Jesus, son of God. Otherwise she would have been merely an ordinary woman giving birth in a theological context which the church had decided would spread original sin into the next generation. Jesus had to be free of original sin (it would have contradicted his image as God) and so the chain had to be broken before it got to him. As one contemporary observer noted, the doctrine of the Immaculate Conception therefore "served more to protect Jesus' image than to honor Mary."

This whole theological construct in turn then raises interesting questions about the status of any descendants Jesus may have sired, running potentially down to our own day—are there humans free from original sin walking among us today? Perhaps questions such as this are the simplest and clearest explanation as to why the very early church began to edit Mary Magdalene out of the Jesus story so quickly (see Chapter 6). With the essential disappearance of Mary Magdalene, a lot of conundra and thorny questions disappeared as well.

● NOTE ON CHRISTIANITY VS. RELIGION

If one wants to draw a distinction, and thus to maintain that Christianity is not 'just another religion,' there are a few pegs to hang one's hat on, but they get intensely theological immediately. For example, Christian apologists like to point out that religion *per se* (general human religion stretching back to the limits of history) is often a matter of attempting to bribe the gods in order to achieve whatever is held out as salvation. An argument along these lines might look something like the following.

This 'bribery' of the gods could involve offering sacrifices such as altar offerings or the acceptance of personal suffering and deprivation which are believed to please the gods, or simply prayer in all of its myriad possible forms. In Christianity, however, God is seen as the one making the sacrifice (of his son) for the benefit of the people. The benefits of God's sacrifice are allotted to the people freely. There is no cost or restriction except one— belief. One must believe in this God (i.e. have "faith") and his sacrifice in order to collect the benefit. Belief, however, is also a gift from God, usually called the gift of the Holy Spirit. One can't simply decide to believe, one can only accept (not refuse) the gift of believing when (if) it is offered by God (John 6:44 etc.).

To not accept the gift of faith is to sin against the Holy Spirit, the only unforgiveable sin in the Christian theological system. However, there is a clever little catch-22 built in as well. God does not need to, and evidently does not, offer the gift of faith to all people. So, one must believe (have faith) to be saved, but one can only have faith if it is offered by the Holy Spirit. If it is not offered, one cannot reject faith—although the consequence (lack of salvation) is the same as it is for the person who has been offered faith and then rejected it.

Whatever the shape of the argument, a sharp theological mind can tie you up in knots easily, and just as easily untangle the knot. It is, to some extent, an intellectual game (although by saying so I am not saying that theologians are insincere or ill-meaning).

Non-Christian general religion seems a lot less complicated and at least gives the worshipper a stab at influencing the gods on his own behalf. It should be noted, too, that the ancient gods do plenty of sacrificing for the people in many non-Christian religions. The fruits of these sacrifices are also free to the people even though the people probably try their hands at inducing them (the context is usually agricultural). Of course, the truth is that Christians do their share of trying to influence God right along with religionists of a non-Christian stripe, past or present.

Another theological theme is also sometimes employed to try to distinguish Christianity from other (mere) religions—that of 'revelation.' Christianity is said by this way of thinking to have been revealed directly by God, rather than evolved by the thinking or inspiration of humans as could be said about some other ("lessor") religious expressions. Revelation is a particularly handy theological device because it can be used to cover almost any religious concept. If something has been revealed directly by God himself, who can argue with it? One really can't argue with it—the best one can do is to argue that, in fact, it was not revealed by God—to argue against the dogma of revelation itself.

Obviously volumes could be, and have been, written about such theological tangles and intricacies. But theology is exactly what I wanted to sidestep in trying to focus just on Christianity as a religion—one among many—rather than on its own particular theological system. But theology and religion are difficult, if not impossible, to keep entirely separate. Both are lurking behind and influencing almost any perspective one can take on these subjects. ⌘

67

4.

Doing what Gods are supposed to do: Resurrection; The third day

The Resurrection of Jesus, probably seen by most Christians as the very heart of the religion or of its message, is another area in which Jesus was just one of the gods. Resurrection did not make him unique. It just confirmed that he belonged in the gods' club along with those who got there first. After arranging to be born of a virgin, the next job of a god usually involved staring down death in some way, shape or form, and emerging triumphant. For some of them this was an integral part of caring for (usually by feeding) their people; others were perhaps a bit less altruistic.

Death is part of life goes the facile cliché. Yes, but we humans have never completely made peace with that particular fact of life. Even when our rational selves sigh and admit the truth, there's something on the fringe of the psyche which clings to hope that death can be somehow muted or mitigated, if not avoided. At least we want to ignore it as much as possible.

Enter religion, which makes, or at least implies, all kinds of promises. One, at least in the popular version of Christianity, is that death has already been conquered. If one believes in the right doctrines, phrases them in the approved way, and prays to the right god, one will have eternal life (although one will still have to technically die to collect the reward).

That's a fairly potent pitch. And it's been very effective over the centuries. Everyone would like to live forever, or at least to believe they would live forever. Christianity promises a cure for the death problem. Can Christianity make good on the promise? In the end we may be left with nothing but the question. Along the way we've heard of a few religious maniacs who claim to be eager to fly off to the bosom of Jesus immediately and continue life uninterrupted but on a far happier basis. But the vast majority of us, even those of us who are sincere believers, are eager to hold on to earthly life for as long as possible.

Easter is a real part of the human picture, however. There's no doubt about that. We continue to embrace life and we continue to celebrate its renewal. Humans continue to have children even though they know those

69

children will have to face death, and even though there's a chance the parents themselves might have to suffer through the child's death. When a beloved pet dies we often respond by replacing it, knowing full-well that the new pet probably will not out-live us either, and we'll have to deal with yet another painful death experience. Even aging widows and widowers may end up as new brides or grooms, so strong is the Easter force.

The life force, and our embrace of life, is too strong to let the fear of death sidetrack us from the celebration of life. Easter is real in that sense, from anyone's point of view. But that's not theology or religious belief. Can Easter be real in the way Christianity tells the story? The question returns the focus not to life and death in the abstract, but to Jesus of Nazareth.

● RELIGION AND HOPE

Easter was not invented by Christianity, either as a concept or a ritual celebration. Death and rebirth in the spring had been celebrated by "pagans" for as long as anyone can look back into mankind's past. Christians merely added another dying and rising figure (Jesus) to the long list of chiefs, kings, gods, and shamans who were there before. The usual basis for these 'Easter' celebrations was agricultural, expressing gratitude for the return of the food supply. The biggest shift Christianity contributed was not casting its Easter in agricultural terms, but in purely theological terms— Jesus was not so much the god who died and rose *in order* to feed his people (excepting the Eucharistic allegories), but Jesus was (demonstrated to be) god *because* he rose up from death. Resurrection was not a tool this time around, but a new dogma. Resurrection confirmed Jesus' divinity. A subtle shift, but a key next step in religious thinking.

A lot of ink has been applied trying to understand and explain how Jesus and Resurrection were brought together in the thinking of the earliest 'Christian' community. Many writers boil it down to the idea that those who had followed Jesus during his adult life (often termed his 'ministry') just could not let go of the idea that he had been someone with an extraordinary relationship with God. He was still alive to them. Gradually they came to feel that he was still alive, period.

The concept of dead people being brought back to life by the power of a god was not at all considered impossible in the ancient Mediterranean world. Egyptian magic, which many early Christians saw as a tutoring source for Jesus himself, was credited with achieving this phenomenon. The gods themselves, according to Egyptian lore, were believed to have come down to earth to raise certain individuals up from death at various times. And obviously the Christians' evolving Biblical canon recounted this phenomenon having been performed by (the god) Jesus.

In fact, the concept of the death, burial, and resurrection of the god or the divine man (or King) was probably the most common and shared

70

religious motif in the pre-Christian world, aside perhaps from sun worship. Survival after death appears to be an idea as widespread as humanity itself. It is said by some authors to be even older than *Homo sapiens*; having existed among Australian aborigines and African bushmen.

● THREE DAYS IN THE TOMB

The usual period of burial between death and resurrection in these ancient and widespread religious ideas and myths was three days. Christianity joined this long parade, although the three day concept (and experience) was certainly not exclusive to Christianity.

Furthermore, aside from this nearly universal concept, many people of Jesus' day had seen, or at very least had heard of, humans who had "died," been buried, and "arose" after three days. For practitioners of some types of magic then, and in fact until at least recent times, that would have been almost a routine demonstration. Egyptian Fakirs could reach a voluntary coma of such depth that assistants could bury them alive—sometimes for long periods of time, although the longer the period of burial the more dangerous the exhibition became, and some did die for real in the process. Three days, however, seems to have been well within their safety range, and according to reports by some of them was experienced as rather invigorating after the fact. Thus 'resurrection' after three days was an existing cultural motif in the Mediterranean world of the first century.

Perhaps partially for this reason, among many others (some of which we'll explore), three became an important number in the realm of the ancient mysteries, and thus in the religious contexts which, intentionally or not, carried forward their echoes. The number pops up in surprising places in the Bible, such as the three day period Paul/Saul spent incapacitated (effectively entombed) in Damascus following his 'conversion' until he was healed (resurrected) by a Jesus follower. The 'three' motif appears also in a variety of ways in the record of general human experience, such as tales of the initiation of boys at puberty, and in ancient mythological stories of death to resurrection, with the resurrection reliably pegged at three days following the death.

John's Gospel reports that Jesus, in a discussion after the 'cleansing of the temple' told bystanders, "Destroy this temple, and in three days I will raise it up." The evangelist asserted that Jesus was speaking of his own body rather than the temple edifice, and thus presumably referring to his coming resurrection as experienced by the Christian community. (This would have been a post-resurrection perspective held by the Jesus movement, implying that Jesus had known in advance of his crucifixion and resurrection.)

But what a strange thing to say in this context, and especially what a strange way to phrase it. Wouldn't it have been sufficient to say he had, and could demonstrate, power over death itself? Why did he need the reference to three days?

Possibly he was simply making a verbal link to the stories of death, burial, and resurrection of gods which would have been familiar to his audience, and thereby making a claim to divinity as well as to having power over death. However, there would also seem to be something about the three days which was independently important in this context. Could Jesus have been issuing a challenge rather than making a prophecy?

Maybe we have interpreted this strange episode incorrectly. Maybe Jesus was not looking ahead to, nor referring to, the resurrection celebrated by Christianity, but instead was speaking as a magician. If so, perhaps he was asserting his ability to survive three days of 'death' and emerge intact, in the known ways of fakirs and magicians of the day. That could have been the case even if he were just a human who had no inkling that he would someday be regarded as a god and credited with resurrection. If the passage does indeed refer to the Christian understanding of Jesus' resurrection, then it is very likely that the words were put into Jesus' mouth by the evangelist—that the reported episode was later religious propaganda rather than history.

From the Old Testament probably the most familiar similar story involves Jonah in the whale's belly for three days. Matthew uses it to prefigure Jesus' entombment for three days. This works nicely looking backward in time, but the most intriguing aspect may be why did the author of the Jonah story choose "three" days in the first place. The point could have just as easily been made with one, or two, or four days before Jonah's "resurrection" by being vomited out of the fish. (If my count is correct, the story of Jonah later waiting outside the city, sheltered by a plant sent by God and then losing its protection, also took three days, which may or may not carry any further meaning. One is always left trying to read between the lines to harvest the full religious weight of these ancient writings, especially in translation.)

And, of course, the best known three days in a tomb story to come down to us belongs to Jesus himself. In this case the three day period was reportedly enforced by the Passover holiday and the Sabbath; otherwise Mary Magdalene, by custom, would have gone to the tomb the morning following interment. But some scholars think the sequence of passion events has been scrambled in the Biblical retelling, and thus that Passover might not have played the role reported. Serious scholars tell us that there are good reasons to dispute the idea that the 'Last Supper' was actually a Passover meal, as most Christians have been told. This raises the intriguing possibility that the "three days" were brought into the story regardless of the actual timeline, for unstated reasons the authors saw as important.

Doing what Gods are supposed to do: Resurrection; The third day

Often the Old Testament passage Hosea 6:1-2 is cited as the origin of the "on the third day" allusions ["on the third day he will restore us"]. But this probably takes the passage out of context. Some Egyptologists have linked the third day allusion instead to Osiris who was said to have risen from death on the third day—a likely more solid link with ancient mythology.

In addition to linking Jesus with the Egyptian gods, the three day theme also links Jesus with the tradition of initiation into the mysteries in Egypt. The shadow of Egypt again is being evoked to some purpose we can't really understand from this distance, but which presumably would have been quickly understood by the enlightened people of the day (and maybe even by just the common folk).

We have all proclaimed that we believe this three day hiatus occurred when, in church, we have repeated one of Christianity's major creeds. "The third day" he arose we have avowed. No one ever seems to pause long enough to ask what 'three days' has to do with it. As a number of contemporary thinkers have noted, most people today don't feel the need to examine the details of the religious propositions they profess—something like our modern propensity to sign agreements without reading them carefully.

The death of Jesus is important theologically (at least from a Pauline atonement perspective), the resurrection is obviously important theologically, but why is the interval between them important (aside maybe from the descent into hell idea which has some theological ramifications)? The three day hiatus would seem to have no relevance at all.

Assuming the whole Passover aspect of the 'last supper' to be true, the three days would seem to have been little more than a calendar accident preventing discovery of the empty tomb until the third day. At any rate, it seems a minor aspect totally overshadowed by the huge events precipitating it. So why are we still confessing it as a matter of centrality in our faith?

The Nicene creed provides the usual answer: "according to the Scriptures." Sometimes phrased as "to fulfill the Scriptures," or "as written in the scriptures." This looking back to interpret some statement from the Hebrew Bible as a reference to, or prediction of, Jesus as Messiah was frequently used by the young Christian community to link themselves to the religion of their Jewish ancestors, and thus to provide an authoritative basis for, or answer to a question about, some aspect of the developing Jesus religion.

Jesus himself is reported to have given the same rationale and interpretation, as for example in Luke 18:31-33. Although this referencing back to the Hebrew Bible must be mentioned here, it would be a diversion from our current discussion to pursue it as a topic—especially since everyone seems hard pressed to come up with a satisfactory candidate in the Hebrew Bible for this third day prophecy (some may look to Hosea 6:2 as I've said, but that seems pretty weak to most observers). Perhaps it is sufficient to say that I don't see that topic as actually relevant here on its own, although possibly relevant if pursed in detail on the level of general universal religion.

What is relevant is that the New Testament writers seem almost obsessed with the third day idea as related to Jesus' resurrection.

One does not have to read very far into the New Testament to see this (Matthew 16:21; 17:23; 20:19; Luke 9:22; 13:31, etc.). And the image continues into the Pauline epistles as well, the earliest material in the Christian canon, as in I Corinthians 15:4. It is almost as if "resurrection" and "third day" are joined at the hip in some kind of liturgical formula (or, could it be a magic formula, surfacing from the distant past whether known to the New Testament writers as such or not).

In the year 2000 an ancient Hebrew text was found near the Dead Sea. It is dated by experts to first century BCE and tells of the death and resurrection of a messianic leader, probably Simon of Perea. In it the angel Gabriel says, "I command you, prince of princes, in three days you shall live." Scholars point out that Paul is the earliest source of the tradition that Jesus was raised 'on the third day,' and that therefore the idea was one that he appropriated and then applied to Jesus. Why not? He invented most of what we think we know about Jesus anyway. Even so, most of Paul's religious ideas did have roots in accumulated mythology ancient even in his day, so saying Paul was the first to link the phrase to Jesus does not really explain its religious potency.

Lots of at least equally important aspects of Jesus' life and ministry could be inserted, but instead were ignored in the creeds—no mention whatsoever is made of his miracles, for example, and for people of his own day and context these miracles were likely a key to understanding him. So, it seems the creed formulizers specifically and intentionally threw in a very minor element which does not really need to be there—if Jesus arose from death on the same day, or in two days, the import would presumably have been the same.

Unless, that is, we are being asked to confess belief in something we don't understand; something which echoes through ancient religion and mythology running through Egypt and then the Hebrew Bible—something the creed assemblers may not even have understood themselves, but which they intuited was both germane and of significant religious importance. Three days between death and resurrection, it strongly appears, is elemental and necessary to any discussion of these ancient mysteries. The early

Doing what Gods are supposed to do: Resurrection; The third day

Christians could be trying to tell us something the ancient Egyptians had already told them—but what exactly? The usage of the "on the third day" phrase shows up very early in the tradition, as for example in the "Infancy Gospel of Matthew" in which it appears during the flight into Egypt story. And then we are also told of three hours of darkness "over the whole land" as Jesus was being crucified, as well as numerous other uses of the number three.

It should be noted, briefly at least, that such an obsession with three day gaps can be found in many mythologies, sometimes using "three days" as a ritual span every single time the plot advances. The reasons for this are no more clear than they are in the New Testament gospels. What is most tantalizing, however, is to contemplate whether they could be due to the same or related reason(s) arising from a strong but forgotten common religious insight or imperative.

Of course, some historians have latched onto the tradition of magic to explain Jesus' three days in the tomb, followed by resurrection. Somehow, supposedly, he would have managed to escape death on the cross—perhaps a substitute was found to hang there in his place, or perhaps through Jesus' own magic—and then, after burial, was "raised" at the appointed time, either by prearranged assistance or maybe just by outright magic.

Jesus was known as a magician with some power over death, and he is reputed by many scholars to have been familiar with Egyptian magic. In any case, the idea of a human coming back to life after three days in a tomb would not have been a unique phenomenon in the eyes of the time—it would have been seen as possible, if perhaps not likely.

It has been proposed that the 'third day' theme is reflected in Christian observance of Sunday, because it is the third day from the Friday on which Jesus was crucified. Of course, we can see echoes of this reaching into our own day from the culturally customary timing of the burial of the dead on the third day after death.

The pattern of three days of death followed by resurrection was not only the stock in trade of magicians; it was also deeply engrained in the cultural and religious milieu of ancient Egypt and Israel, and even beyond we are told. We can find similar religious expression described from the general geographical neighborhood. In one, there was an annual 'passion play' in which a young man would enter a cave and lie down on a bed of flowers and herbs as if he were dead. The queen and her priestesses would anoint his body and mourn his death. Then, on the third day, the youth would 'arise from the dead,' marking the annual celebration of new life. This ritual, we are told, was celebrated throughout the Mediterranean world. It was known in Egypt at least as early as 3,000 BCE.

There were evidently Sumerian fertility rites of Dumuzi which spread to Palestine and surrounding areas. The king, Dumuzi, was tortured ritually, killed ritually, and buried, in order to ensure regeneration of the crops and herds. In some of these rites, the tortured king was entombed and then 'resurrected' after three days. As the Greeks and then the Romans gained cultural dominance, rites of other sacrificed Sun Gods became modified, borrowed, and merged into neighboring practices. Lines that are identical or parallel to those in the Old Testament Song of Songs are found in a liturgical poem from the cult of the Egyptian goddess Isis, the sister-bride of the mutilated Sun God Osiris. One writer holds that Jesus, "willingly" assumed the role of the sacrificed pagan fertility/Sun God. (Or perhaps early Christian writers were merely willing to paint him into that role whether or not he assumed it for himself.)

Joseph Campbell relates a story about a man who tried (unsuccessfully, as it turned out) to become a shaman through all the prescribed rituals. The candidate is quoted as saying "I am to lie there like a dead man for three days, [mutilated, and then]...On the third day I shall rise again."

For the ancient Egyptians resurrection was thought to be achieved after a period of three days, say the experts. They say that the phrase therefore has no chronological meaning but is intended as a theological statement when used in our scriptures—another instance of claiming Jesus was a god because of similarities between him and other gods. The general (not individual) resurrection of the dead which Judaism expected was to occur three days after the end of the world.

A good amount of space is devoted to the three day question by Edward Schillebeeckx in his massive book *Jesus*. He pulls the question back from all the areas mentioned above and places it entirely within context of the place of Jesus in his own religious and cultural experience. He describes the Jewish notion that a dead person is "well and truly dead only 'after three days.'" Rising on the third day would then imply that Jesus had risen not after an illusory death, but after he had truly died. Schillebeeckx calls the third day the "decisive day," the "conclusion of the matter."

If Schillebeeckx's theological explanation does not satisfy, we again must ask what was the basis of this three day pattern? Perhaps it went to the heart of Egyptian religion—to the sun itself. And here's where it seems to me we finally get some helpful insight.

The ancients were skilled astronomers and were well aware of the winter solstice, the low point of the sun as viewed from the northern hemisphere. When the sun reached its low point in the sky in late December, it seemed to linger without further movement for three days. After these three days it again could easily be seen beginning to climb from the horizon. In popular culture of the time, this was seen and understood to be the 'death' of the sun (when it reached its lowest point on the horizon) followed by three days entombment and with no movement (except for its nightly passage through the underworld). Then, on the third day, the sun 'arose' from death and again began its ascent in the sky. This is as likely an explanation for the 'third day' language as any, and given Christianity's ultimate dependence on ancient Egypt, probably the most likely explanation of all. And recalling that Christianity early-on regarded Jesus as one of the Sun Gods provides an extra link between him and this perception and understanding of the winter solstice.

Before leaving 'the third day' question, it should be noted that the theme also appears in the New Testament beyond topics of death and resurrection. The evangelist known as John began his account of Jesus' ministry with John the Baptist and then writes, "The next day [John] saw Jesus coming towards him." He continues the account by twice more using the phrase "the next day." Then he begins to recount the story of the wedding at Cana by writing, "On the third day." (John 2:1)

Why? By his own account, if literally trying to be accurate about the days involved, the Cana story would have occurred on the fourth day. Also, there would seem to be no special reason for noting the number of the day to begin with—he could have written simply "later," or used his "next day" phrase again. Did "on the third day" have some significance beyond arithmetic? Was the writer signaling something (a transition perhaps) that is no longer obvious to modern readers? The next time John writes "three days" the words come directly out of the mouth of Jesus. To me, the "third day" language in the New Testament is enormously intriguing, and my suspicion is that it may hark back in some way to the ancient Egyptian mysteries. What I do not believe is that it was used casually or that it was ever without some kind of ritual significance when it was used.

These questions also go back to similar Old Testament language. When the Lord told Moses that He wanted to speak within the hearing of the people (Israel), He said "be ready by the third day; for on the third day the Lord will come down upon Mount Sinai." So Moses told the people "Be ready by the third day; do not go near a woman. On the morning of the third day...Moses brought the people out of the camp to meet God." (Exodus 19: 10-16)

Again, there seems to be no explicit purpose to three days, as opposed to fewer or more. Some time was needed—the people had to clean their garments and otherwise prepare—but why 'the third day?' If it did not appear so frequently in the Bible, the phrase would probably not catch our attention here. But it is this frequency itself which adds a mysterious element to the words, and it is the involvement of Moses, the greatest

77

Biblical magician before Jesus, which further adds a vague sense of the presence of magic.

Maybe this language of the three days could be fairly benign, such as a fragment of liturgical text which would fall easily on the ears of people of that time, bringing the comfort of familiarity and memory. Maybe it was simply a reference to Egyptian religion, used to bolster or magnify some claim or association the writer wanted to make. Maybe it was a bit more mysterious or even slightly darker, as in a magical formula. Whatever this constantly repeated phrase was, however, its use was not an accident.

And, when pondering the three days language, we should remember that in the initiation rites of ancient Egypt, the candidates were kept for three days in some sort of trance or catatonic status representing death, before being returned to consciousness, i.e. resurrected. This is certainly an important factor to take into account in trying to de-code the three days between death and resurrection concept. But this pattern, in turn, was likely influenced heavily by the sun's apparent three day entombment at the winter solstice. Therefore I would assess the sun's turn on its 'hinge' (see Chapter 10) as the ultimate key to understanding the mythological three day gap between death and resurrection.

● JESUS AND EGYPTIAN MAGIC

Some have suggested that Jesus' contemporaries viewed his miracles as a means of grace—as a way for God to bring healing and order into a world of disease and chaos. The longing for such divine intervention in order to give humanity some sense of control over the uncontrollable is hardly just a thing of the past. Many modern people have found themselves tempted by the proverbial Faustian deal with the devil when they faced a crisis. And when the person is religious, a crisis often enough brings a promise to God or a favorite saint if relief will only be provided. Luther is said to have promised to become a monk if St. Anne spared him from a violent storm as he rode horseback from Erfurt. And he even made good on the promise— for a time.

Margaret A. Murray, speaking of ancient Egypt but putting her finger on a universal reality, has written "It is almost impossible to distinguish with any degree of certainty between the practices of magic and the ritual of religion."

There has traditionally been some sort of connection seen between Jesus' magic and Egypt. A number of non-canonical texts tell stories of Jesus going to Egypt in order to study magic during his non-public years, to the extent that a gospel writer who did make it into the canon (Matthew) also included a visit to Egypt. Some scholars think this story in Matthew's gospel was totally invented (no records of a universal taxation or a slaughter of the innocents exists for the period or geographic area in question they say) and oddly was placed in Jesus' infancy when he was not yet able to be a student. But, for some reason it was felt to be important that a visit to Egypt should be included, no matter how convoluted the storyline. Egypt was needed to explain something that was either widely known about Jesus in his time and therefore could not be ignored, or to answer questions of sufficient substance that arose later. Or, of course, for the simple reason that some period of time in Egypt was included in all of the stories which had come down orally to the writers who set out to encapsulate Jesus' life and ministry in text.

So Matthew could have felt he needed to include Egypt in Jesus' pre-ministry story, probably because he knew it was a truth which belonged there. Why he inserted it into the infancy period is confusing, and may have reflected Matthew's desire to downplay the impact somewhat.

These Jesus in Egypt stories are great in their variety and fascinating in their fantasy. One man, Elieser ben Hyrkanos, claimed that Jesus had tattooed the magic formulas which he had learned in Egypt on his own body. When asked what should be said of something like tattooing oneself with magic formulas, he gave the answer that it was only Jesus who had done this, and he, of course, "was a madman." Often, as we've just seen, these Jesus in Egypt stories were used as anti-Christian diatribes.

An example of a non-canonical text which connects Jesus to Egypt is the anti-Christian work "The true Word" by the second century philosopher Celsus (whom we met briefly in Chapter 2). He says Jesus, before his public ministry and because of poverty, found work as a servant in Egypt and there acquired magical powers "on which the Egyptians pride themselves, [then] returned to his own country where his sorcery won him a great following, by means of which he proclaimed himself a god."

The idea that Jesus traveled to Egypt while a young man in order to learn magic is a widespread theme, and commonly used in later Jewish polemics against the Christians. It has even been proposed that Jesus was not a follower of Judaism at all, but a pagan priest of Isis. (We'll see later that same exact charge, or maybe just proposal, was made about Mary Magdalene, who was perhaps Jesus' mate. That might have made for a rather dynamic marriage.)

In the time of Jesus, and in his Jewish milieu where the dead had to be buried before sunset, another phenomenon had to be accounted for which we would not anticipate in an age where embalmment or cremation is the norm. It is often called resuscitation and refers to the occasional mistake of burying someone prematurely, in haste to meet the religious deadline.

For this reason, a close family member, most likely a spouse, would visit the place of burial soon thereafter to make sure there had not been such a resuscitation. This could also be combined with other customs such as

79

anointing of the body. One of the best known episodes in the New Testament is just such a visit to the tomb when Mary Magdalene goes alone to Jesus' burial place to verify his death and to anoint his body (for which presumably there had been no time when Jesus was hastily buried after being crucified).

Can we know anything about Jesus' resurrection with historical (rather than religious) certainty? For one thing, we know that the concept of three days in a tomb followed by resurrection did not originate with Jesus or the early Christians. It was actually a fairly common theme which had been around for a very long time, coming down to Judaism from Egypt but also reflected in various ways by other neighboring cultures.

A second thing we can know with relative certainty is that, at least according to the Bible itself, Jesus was not the first person to be resurrected following death. There was the daughter of Jairus, there was Lazarus (if we look at him as a human and not merely code for discussing initiations)—it is not an easy choice to decide if these resurrection stories were offered as history or as matters of faith (or magic) by the Biblical writers, but it is safe in any case to say that the Bible claims that resurrection after death did not begin with Jesus, and therefore did not belong to Jesus uniquely. There is even such a story of a dead person returning to life in the Old Testament: 2 Kings 4:32-37.

Of course, all of these people had to face death a second time—because they were still mortals. So theologians could, and did, argue that their 'resurrections' were not the same as that of Jesus—who was (presumably) already immortal in any case. It is interesting to note, that by proclaiming that the resurrected Jesus ascended into heaven as witnessed by an audience, the church has nicely avoided the question altogether. Ditto, it seems, for Elijah, Enoch, and Noah riding their fiery chariots into heaven.

Many scholars focus on the, as we might call it, community aspect of Jesus' resurrection, i.e. that the resurrection was a fact in the hearts and minds of the Jesus community which resurfaced after its apparent defeat, and that this may be the only 'historical' reality available by which to study this resurrection. Morton Smith commented on the "psychological inability" of Jesus' disciples to accept his death, and suggested this resistance caused them to hallucinate.

We should here give at least a fleeting glance at the reason(s) for the death of Jesus, without which there could be no resurrection. The most obvious reason is simply that he was a man, and all men must die from one cause or another. But the church sees him as the incarnation of God, and therefore the question becomes a matter of theology.

The traditional view the western church has bequeathed us, mostly from Paul, is that propitiation had to be made for man's sinfulness (or sinful

80

nature, i.e. 'original sin'). In this view, the only sacrifice strong enough to accomplish the task was evidently if God sacrificed himself. In this viewpoint the picture of God the Father is not very appealing—angry, bloodthirsty, stubborn, violent, sadistic, and not very imaginative. This is the very opposite of the God we met in Sunday School, and these warring images ripple throughout the religion, or at least through its shifting theologies. This is, however, a very ancient image (idea) which had been applied previously in human religions.

When discussing Jesus' birth and apparent triumph over the death, at least a quick word should be inserted about Apollonius of Tyana, because the two figures, he and Jesus, are so often compared and evidently had such similar careers—and not least because some think the Jesus story was inspired by and modeled on that of Apollonius. The two were at least roughly contemporaries, and Apollonius was also known and remembered as a miracle worker. It is not necessary to detail his life here, but in the context of this and the previous chapters, two points need to be mentioned—that Apollonius was thought to be fathered by a god rather than by a human, and that he escaped death and ascended directly into heaven—and thus shared with Jesus the miraculous experiences at the beginning and end of their earthly lives (although Jesus did not escape death, but was said to have conquered it).

Again, Jesus is not unique in those aspects. With so many similarities, why do we know of Jesus today but few of us have heard of Apollonius? Some suggest it may be because Jesus had a better publicist—Paul—whereas Apollonius' biographer, Philostratus did not have the ability of Paul to be able to turn just one among many holy men into the savior of all mankind who would be adored by billions.

This perspective is interesting also because many commentators note that this Greek philosopher, Apollonius, had as his chief biographer the highly educated Philostratus working under contract to the Empress. Jesus, on the other hand, had to settle for his story being told at the beginning by a group of uneducated apostles, or recruited followers, most likely fishermen by trade. But Jesus also, in fairly short order, acquired a would-be apostle who was highly educated and sophisticated in the ways of the Greek philosophical world. It's probably no wonder then that the Jesus story which endured was the one written almost entirely by Paul, not the original one passed down from Jesus' "uneducated" earliest disciples. (Evidently Jesus himself was seen as uneducated as well: John 7:15.) And also no wonder that the Jesus story which endured ended up looking so much like the Apollonius story. Paul's version of the Jesus story fit in with the intellectual milieu of the day and could therefore more easily gain attention and credibility than vague gossip from a bunch of rural tradesmen.

Apollonius does make some observers of Christianity a bit uncomfortable, in any case. If one is claiming that a specific man in a specific place and time such as Jesus is actually God (theologians term this the "scandal of particularity"), it is not an especially encouraging development to find a near neighbor in both time and place who claims a parallel career and divinity as well—and was followed by nearly equal masses of believers at the time. Was there something in the water around there?, one might well ask.

The Christianity story rests, technically, not upon the miracles allegedly performed by Jesus, but upon the claim that his life shared and recapitulated the events in the lives of many gods who were born on December 25, died, and rose again for the salvation of mankind. And again, we find the model in Egypt, where Osiris was another god who dies and is resurrected; sharing in man's inevitable destiny to die, but demonstrating that the road does not end there, at least in the hopeful view of the priestly class who perpetuated this mythology.

Before leaving the subject, we should at least briefly note what likely was Jesus' own view on the subject of resurrection. Jews of Jesus' time believed that on the 'last day' the dead would be raised (as a group), although many people confused the idea with a literal physical and individual resurrection. But the Jewish idea of resurrection at the end of time does not involve collecting the physical remains and watching them come back to life.

Scholars tell us this was a belief in a spiritual resurrection, not a physical resurrection. Which may shed light on the end of St. Mark's gospel. His Easter morning passage, you will recall, states only that the women found an empty tomb, and then stops. After so many centuries of the development of the Easter story, our ears or eyes can read Mark's empty tomb conclusion and see or hear resurrection of the body—the tomb was empty because Jesus was no longer dead; he had walked away. But for people of the time, including Jesus' family and followers, the first instinct seems to have been that someone must have stolen the body. The physical resurrection idea we've been raised to believe, or at least to hope was true, took quite a long time further to develop in Christianity.

The Jewish, and thus early Christian, idea of resurrection was communal (it involved all the dead) and only after earthly life was finished for all people (at the "end of days"). It was not individual and instant. One did not immediately fly off at the moment of death to dwell in Heavenly bliss—that idea somehow inserted itself into Christianity along the way (comforting to many, perhaps, but not actually what Christianity officially promises). The resurrection Jesus spoke of in the Bible was not individual, but collective; see John 5:28-29. Nor was it an immediate aftermath of death, but was to take place at "the last day" as Jesus is quoted as saying clearly. See John 6:40 and 6:44.

That said, however, the process of such individualistic life-after-death beliefs had already begun to surface in Christianity's parent religion by the time of Jesus. The concept was never carefully defined in Judaism, however, and therefore we don't know much more than that it involved "eternity in the World to Come." How close that comes to the mostly later Christian idea of resurrection is therefore difficult to gauge. It is intriguing, though, to note that this later idea of individual resurrection could have developed in the Judeo-Christian imagination simply because people wanted it to be true—almost as though religion could become a democracy wherein the major themes could be determined by popular vote—a reminder that religion does, in fact, arise from human needs, fears, yearnings, etc.

Slightly before Jesus, the great Rabbi Hillel wrote, "One who has acquired Torah has acquired eternal life in the world to come." The exact details of the 'Resurrection' and its shape have generated plenty of different ideas, and arguments, for Christians from their early history through long ages since. Evidently this debate even influenced the structure of our Bible. "The Letter of Barnabas" and "The Shepherd of Hermes", which once were considered part of the canon of the Christian scriptures, were dropped from it because they opposed a bodily resurrection. That idea by then had evidently gained some popularity. Many Gnostics called it 'the faith of fools,' and claimed the resurrection was a purely spiritual event. Religious people, however, have always gravitated toward doctrines which fit their own hopes.

Of course, most people would still prefer that instant and individual life after death, or the Sunday School version of resurrection, were true. That's probably why the notion of flying off to 'be with Jesus' at the moment of death is thought by so many people to be the actual Christian teaching (and appears in the first few lines of so many newspaper obituaries). A lot of people want to believe that reported Near Death Experiences provide proof that the soul survives the body in death. But science has increasing evidence that brain activity does continue for a time after clinical death, so visions remembered by revived people after a few seconds or minutes of technical death are probably not evidence of being stopped on the way to Heaven and then returned to earth.

The bottom line, then, is that concepts of the divine figure being born of a human virgin and of rising from death after three days are not unique to Christianity.

They are totally derivative from general religious ideas stretching back into the mists of human origins, and concentrated during the Hebrew history and early Christian period in ancient Egypt, the source of so many

Judeo-Christian ideas. It is a big assignment to find anything truly unique in any established religion, because mankind has been seeking and imagining truth and explanations, and experiencing religious ecstasy, for so many eons.

Most of the difficulty we experience in trying to talk about topics like this (in addition to piety, or to the fear that God will 'smite' us if we get it wrong) is the tension between the work of the historian and the work of the priest or theologian. The historian may be interested in the spiritual and religious heritage a specific individual (such as Jesus) bequeaths to future generations, but that is not his work—his work is to separate such an inheritance from any verifiable or at least reasonably acceptable evidence and then to base his conclusions on that evidence.

So when an historian tackles a question such as "did Jesus rise up from death," he is not trying to answer a religious question, but a historical one. He looks around for evidence. He sees that all historically existing humans die, even though some 'gods' are believed not to have died, or to have died just temporarily.

Therefore his conclusion must be that, in the matter of Jesus, whether the man lived is a question to be explored and answered in terms of historicity, whereas questions about his resurrection must be left to the priest and theologian. Resurrection simply does not belong in the vocabulary of the historian. For a historian, the life (existence) of Jesus, if the historian has concluded that Jesus did live as a human, ended with his death—period. There can be no other answer from a historical point of view. The priest or theologian is free to answer the question differently.

There is historical evidence that followers of Jesus believed that he rose from the dead, but there is no historical evidence that he actually did so.

History simply cannot answer this question for us. If we choose to believe that Jesus rose from the dead, we are acting in the realm of religion and faith, not in the realm of history. Belief does not constitute actual history, even if belief turns out to be accurate (which means we're going to have to wait for any answers about resurrection, after-life, etc.). Such answers simply cannot be verified (historically) during this current life.

Seeing with the eyes of faith is not the same as reading history.

To conflate religion and history is to cheat both. They each have their own distinctive truth to tell. Historically Jesus, as a man, could not have risen up from death. Religiously, as a god, he did. We need to learn to leave it at that (unless, perhaps, we're professional theologians).

As to whether Jesus actually arose from death, as noted above, it is worth remembering that the oldest (and for a significant period in early Christianity, the only) gospel, that of "Mark," claims only that his tomb was empty on Easter morning. An empty tomb may suggest the idea of resurrection to some minds, especially by our stage in the development of Christianity, but it is not at all the same thing as actually claiming that resurrection has literally taken place.

What Paul paints as the central story of Christianity, that of Jesus' death and resurrection, is greatly influenced by ancient Egypt in general, in addition to fairly obvious similarities in the Isis/Osiris mythology. In this resurrection story, could it be that we are being told something which lies beneath the surface events which it describes? After all, Jesus himself told his disciples that he taught in parables intentionally to obscure the meaning to the uninitiated—to those who have eyes, but see not.

Such vagueness seems to be a mainstay of religion in general, with priests or priestesses speaking for the gods giving messages that normally came veiled in ambiguity and obscurity. And we are told that Moses put a veil over his face, symbolizing his unwillingness to reveal the mysteries imparted to him during his Egyptian initiation.

This approach, teaching in allegory and hidden meanings, was the way religion was handled in ancient Egypt. Clement of Alexandria is quoted as saying, "The Egyptians do not reveal their Religious Mysteries promiscuously." And Plutarch talks about pharaohs who rise from the military (instead of inheriting the throne by the birthright to marry the pharaoh's daughter and therefore as royals having been already familiar with the needed material) who are then immediately brought to the priests to be instructed in arcane theology, which conceals the mysteries under allegories.

The church father Origen is quoted in a similar vein, "The Egyptian philosophers have sublime notions with regard to the Divine nature, which they kept secret, and never discover to the people but under a veil of fables and allegories."

An important aspect of resurrection (of Jesus) faith to remember is that we're looking at a concept which took some time to develop—resurrection faith was essentially a story in the process of becoming; a looking back and reconsidering, rather than a flash of the moment discovery. The resurrection of Jesus could be termed a *decision* of the church just as accurately, or even more accurately, as it could be termed an *experience* of the church.

One the Biblical scholars has written that the resurrection was not a single event, but a protracted series of visionary experiences occurring variously and in widely different places over an extended period. In Paul's case it came several years after Jesus' crucifixion. She also reminds us again that the claim by relatively early Christians that Jesus had been raised from the dead "tells us nothing directly, of course, about the historical Jesus himself."

● A PRACTICAL ANSWER

So, how do we answer what may be this book's most intriguing question: Was Jesus an actual man who lived in history, or a collection of religious myths and allegories? Was he flesh and blood, or just a story?

Even if he were a flesh and blood man (take your own pick on a scale of likely to unlikely), he was *also* a story. Whatever elements from the New Testament gospels might be actual biographical details of a real human, they are accompanied and overlaid, essentially obscured, by a rich trove of religious allegories and mythology which are applied to him in addition to those biographical elements. What we have ended up with most likely is a jig-saw puzzle full of pieces which fit together with varying degrees of ease and difficulty.

It's very possible that he was both a real human and then later a religious myth, of course. But that approach begs the question. And it's not a very satisfying answer for anyone really interested in the question.

For practical purposes we have to look squarely at what information we have access to, and then evaluate it for accuracy.

Most of what we are told about Jesus which would fit into a believable human biography is not verifiable. On top of which real humans have both a human mother and a human father, just for starters. And, alas, real humans end up with obituaries rather than worshipers proclaiming them to be living gods.

The Jesus whom the Biblical evangelists thought they were writing about may have shared these and other real human traits with the rest of us. But if so, those human traits have been hidden in their writings, or perhaps intentionally obscured, behind a fog of religious history and dazzle.

The bottom line is that the Jesus *we know about* is almost entirely a jumble of religious stories, traditions, titles, and ideas. And even the authors who tell us these things wrote them well after the supposed facts of the life they tried to write about—all of this story was written in retrospect, and none of it was written by a reporter with first-hand experience of this Jesus. (The shorter letters [epistles] near the end of the New Testament use names we associate with Jesus' companions [James, Peter, John, Jude] but scholars generally feel they were written by later figures who simply appropriated the more authoritative names. In any case, they don't deal with biographically related material for Jesus. Wouldn't it be helpful if we had at least one gospel written by a person in Jesus' inner circle during his lifetime, rather than all of them having been written by members of the following or a later generation and relying solely on oral history?) The aspects of the Jesus story which might fit into a credible human biography are therefore few, and many of those meet with scholarly skepticism as to their historical accuracy.

Does that mean that the Jesus written about in the New Testament never lived? No. It merely means that we have extremely little significant information about him of historical worth if he did, in fact, live. Most respected authors on this subject seem generally agreed that there *was* an actual man behind the story, by the way.

What we have instead is a portrait of a man who sums up in himself the long mythology of both ancient Egyptian and Hebrew religious experience, terminology, and tradition. So that is the Jesus we know about. Whether this Jesus was a *historical* figure or not, it is safe to say we know him almost entirely as a *religious* figure of at least some probable invention.

Therefore the only practical answer we can safely give to the question is that the Jesus *we know* was a religious concoction rather than a man, even if the story was built up around an actual man. We know about a religious figure named Jesus, but we don't know a man of the same name from Nazareth. So did Jesus exist as a man? Probably not the Jesus we know from the Bible.

The Jesus we know was channeled through the men who wrote the New Testament. We have essentially no other sources. These men had no interest in writing history or biography, and had no reason to attempt either. They were making a religious and theological argument. They gave us a Jesus who became God, or was God all along. The Jesus who was just a man, assuming he existed, is basically lost to us.

The Jesus who does emerge from the New Testament gospels is a miracle worker or, put another way, a practitioner of Egyptian magic. The writers spend so much space and effort telling us of miracle after miracle that it is difficult to escape the notion that they viewed these miracles as the essence of his life's work. We are not left with much of a biography of this man Jesus, but we are left with a Biblical character who Morton Smith insightfully called 'Jesus the magician.'

● NOTE ON CHRISTIAN BELIEF IN THE RESURRECTION:

As mentioned earlier a lot of Christians believe that at the moment of death their 'souls' will *immediately* fly off to take up residence in Heaven. There are Christian sects which label their funeral services "Homegoing Celebrations" or otherwise paint them as victory laps of some kind. Evidently the 'homegoing' terminology is used widely in the religious ethos of Black Americans, as well as some white Evangelicals. A friend recalls attending a funeral for a business associate in a mostly white fundamentalist church at which everyone who stood up to give a remembrance began with a statement like "I'm *jealous* of Mary Jo. She's home now."

And I remember with some pain my father's funeral at which a newly ordained pastor began her sermon with the announcement: "Don't worry about Roy. He's with Jesus now." I was suddenly disappointed in the quality of our denomination's theological education for its clergy, as well as feeling that my dad's life and struggles had suddenly been reduced to a cliché—dismissed as nothing more than a race to death so that an extremely suspect religious idea could once again be proclaimed in lieu of a seriously prepared sermon.

Who gets to decide what a religion stands for and teaches? If a long-standing tradition says one thing, is that the answer for all time? Do the answers legitimately evolve with time, like the way a language is used or the shape of what a political party stands for? Is Christian belief a matter of democracy? If so, who gets to vote? When a synod of bishops declared a belief to be orthodox many centuries ago, should mass popular Christianity (or even a modern synod of bishops) now have the power to revise that verdict—to alter the balance between what is "orthodox" and what is "heresy"? Does the Holy Spirit who inspired one set of beliefs in the past, change His mind with time and come to inspire a different set of beliefs in a younger generation?

On the question at hand, resurrection of the dead, I'd feel fairly safe in guessing that no layman I've ever met conceptualizes the Christian belief as communal (all the dead arise at the same time rather than individually along the course of history) and "at the end of time" rather than at the point of the individual's death. And probably a fair number of seminary graduates are in the same boat. Who's right—the long trajectory of the Judeo-Christian tradition or the current consensus among those who label themselves Christians? (When I say "right" here I'm not speaking of scientific or real world facts, but of a definition of Christian belief. In other words, do contemporary Christians get to alter long standing doctrinal positions because their own version is more attractive or comfortable?)

And for that matter, as long as we're asking questions admitting of no quick answers, does it really matter? Whatever one believes as an individual, or whatever the church does or does not teach, nature will decide questions of life and death by its own laws—or perhaps the laws given to nature by the creator if you prefer to look at it that way. If such a creator God wants to intervene at the end of days, or even at multiple steps along the way, it will not depend on what any individual believes or what any church body teaches. God is not responsible for adhering to church doctrine or a variant interpretation of church doctrine; rather it's the church which is supposed to match its dogma to divine purposes to the extent that may be possible for humans.

Jesus is reported in the Bible to have said to a neighbor hanging on a cross to his side, "today" you will be with me in paradise. It's understandable that we instinctively want Jesus to have really spoken such words and for them to mean what we assume they mean. But it is highly dubious that a religious Jew (let alone a Rabbi) of that time and place would have done so.

It is apparent that most people who call themselves Christians wish that their religion afforded them instant and individual relief from death. The remaining question is whether all that wishing over all those centuries has actually delivered such a religion to us. Does religion ultimately evolve into what we want it to be? Does the apparent fact that most contemporary Christians believe that at the moment of death the soul flies off to some form of paradise mean that this is now the Christian position on the matter?

● NOTE ON THE RESURRECTION IN MARK'S GOSPEL

In writing that Mark's Gospel stops short of asserting the resurrection of Jesus by saying only that his tomb was found empty, I have followed the lead of several recent scholars, and mostly because I suspect they have put their fingers on something important. But to say not everyone agrees with this evaluation would be an understatement. The objection comes from people who think Mark declares the resurrection before he gets to the end of his story, not in how he structured the story's conclusion.

I've already acknowledged in passing in the above text one segment of Mark's gospel which would seem to point in another direction. Mark 16:6 tells us that when the three women found the tomb open they were greeted by a "young man" inside who said, "Do not be amazed; you seek Jesus of Nazareth, who was crucified. He has risen, he is not here..." (you may recall that in chapter 2 I mentioned that some observers connected the young man who ran naked into the night with the young man in the tomb on Easter morning).

This is indeed a statement of faith on the part of the author of Mark's gospel's, a ritual tying together of crucifixion and resurrection which is a unifying theme throughout most of the New Testament. But here it is evidently written by an author perhaps two generations down the road from the time of Jesus who may have heard about the young man's words from oral sources but did not hear them for himself, nor did he hear them from one of the three women whom he seems to claim had heard them directly.

These words from the young man in the open tomb are clearly one of the 'confessional' insertions into New Testament text, there to assert a religious point and not necessarily trying to make a historical claim—whether inserted by Mark himself or by someone later trying to correct Mark's omission of the resurrection idea which was by then gathering strength and finding its narrative. Many scholars have pointed out that the resurrection idea took some time to develop, and that a lot of editing of Christian texts was going on already during this early period.

The fact remains, though, that Mark stops his story at this point of the empty tomb. The final characters in his gospel are the young man and the three women. Neither a risen Jesus, nor the corpse of a crucified Jesus, makes an appearance after this point. We are, indeed, left with only an empty tomb, which is the point being made by the scholars I've followed.

Furthermore, Mark's failure to push ahead with the resurrection story, in contradistinction from his fellow gospel writers who came along even further down the road, is underlined in his last verse. The women had been instructed by the young man to "go, tell his disciples and Peter that he is going before you to Galilee; there you will see him as he told you." But Mark reports that the women ignored this order. They "fled" and "said nothing to any one." Mark simply closes his story at the empty tomb.

Whether he was making an assertion by doing this or not, whether he was the author of earlier material in his gospel that says or suggests that resurrection was involved or not, it is still true that those who say his gospel does not go beyond an empty tomb are correct. There must be some reason for this. It wasn't that he was out of material, especially since we have likely evidence that his original gospel was longer than the version we have in the canonical Bible.

And whatever conclusion you may want to reach, it is pretty much beyond any disagreement at all that Mark's telling of the story represents the earliest New Testament version of resurrection that we have short of the genuine letters of Paul. The Easter morning scene Mark paints, therefore, is probably as close to the historical truth of the matter as we can get. The subsequent gospels were written after the concept of the resurrection had begun to reach a level of universal doctrinal acceptance in the church—and their enthusiasm for the concept also then begins to color the way we perceive earlier material such as Mark's gospel. We assume that Mark believed exactly as did the Christians for whom John's gospel was written, whether Mark spelled it out in detail or not. But in an era when Christian "truth" was evolving, is that necessarily the case? ⌘

5.

A Goddess in the Men's Club?

What is God's gender? Christians accustomed to thinking of Jesus as God probably hesitate little in assuming that it's male, or at least hesitate little in using male pronouns to talk about the ultimate deity.

Yet general religion (ancient religious mythology) has always posited a great female goddess in charge, usually in combination with an equivalent male god. In the Mediterranean world this great goddess was usually inspired by, and modeled on, Isis, the Egyptian Queen of Heaven. Isis had her doppelganger in the religious scriptures of the Hebrews, and thus also in due course in those of Christianity, in addition to her solid lofty place of worship among pagan religions. Yet by the period of the writing of the New Testament, this ancient goddess came to be identified with the man Jesus (or the god-man Jesus, if you prefer). So the gender question got a little scrambled.

What is God's gender? There are a lot of ways of looking at this question, and none of them is especially simple or easy. Many throughout the ages have concluded that the answer is probably both male and female at the same time (which was also expected to be reflected in the psyche-personalities of the priests of these gods on earth). But even androgyny doesn't suit those who say we should not think of the gods anthropomorphically in the first place.

The gender tension started early for Christianity. The female half of our race seems to have gotten off to a religiously rough start as early as Eden in the Judeo-Christian tradition. The first woman in our Bible was an afterthought to the first male and then she was blamed for leading Adam, and thereby the whole race, into "original sin." She got her husband and herself kicked out of paradise, the story goes, and God has had misgivings about the human race ever since. That's even why God had to eventually send his own son to take the punishment for disobedience on our behalf, the Christian line has it.

There is some evidence in ancient religious art to suggest that the 'tree of good and evil' in the Eden story which was prohibited to the first

91

humans lest they become like 'gods,' was thought, at least by some, to be the *Amanita muscaria* 'magic' mushroom, which many people through the ages have felt indeed does open human eyes to things known only to the gods.

Anyway, the Eden episode was quite an accomplishment for the 'first' woman. And it sent repercussions rolling down to this day, traditional theology would maintain. As a consequence, women have mostly been viewed with a jaundiced eye in the Judeo-Christian tradition as it has grown. Negativity toward women has been a significant, albeit unfortunate, legacy of the Christian church to human civilization.

Iconic Christian teachers such as Thomas Aquinas argued that if a girl were born instead of a boy, it was because the father was ill or in a state of sin when she was conceived. He said all women were "birth-defective" and that only males possessed souls.

At the very beginning things may have been more balanced, however. Such negative views of the female half of our race were apparently a late development in general religious thought because evidence can be found that the earliest roots of even the Judeo-Christian tradition contained female gods, as well as male gods with female spouses. Scholars have found evidence, including archaeological findings and largely hidden echoes in the Bible, that the original religion of Israel was characterized by worship of goddesses. Some say Yahweh at first had a spouse (perhaps named Aserah). Eventually both the male and female principals were apparently merged into the concept of just that one god, Yahweh.

Aserah notwithstanding, the Judeo-Christian tradition has been welcoming to male deities and apparently devoid of female deities for as long as it can easily be traced. (That is, unless you decide that humans who became 'saints' should be considered mini-gods; in which case, suddenly, we have an abundant supply of divine females.)

In this negative view of females Christianity diverged from a more universal religious norm, however. God had traditionally been seen as both masculine and feminine, or as androgynous, and probably had been thought of as a woman long before being seen as male—females were the creators, after all; all new life came from them. The church father Origen referred to God as both feminine and masculine. Even that ancient symbol of god, the sun, was once seen as both male and female, or at times simply as female. Jesus, too, in the Gospel of Thomas is quoted as teaching "when you make the male and the female one and the same," that is when you enter the kingdom of God.

This conception of God as both male and female, father and mother, may have faded dramatically as Christianity marched along its lengthy history, but it has certainly not disappeared completely. Our mystics have always known this key truth. And none more so than Julian of Norwich, the English female mystic of considerable current interest—and the first woman known to have written a book in the English language.

Julian speaks of God as "our Mother as well as our Father. God rejoices that he is our Father; and God rejoices that he is our Mother, and God rejoices that he is our true spouse, and that our soul is his beloved wife." Christ, she writes, is "our Mother, brother and savior...our kind Mother, our gracious Mother."

● HOLY WISDOM

But there is a female god who did manage to survive inside the Judeo-Christian tradition.

She's a largely unknown Biblical character to modern Christians because for centuries she's been largely ignored. You may well have heard of her only indirectly—because of the name of the great church (now a mosque) in Istanbul (Constantinople): Hagia Sophia ('Holy Wisdom,' or 'St. Wisdom').

This is the goddess known as Sophia, the *sui generis* spirit whom we're told at least participated in the creation of all that exists. At various stages of Christian thought, this female god, Sophia, has also been identified with Jesus, the Holy Spirit, and by some with Mary Magdalene. We probably know her better by her simple translated name 'Wisdom'. She is almost certainly modeled on the Great Goddess mythology of the ancient near east, which in turn was almost certainly inspired by Isis, the great Egyptian goddess. She can probably safely be seen as Isis translated as a concept into Hebrew religion.

● EGYPTIAN ADVANCEMENT LOST TO CHRISTIANITY

We probably have a remnant of this orientation in the matriarchal conception of Jewish identity which traces ancestry through the female line, rather than the male line as it does in our European originated culture. This, as was so much in the Israelite culture and religion, was owed to ancient Egypt, where all landed property descended in the female line from mother to daughter.

This even extended to kingship—the rightful heir to any pharaoh could only be his daughter. So if the son of a king wanted to inherit his father's place, he had to marry his sister. "The Great Wife" of the king was the king's heiress and it was only because of marriage to her that her husband was king, or pharaoh. The king did not even have to be of royal blood. His status in society was not a key to his succession, but if he married the queen he immediately became king. The queen was queen because she was born the daughter of a king. The king was king because he had married the queen.

Ancient Egypt thus gave an importance and standing to women which sounds almost modern to us, but its basic feminist contribution was to maintain a female near, or at, the top of its major gods—the cult of the great goddess Isis. The Isis cult then spread throughout the ancient Mediterranean world, and eventually it seeped into Christianity in disguised ways.

We will note in Chapter 8 the importance of the pharaoh Akhenaten in crystalizing the theological concept of monotheism. It seems he may have also played a similar role in the elevation of women as important religious figures who could stand and act alone, without authority derived from a husband or son. As with the concept of monotheism, this growing status of women was probably trending before Akhenaten, but it seems safe to say he became a key figure in encouraging and promoting it.

As Amenhotep IV (before changing his name to Akhenaten) he built temples at Karnak with extraordinary features. Much of the decoration revolved around the king's wife, Nefertiti, and omitted the king himself, both aspects being very unusual. And these decorations illustrate the queen (sometimes along with her daughter) performing rituals that had theretofore been reserved for the king.

With so many Egyptian religious features incorporated into what became Christianity, it seems a shame this inclusion of women in priestly and liturgical roles was lost for such a long time. The difference it could have made if Christianity had not deviated from this course is so profound that it is almost impossible to visualize.

A legend about women and religion (magic) from aboriginal South America tells about witchcraft that was known only to the women, while the men lived in fear of them and were totally under their control. The men, we're told, finally solved this problem when they simply killed off all their females—only to realize later to their chagrin that they now had to wait for the remaining female infants to grow up in order to find brides for themselves. It's a startling and somewhat amusing anecdote from prehistory, but the point is only that women once did hold primary positions in the religious and mystical rites of their communities. Magic back then was what we today would call simply 'religion,' and the females were in firm control of it, at least in some places and times.

When I was a boy the idea of women as Christian clergy was almost nowhere to be found. Women could be lay parish workers, or Deaconesses in some Protestant groups, or as they had been for centuries in the Catholic tradition, nuns. But church leadership was pretty much a patriarchal affair. Seminary was for young men just out of university—I recall the great novelty of having a young Deaconess join classes at my seminary, even though she could not realistically expect ordination at that time. I could sense she was in the vanguard of change in the church, but I could not have imagined how quickly that change would come.

Had women always been so sidelined in the infancy of Christianity? Probably not. Scholars point out that the Nag Hammadi materials discovered last century in Egypt might preserve memories of an age when women were far more important in the 'Jesus movement' than subsequent writings indicate. Women were prophets, leaders, and even bishops, evidently. There is a substantial literature which now argues that women played a critical role among the earliest followers of Jesus. This may have even been the case as long as a century into church history.

Partially (maybe largely) to help supply the missing feminine aspect in the Jesus story, the western catholic tradition eventually built an ever more elaborate cult of the Virgin (although to do so it had to squelch an equally powerful tradition of Mary Magdalene to make room).

For centuries Mary the Virgin mother was the only major female on the ecclesiastical landscape, although there were some saints and lots of nuns. Yet Mary's stature was derivative. She may have been the Mother of God, as even Luther insisted, and therefore worthy of veneration, but she was not herself God, despite some thought along the way that she should be seen as Co-Redemptrix (a title which a few have thought should be ascribed to Mary Magdalene also).

Historians and psychologists see the ultimate roots of the cult of Mary the Virgin as a continuation of the primordial mother goddess legacy of ancient general religion, and the workings of the subconscious human mind. Even so, females, along with their feminine qualities were still missing from the main religious stage in their own right.

And this misogynistic bias was not just some quirk of the newly emerging Christianity. It was an integral part of the whole Judeo-Christian tradition from which the Jewish sect of Christianity arose.

Even though women are known to have supported rabbis with money, possessions and food, much like Mary Magdalene is thought to have supported Jesus' ministry, their participation in the actual ritual practice of Judaism was minor at best. Women were allowed to read from the Torah at services in the congregation, but they were prohibited from reciting lessons or sermons. A first century Rabbi is quoted as saying, "Rather should the words of the Torah be burned than entrusted to a woman."

In Egypt we encounter similar disgruntlement at the idea of a female becoming Pharaoh, as when Nefertiti succeeded Akhenaten (he had named her as co-regent), and she seems to have taken the name Smenkhkara in the thirteenth century BCE.

The Egyptologist establishment felt a mistake must explain the situation of a (gasp!) female pharaoh. So it was speculated that a feminine-looking prince had stolen Akhenaten's affections and had thus displaced Nefertiti before the old pharaoh's death. Some have described this idea as similar to the Roman emperor Hadrian falling in love with the beautiful youth Antinous, and later, after the youth's suspicious death, promoting him to the rank of a god. One author reports that *The Sunday Times* of London commented in the twentieth century on this Egyptian succession theory as "better gay than female."

How time can change things! Female clergy in the non-Roman western church are now commonplace—if there are any surprises left, they involve an area of church life where women have not yet made great progress, although in some denominations they have already risen to apparent dominance. We've had a female Presiding Bishop in both the Anglican and Lutheran communities in the United States, and we've had a Pope (of the western church), Francis, who, without actually giving an inch in doctrine or organization, has seemed genuinely aware of, and even sympathetic to, the concern of women to serve the church in expanded capacities. (According to legend we've also had a female Pope a long time ago, but if so it didn't do anything to advance the position of women in the church; maybe it even slowed things down on that front.)

It almost seems that the only unassailable male stronghold remaining is the Godhead itself—but could we have been wrong on the assumption that the Godhead is male? Maybe God was actually just as much 'female' as 'male' all along in our tradition, but the concept for a long period was obscured by other concerns.

The word Goddess is about the last word I would have associated with the Judeo-Christian tradition as a young student of religion at university, and then even at seminary. For starters, we were monotheists, and the position of the one god was already taken—by a god we assumed without further question was male (although perhaps a bit of a challenge to understand mathematically because he was a Trinity of, undoubtedly, male gods).

● WISDOM AS SOPHIA

So it may come as a revelation to some that the Bible presents us with a female figure, Sophia (Greek for "Wisdom"), with the status of a Goddess, and the role of creator of all that exists—a rather lofty position!

Think of the exquisite hymn at the beginning of the gospel attributed to John ("In the beginning was the word..."). Scholars feel this was originally a hymn to Holy Wisdom. If you substitute "Wisdom" for "Word" or "Logos" and read it again, you will have a good, and elegant, summary of Wisdom's (Sophia's) role in the Judeo-Christian Biblical tradition.

Sophia in the Hebrew scriptures is a highly developed personification of God's presence and work. Sophia existed before the world was created. She herself was the first of God's creations, and then she presided along with God over the rest of creation. Therefore creation is portrayed officially as not simply a male activity. As understood by primitive people stretching far back into prehistory, creation is thus recognized as a uniquely female assignment—new life comes from females, although males may be of some assistance.

The tradition has consistently identified Sophia as female. In the "Wisdom of Solomon" (situated in the apocrypha, non-canonical, group of scriptural writings) she is referred to from the beginning as "she." "For she knows and understands all things, and she will guide me wisely in my actions" (9:11).

She is also at times treated as a separate being from God (the Father): "Give me the wisdom that sits by thy throne (9/4)....With thee is wisdom, who knows thy works and was present when thou didst make the world....Send her forth from the holy heavens, and from the throne of thy glory send her" (9:9-10). This is also true in Ecclesiasticus, "Wisdom was created before all things" (1:4). Most of the wisdom literature treats her simply as the "first born of all creation." (A sort of reversal of the Eden story where the male was created first.) The Wisdom of Solomon, written in Egypt, pays homage to Sophia's role in creation.

A similar figure can be found, not surprisingly, in Egyptian religion, again connected with creation and again female. The Sun God in Egyptian religion was seen as the creator who created himself. But there was always a female component deemed to be necessarily involved in creation. In fact, the sun, which was Egypt's main god, was seen as androgynous. At the center of the sun's cult, in its own city Heliopolis, the sun was characterized as "the mother and father of all, and the great He-She," and the "beneficent mother of gods and humans," historians tell us.

The story of Sophia runs through the Hebrew Scriptures and then into the history of the Christian church in ways strange and obscure. At the politically (and greed) based dissolution of the Knights Templar in France, the order was accused, among other heresies, of worshiping Sophia, although under another name. And much earlier the Gnostics had worshipped Sophia as the feminine element of God, as the Nag Hammadi discoveries in Egypt have shown.

● ISIS AS SOPHIA

Where did the Hebrew idea of Sophia/Wisdom originate? Scholarly opinion is nearly unanimous in feeling that the major influence came from a non-Biblical female goddess and that the Egyptian goddess Isis, in her Hellenized form, is the most logical candidate. And to boot, much of the

Bible's wisdom writings had appeared first in Egypt either nearly verbatim or in similar language.

Scholars believe that Jewish authors simply took the characteristics of the great mother goddess Isis and painted them on their Sophia figure. It wasn't Isis, but God's wisdom which/who should be exalted. Isis, rival to Yahweh in the minds of the populace, is thus at least somewhat neutralized.

In other words, if the Israelite people find the Egyptian goddess attractive, as do their neighbors in other lands, then we come up with our own goddess who has the same capacities and attributes—'anything your goddess can do, ours can do better' (or at least just as well). This approach has been a basic and repeated Judeo-Christian response, leading to an early Roman Pope instructing Christians to simply "baptize" the opposition's ideas, shrines, etc. by turning them into Christian ideas, shrines, etc.

Some of the great Christian edifices in Europe, and even in the New World, have been constructed intentionally and directly on top of pagan holy sites, thus "baptizing" them and neutralizing (or incorporating and appropriating) their holiness. One of the most vivid and accessible examples of this which is easily available to tourists is the Basilica San Clemente (St. Clement's), in Rome where a first century pagan temple of Mithras, a Persian all-male sun-cult which rivaled Christianity in Rome during the first century CE, was discovered beneath the church and is being progressively restored and made available to visitors. Even in the Americas sites which became holy to Christians have been discovered to have once been pagan holy sites.

In Egypt, the creation of life was attributed to Isis. She was sometimes styled 'oldest of the old' or 'eternal mother,' and usually labeled 'Great in Magic' or 'Queen of Heaven.' Eventually she had risen above all of the other goddesses of Egypt, and eventually her cult spread throughout the ancient near east, far beyond Egypt. Politically her role was divine mother of the reigning pharaoh. We are also told that Isis knew the secret name of God (the sun), and thus came to share and possess God's key to power.

● JESUS AS SOPHIA

A certain androgynous aspect can be felt in the way Jesus was treated in New Testament writings, not least in the way his closest female disciple (lover? wife?) Mary of Magdala was nearly erased from the record. Jesus was seen as the incarnation of Wisdom, a female figure, and Jesus was seen as the equivalent of the sun, an androgynous or female figure. Attempts at getting everything to square up neatly during Christianity's first century(s), with ideas and beliefs still developing, must have been difficult work, yielding various degrees of success.

So, unfortunately perhaps, this female figure Sophia eventually came to be identified mostly with Jesus, a male figure, (or sometimes with the Holy

Spirit, a presumably asexual figure). This identification may have pushed us further into a patriarchal framework for Christianity. Jesus was first seen as a wisdom teacher, or the messenger of Sophia. Then he was seen as the very incarnation of Sophia. Among the four gospels, Matthew offers the strongest Sophia Christology.

Of the many ways Jesus is portrayed or could be perceived in the New Testament, one of the easiest to understand is that he was a wisdom teacher. Wisdom in the Bible is a path, a way. It is not smartness or cleverness. Rather, wisdom teachers usually teach "the way" that people should follow and live. See, for example, Mathew 7: 13 & 14.

Statements made about Wisdom in Jewish literature, sometimes hymns, are repeated about Jesus by Paul in his letters, solidifying the association between Jesus and Sophia. The great Egyptian (Alexandrian) church father Origen said wisdom was the truest designation of the nature of Jesus.

Jesus himself is quoted in our Bible as proclaiming "I am the way" (John 14:6) and thus, at that point, going well beyond his role of wisdom teacher and claiming a divine (and perhaps magical) role instead. In any case, it is obvious that Sophia's role has now been transferred to Jesus in the minds of John's community—the feminine had been subsumed by the masculine, or so it would appear. Maybe this community felt these things in an asexual, purely allegorical, way; maybe it felt Sophia was strong enough to bear both the feminine and the masculine; maybe it just didn't care or even notice.

The transfer nonetheless had been made. Perhaps Sophia's rightful successor in the new Christian milieu should have been the Holy Spirit, or Mary Magdalene, as some have suggested, but instead it became Jesus.

Paul, in Colossians, quotes an early hymn which merges Sophia and Jesus: "He is the image of the invisible God, the first born of all creation; for in him all things were created in heaven and earth, visible and invisible...all things were made through him and for him." Jesus was now being given Sophia's role.

"Christ...the wisdom of God," I Corinthians 1:24. "What is the wisdom given to him?" Mark 6:2. "I will give you a mouth and wisdom, which none of your adversaries will be able to withstand or contradict." Luke 21:15. And we are brought back to the beautiful hymn to Sophia at the beginning of the gospel of John, now reassigned to Jesus as the "Word" or "Logos."

How much did we lose with that shift of a female Sophia to a male Jesus? The shift further obscured the Bible's great goddess and thereby helped shift the whole of the emerging religion toward a male bias. But on the popular level my guess is that most lay people, without really thinking about it, view Jesus as a fairly androgynous figure anyway. He is nearly always presented to us in church-sponsored and church-preserved art (in the West, at least) as a rather pale hippie-like Scandinavian-looking guy in a flowing gown. The long-haired and bearded figure used ubiquitously today did not become established until the eighth century. Before that Jesus was usually portrayed as beardless, with short hair, and wearing a Roman tunic. The Bible also seems to underline the gentler, more feminine, qualities of Jesus' personality—his caring, tender, nurturing side (not that it lacks apparent explosions of testosterone as well at some points).

Anyway, the role of wisdom teacher was the first assigned to Jesus. After that, he gradually became supernatural—a god, just as Sophia was a goddess.

It must be noted here again that there is a strong school of thought which sees Jesus (or the Holy Spirit) as not the proper successor figure to Sophia. Instead this way of thinking believes that honor should belong to Mary Magdalene. The Gospel of Philip from the Nag Hammadi texts is a primary source which sees Mary as divine wisdom; as Sophia.

That Wisdom/Sophia, identified in the Bible as the creative force ("without whom nothing was made that was made") should also then be consistently identified as female/mother is not much of a surprise. The ancients may have experienced some confusion about the finer points of the human reproduction process, but it was clear that females brought forth each new generation and therefore that all creative endeavors must involve a mother.

This early identification of Jesus as the incarnation of the goddess Wisdom, perhaps reached its zenith in the Middle Ages when it blossomed into a piety which sounds strange to us today—speaking of Jesus as 'mother.'

St. Anselm of Canterbury is a somewhat odd example of this piety. First he objects to God being called 'mother' because of supposed male superiority and also because he thinks that the father contributes more genetically to the offspring than does the mother (which some scientists today think is probably the exact reverse of the actual genetic reality). However, he then glides easily into speaking of Jesus as the mother who loves, using the analogy of the hen gathering her chicks beneath her wings.

Anselm is quoted: "But you, Jesus, good Lord, are you not also a mother? Are you not that mother who, like a hen, collects her chickens under her wings? Truly, master, you are a mother. For what others have conceived and given birth to, they have received from you...It is then you, above all, Lord God, who are mother."

This sort of language was frequently associated with the monasteries, and Bernard of Clairvaux also used it to describe Jesus as 'mother,' writing, "suck not so much the wounds as the breasts of the Crucified...He will be your mother, and you will be his son."

Jesus as a wisdom teacher (or as the incarnation of Sophia, stated in code) runs heavily through all four of the gospels, but, as I've said previously, is a major theme especially in Matthew.

● CHRISTIAN ARITHMETIC

The ancient Sophia mythology poses a little glitch to Jewish monotheism by giving us a goddess who participated in creation but was not herself Yahweh, Israel's "only" god. It then does Christianity the same service by suggesting that Jesus, by identification with Sophia, was a god, although not "God the Father." Or by introducing a "Holy Spirit" which is a god but also not the only god. Of course, all of these ideas have long roots and were developed over long periods of time, so to reduce them to a couple of sentences may do them some injustice.

Nevertheless, Christians ended up with a "three in one" god, or a "one god in three persons." Try explaining that to a school kid learning arithmetic, or for that matter to almost anyone trying to understand Christianity and trying to take it seriously. Religion professionals have done a lot of explaining on this score, some of it rather fanciful, but none have actually claimed (to my knowledge, at least) that one and three have the same numeric value. So the Trinity becomes another mystery which the Christian adherent is obligated to believe, but not obligated to understand. A good deal of the clerical explaining comes down to little more than 'God is omnipotent so He can organize Himself in whatever way He wants.'

It's all a little like trying to understand "Big Ten" arithmetic in 21st century America college sports, where ten currently actually means fourteen (or for that matter "Big Twelve" arithmetic where twelve actually means ten—for the moment at least; the numbers will probably have mutated again by the time you read this book and indeed the Big Twelve has already started the process anew before I can even finish this book). The football gods are evidently as hopeless at arithmetic as were the guys who first tried to explain Christianity to us.

The Gospel of Thomas tells us that Jesus himself may have tried his hand at an explanation: "Jesus said: Where there are three gods, they are gods; where there are two or one, I am with him." Well, that certainly clears things up, doesn't it?

A rational person could be forgiven for feeling that the Trinity doctrine results from a 'monotheistic' religion which simply has too many gods to accommodate at once. But we still need to find some kind of reason that we may have ended up in this mathematical bind. As with so many aspects of Christianity, the seeds may have been planted in ancient Egypt.

Somewhere along the way, the Egyptians started to group depictions of their gods in threes. Scholars understand this phenomenon from different perspectives, with some assuming the motivation was simply a desire for symmetry. But so many Egyptian religious ideas and practices surface again in major or minor ways in Christianity that these trios of gods are also likely to have been a theological influence on successor religions.

The trios were portrayed as family groups—a father, always the main god in the grouping, a son of god, and a mother goddess.

When this grouping gets translated into Christianity we have the divine family with the Holy Spirit in place of the lost Sophia (and on the way to erasing almost all other feminine figures to make way for the Virgin—the safest choice to represent the feminine in Christianity without threatening male domination or egos). The idea that the Holy Spirit could represent the continuation of Sophia and her work has been articulated by many, although the consensus probably points either to Mary Magdalene or to Jesus himself, as we've noted. In any case, the Trinity is safely seen as a family unit of gods, just as were the Egyptian trios. It is interesting as well to note that these Egyptian trios of gods likely influenced other near Eastern religions as well.

Harold Bloom, the Yale humanist, wrote that "Tritheism is imaginatively as appealing as any other polytheism," and "Christianity remains polytheistic from the Gospel of John down to the contemporary United States."

Many other scholars and observers agree. Christianity was founded by a man who felt justified to appoint himself an apostle of Jesus despite having no qualifications, and despite violating the Zodiacal cap of twelve for the apostolic club in doing so. The religion he founded continues to feel free to describe itself as monotheistic despite the lack of any real evidence in that direction.

One aspect of Egyptian religious practice which we, from our (quasi?) monotheistic perspective, would find strange is that everyday Egyptians of the period were free to choose the god they wanted to worship out of the hundreds of candidates recognized along the Nile. But then observe, for example, the pious Catholic matron of today (or at least just a generation or so past) faithfully praying her Rosary at daily Mass, loyally active in the Rosary Society, and probably with art depicting the Virgin in her bedroom and kitchen. Even though the church has tried to teach the difference between the worship due to God and the lesser veneration which can be paid to the saints, when the message reaches the pew, choosing which 'god' or 'goddess' to give first devotion to is not necessarily a thing of the past.

That women are once again beginning to fill their ancient role as priests may (should?) help us more fully understand and embrace the essential aspects of religion which have been obscured of late (just a few handfuls of centuries!).

● TODAY'S HOLY WISDOM

In large measure we've lost the goddess bequeathed to us by the Judeo-Christian tradition: the goddess Wisdom/Sophia. Just by neglect—she's still in our scriptures, of course. But generic religion demands at least one goddess to stand with the gods, so Christianity had to comply by some means. It did so by evolving the humble mother of Jesus into the Blessed Ever-Virgin Mary, and installing her as the new "Queen of Heaven," replacing the Egyptian goddess Isis.

In the East, in the Orthodox churches, this adulation of Mary is said to be still nuanced and historically layered. In the West, among Roman Catholics, it is not as nuanced as the official church line wishes it were. It has pretty much become an official arm of the church, and Mary has become pretty much part of the godhead despite the responsible efforts of some theologians and popes to draw the relevant theological distinctions. Among Western Protestants Mary is a beloved figure, but beloved in the uncomplicated, almost innocent, way most Protestants love Jesus, i.e. theologically naïve and Sunday School simple.

Most Protestants may not even be able to recognize Mary when they stumble across her. They can sing their much loved hymn "For All the Saints" and sail right through the second verse without realizing they are acknowledging the Virgin as the primary religious figure short of the Trinity itself. "O higher than the cherubim, more glorious than the seraphim…Thou bearer of the eternal Word, most gracious, magnify the Lord."

Christianity is a Johnny-come-lately religion. Its many predecessors have been packed with virgins and goddesses. Christianity is simply carrying on a very long-standing religious tradition by inventing its own chief virgin and treating her as a goddess.

So Christians still have their goddess. But among some of them, she walks heavily veiled, blending somewhat into the background and yielding the stage wholly to her son. While among others she has taken over center stage herself and casts a shadow on her son. An innocent party looking at Christianity today could be excused for a bit of confusion as to which figure, mother or son, was the god. And in fact, taking into account the very deep roots of Christianity, reaching back far beyond Judaism, maybe it's most honest to stop trying to claim a distinction. Christianity ultimately is a religion, and religion will have its goddesses. It will also have its hero-savior. Christianity, despite the sometimes fevered efforts of theologians to draw distinctions, has both.

It may be a fair question to ask why the gender of a disembodied being, such as a god, even matters, let alone whether or not such a being even has a gender. And as to Sophia, the simple way to see her is as the Jewish, and ultimately the Christian, answer to Isis.

For the Roman, or Catholic, portion of western Christianity it seems reasonable to posit that the dominant story-theme has been a thirst for the great Goddess, the Mother Goddess of ancient religion even before Isis. This is actually a universal theme in mankind's religions. In the specific Christian version we started with a man who gradually came to be regarded as a god, which in turn yielded an opening to take a new look at the man's mother. She then became a viable candidate for the needed update (for a specifically Christian version) of the universal Mother Goddess. And over time she started to fill those shoes so successfully that there's now a question as to whether it's the mother or the son who is the most god-like, and most worshiped, of the pair.

The Bible story which accommodates this most succinctly is probably that of the Annunciation, when the humble maiden Mary receives an emissary from God and learns she has been chosen from all the women on earth to bear the child of God—in effect that she has been chosen to be God's wife. Well, 'Mrs. God' is a pretty steep promotion for a poor country girl. It's no wonder that she was now herself on the road to becoming a Goddess. Christians were now yearning for their own Isis, as had religious groups at every step along the way from depths of pre-history. ⌘

6.

Did Jesus have a Girlfriend?

As long as we're talking about gender, we may as well plunge all the way into the topic and have a look at the big sexual question dangling in the New Testament—did Jesus participate in human sexuality? Perhaps we had a hint, or even a solid clue, in Chapter 2. But speculation has traditionally focused elsewhere—on the mystery woman of the New Testament: Mary Magdalene.

The two women closest to Jesus have both been accused of deserving Nathaniel Hawthorne's Scarlet Letter—Mary his mother, and Mary of Magdala, his foremost disciple (student) and maybe his mistress, or even his wife.

Of the two, the mother being described as an adulteress would shock far more people. For one thing, it could make Jesus not a miracle baby, but a bastard. For another, Mary has been venerated (essentially worshiped, actually) by untold generations of Christians as the Blessed Virgin Mary, the most innocent and pure human ever to walk the earth (aside, perhaps, from her son).

But stories about Mary the mother that ran in other directions circulated as well. A guy named Celsus (and a number of others who wrote in a similar vein) wrote that Mary was kicked out of the house by her carpenter husband because she was an adulteress and that the real father of Jesus was a soldier named Panthera. Celsus claimed that Jesus came up with the 'virgin' bit himself (so he could claim to be a god) and that Jesus later went off to Egypt as a hired laborer where he picked up his magic tricks.

The New Testament actually does confirm Egyptian involvement, although it leaves the timing and duration ultra-vague by placing Egypt in the infancy narratives. A number of scholars suggest that may be just a sop to the truth because, although Jesus' connection with Egypt was too widely known to be entirely ignored, the evangelists, for whatever reasons, did not want to pursue it in detail. Or maybe they simply *could not* pursue it in detail by their time—maybe too much of the story had already been lost, and all that remained was the knowledge that there had been an important connection with Egypt which at least needed to be acknowledged, however vaguely.

That Mary Magdalene, on the other hand, might deserve a Scarlet Letter would surprise considerably fewer people. The idea has become part of popular culture even though it showed up one day without any rhyme or reason, and has only fairly recently (1969) finally been disavowed by the Vatican. Pope Gregory the Great decided on his own that the Magdalene was a tainted woman. About 600 years into the Christian era he preached a sermon labeling Mary as a prostitute possessed by evil spirits. Nobody really knows with certainty where he got the idea or why he preached the sermon. Anyway, despite the Bible telling us that she had a prominent place in Jesus' circle, Mary was now saddled with an unsavory reputation. She became the great penitent. (Gregory's inspiration likely came from the New Testament story of the woman who anointed Jesus with costly ointment and dried his feet with her hair.)

Maybe Mary's sin in Gregory's eyes was merely that she was female. (In grudging fairness to Gregory, I need to admit that *if* the identification of Mary Magdalene with the woman who anointed Jesus' feet with precious ointment is accurate, then the Bible does indeed paint her as a sinner, at least in Luke 7:36-50. However, that identification, while widely held, is basically conjecture.)

Christians, officially at least, have never been very big on sex. Even today, some people with the keenest religious zeal dedicate themselves to lives of celibacy as nuns, monks, priests, or just plain religious nut cases. And it's not difficult even today to find entire church groups which preach and teach as though sexuality is the worst 'sin' possible. The whole attitude has many roots (notably from Clement of Alexandria as noted in a previous chapter), but it got a big boost from the get-go with St. Paul, and not much later from generations of Christian hermits who moved to the Egyptian desert to avoid any fleshly lusts. Some of them even moved up to tiny platforms on top of poles where temptations of the flesh were presumably minimal, or at least extremely inconvenient.

So it's no big surprise that most Christians assume that Jesus was probably asexual, or in any case was above sexual temptation and absolutely was beyond sexual activity. That is, when the idea of "Jesus" and "sex" come together at all, which we can probably safely assume for most Christians is a rare to nonexistent happenstance.

The New Testament does scatter a sprinkling of women here and there among all the men who populate its stories. But they are few and rather obscure. Speaking lines are rare. Jesus is not painted as a male chauvinist; in fact at points he is described as standing up in defense of a female. But he is certainly not portrayed as interested in females on a sexual level; at least as the edited texts have come down to us.

This has given some theologians a headache. If Jesus was true man, as well as true God, he must have felt the same sexual urges that every man has felt. But does that then mean God feels sexual urges? Very quickly it gets a little complicated as you can see.

Anyway, it's likely that the guys who wrote the New Testament skirted the issue intentionally. Avoid the subject and hopefully it will go away. So we are left with the portrait of a Jesus who did have a few women in his life, but they were apparently at some distance, not necessarily always physically distant, but surely always erotically distant it would appear. He's even painted at one point as saying some things about his mother which seem a little harsh to our ears.

Then at some point along the way theologians and religious historians began to look at things and tried to find reality hidden in the cracks. The "historical Jesus" must have been a sexual being they reasoned (if he was a "true man", although there have been sober theologians along the way who believed he might not have been a man at all, as we've seen) and they found hints through something called "textual criticism" which suggested that the Biblical story had probably been heavily edited. The man Jesus had been portrayed for effect—to make this or that point espoused by one or another theological point of view, or faction, along the way.

This not only freed up to an extent the taboo against thinking that Jesus might have a sexuality, but it also uncovered some likely evidence that Mary Magdalene played a far larger role in his life and ministry than the canonical scriptures had made obvious. With that came the increasingly open assertion that Jesus and Mary could have married; that Jesus had a wife and thus maybe even children.

That idea did not sit well with every pious Christian, but at least it was somehow an idea which left Jesus on a lofty perch. Marriage was not only common in Jewish culture of his day, it was expected, almost demanded, and especially so for a rabbi like Jesus. And through the ages since his time there have been no shortage, shall we way, of pious religious men who have married women. So the net result of the idea was well within cultural norms even if it was still unsettling to some pious souls. The Jesus walking around Galilee may have had a speaking acquaintance with sexual feelings, but if he was married he was not sinning; everything was at least socially sanctioned. Marriage was expected of an upstanding Jewish man of the period (but then so was fatherhood, so the whole question still has some loose ends).

And the idea of a married Jesus took hold later in another way, although one which took quite a few steps beyond normal. There have been troves of nuns who claimed they were married to Jesus, especially during the

Middle Ages (which could be seen to make him an adulterer or at least a sexual athlete). Historians tell us that the ranks of these spouses (usually "brides") of Jesus even included a few men along the way (which I guess in today's lingo would make him "bi").

Later, however, some observers began to speculate that maybe Jesus and Mary Magdalene were a couple but may not have married. This idea seems popular today with a number of writers, and of course we have no proof in either direction. So now the idea that Jesus had sex outside of marriage was posited. This returned "sin" into the equation and with it more opportunity for scandal—more opportunity for pious souls to take offense. Jesus could now be seen as a potential adulterer.

Like you, I have no evidence whatsoever about Jesus' relationship status. But we can be, and probably are, somewhat intrigued by the possibilities as have been many generations of people familiar with the Christian story. And there is a rich vein of extra-Biblical lore surrounding the Mary Magdalene theme which is fun to know about whether it could ever be pinned down as history or not.

● THE OTHER MARY, OR THE MAIN MARY? WIFE OR HARLOT?

Mary Magdalene has been riding a recent wave of attention from Christian feminists and from the 'liberation theology' folks. She's always been flirting with some sort of center stage appearance, but always somehow remained hidden in the wings. It was easy to have the feeling she must have played a much more prominent role than the skimpy one painted in the New Testament, and many have reached that conclusion. But there was a touch of frustration. She remained basically off-camera, at least if one's primary reference was the canonical New Testament. Later discoveries of ancient texts opened the curtains wider and did give her a starring role.

It seems likely that this Mary was hidden on purpose in our New Testament. To some extent we can only guess why, although the emerging discoveries of other period texts, such as the Gnostic gospels, give us pretty unmistakable hints. Likely the initial reason was the tradition of male dominance in place in the culture of the time. Mary was not only, it seems clear, Jesus' favorite woman and a close follower of his, but evidently also the most attentive and discerning of his followers—his best student. She got the message, and she understood it, apparently better than did Jesus' male followers, including the vaunted twelve. It's apparent too that the twelve were jealous of her position as Jesus' favorite and quickest learner, especially Peter, the evident official leader of the group of twelve.

Mary herself is painted in extra-Biblical sources as understanding full well that she knew the master's message better than the rest, and that she really should be the leader of the group. Peter won out, of course—he was male.

Although the cult of the Virgin (in this case it's her turn to be the 'other' Mary) developed over a long period of time, it's possible that even as early as the time of the gospel writers there was beginning to be a sense of rivalry between the two Marys in the minds of the early Christians. That was quite probably another reason for Mary Magdalene to be gradually shoved to the sidelines. Then there was the matter of sex. If the Magdalene and Jesus were romantically involved there might have been motivation to mute that image in the face of the growing Christian sex-negative posture.

But who was Mary Magdalene? This question always swirls around her name, much as we find it so difficult to answer the same question about Jesus himself. Smithsonian Magazine tells us that, "In one age after another, her image has been reinvented, from prostitute to sibyl to mystic to celibate nun to passive helpmeet to feminist icon." She is a major figure in the early Gnostic texts where she is portrayed as a constant companion of Jesus and an "apostle" right up there with the twelve (although technically she could not have been an apostle because Jesus had already chosen his twelve). Some thought maybe she even out-ranked Peter, not to mention being at least a spiritual companion to Jesus if not a spouse.

The Evangelist John treats her as essentially the very founder of Christianity by telling us that she was the first to witness the empty tomb and the first to encounter the risen Jesus. Clearly, if one is a believer, she is portrayed as the first to experience what Christianity claims as its central truth (the resurrection), and thus she is the channel through whom first the apostles, and then the world, came to know of the resurrection of Jesus.

If one is not so much of a believer, she is nevertheless the first to propound the story of the resurrection. Either way, it is Mary Magdalene who is the link between the resurrection and the church. She had the front row seat and was said to be the first to whom the risen Lord disclosed himself—she has frequently been called the 'Apostle to the Apostles' although that amounts mostly to being just a cute phrase because, as I need to keep emphasizing, it was technically an impossibility. (I see the twelve apostles as a Zodiacal influence on nascent Christianity, as do many if not most sober observers.)

Some modern feminists, as noted, have stated that Mary Magdalene has a better claim than Paul to being the founder of Christianity (although that would have to be basically an historical argument rather than a theological one). But thanks to the twists and turns of the evolving Christian viewpoint (theology and mythology) as well, probably, as the twists and turns of the human male ego and psyche, most Christians for centuries (certainly since

Pope Gregory the Great) have understood Mary Magdalene as a great sinner who spent her life seeking forgiveness.

Mary Magdalene's recovery has been long and slow, but she is again finally being seen as Jesus' primary female disciple, or even primary disciple—period. And more than that, as a leader of the early church in her own right. And in some quarters as even more still—as the incarnation of Holy Wisdom (Sophia). She was part of a trio of Marys who walked with Jesus in the Bible's telling, the others being his mother and his sister. Wherever one starts in trying to discover Mary's story, one inevitably arrives at the mystery of Mary Magdalen's precise relationship to Jesus, which evidently has been a source of fascination from the very beginning of the Christian era. The Greek word for 'companion' used to describe her generally suggests a sexual relationship many scholars say, although others argue that it could mean merely a consort, whether sexual activity is a factor or not.

Thanks to Dan Brown's novel "The Da Vinci Code" most of us are now familiar with the concept of Jesus as a married family man, whether the idea seems preposterous or plausible, heretical or joyous.

Scholars for some time have speculated that Jesus' "beloved disciple" (a major figure in the Gospel by John) might not have been one of the twelve after all, but rather his close companion Mary of Magdala. In which case John's gospel was probably intentionally rewritten, or edited, early-on to make the beloved disciple into a male figure. Then, to add the practical to the 'romantic,' Mary is also thought by some to have financed Jesus' itinerant ministry.

The working assumption of Biblical scholars for a long time has been that the Evangelist John was himself this 'beloved disciple.' However, some scholars believe Mary Magdalene may have been the actual author of the fourth gospel, as well as the actual 'beloved disciple' referred to therein. Misogyny led the early Christian community to edit out her "beloved disciple" role, these scholars believe, so that the figure could become male. (Just to add another pinch of further confusion, some scholars suggest this 'beloved disciple' was actually James the Just, Jesus' brother.)

In the Gospel of Mary (Magdalene) from the early second century CE she is said to have received secret revelations from Jesus that were above and beyond those received by the twelve, and after Jesus' death she seems to have felt she should have a leadership position in the Jesus movement, although Peter and others objected, as we've seen.

Peter, however, is also quoted in the Gospel of Mary thusly, "Peter said to Mary, 'Sister, we know that the Savior loved you more than all other women.'"

In any case, Mary Magdalene played a major role in the life and ministry of Jesus, and the earliest Christians probably knew of her much more than they did of Mary the mother. For a long time, the Magdalene was the more prominent of the two Marys for early Christians.

Scholars tell us that Jewish culture in Jesus' time almost required an adult male to marry, or at least would have painted Jesus as a distinct oddball if he didn't have a wife. Still, in all the material from various authors which made it into the canonical New Testament, there is not a word about his having a wife or children. Even the Gnostic gospels are silent on this topic. From our distance it's a little difficult to evaluate this silence. Was it so taken for granted in that time and place for a man to be married that there was no point in wasting words saying that Jesus was married? And we need to remind ourselves again that the object of the New Testament writers was not to provide a biography for Jesus, but to stake a religious claim about him. Maybe those writers simply saw no purpose in writing about his family life because it didn't advance their objectives.

The French scholar-priest Jean-Yves Leloup (a *nom de plume*) makes two interesting points in this regard. A) Jesus might have had "an obligation" to be married because he taught in synagogues, and unmarried men were not allowed to teach in synagogues because they were "disobedient towards God" [as viewed from the command in Genesis to "be fruitful and multiply"]. B) If Jesus did not have a normal human sexuality, was he really fully human? It would have implications for understanding the doctrine of the Incarnation if he were not fully human—sexuality itself would be then unredeemed.

As to the famous wedding at Cana, some writers have speculated that Jesus was himself the bridegroom, and therefore that the passage is another allusion to his 'secret' marriage to Mary Magdalene. St. Jerome, for what it may be worth, proposed that the Cana marriage was between Mary Magdalene and John the Evangelist. One writer in discussing this topic refers to "Mary Magdalene the sorceress," which might make her an ideal mate for Jesus the magician, and in any case links her to Isis, the great Egyptian goddess who was "great in magic". That linkage of Mary to the Isis cult shows up in the thinking of several writers and even in the legends that Mary spent the final years of her life in France.

To give just two quick examples of biblical clues that Mary Magdalene and Jesus might well have been married, Mary is remembered in the gospels as going to Jesus' tomb alone early on the first religiously available day to verify the death and anoint the body. This was a task reserved for close relatives, and, if possible, for a spouse. The anointing of a king is another rite reserved in that period for a spouse, and Mary Magdalene is seen by many scholars as fulfilling that rite in our gospels when she anointed Jesus' feet and dried them with her hair (assuming that woman was indeed Mary). That sort of physical contact would not have happened between an unrelated adult man and woman in the social and religious context of the time and place, it is noted by scholars.

● A MYSTICAL UNION?

As somehow should be expected, the love between Jesus and the Magdalene has attracted the attention of a lot of new age and spiritualist type writers who posit various types of relationships in place of standard-fare love and marriage. The combination of sex and a mystery love story embedded in the western world's dominant religion is just too much to resist, apparently.

Mostly, it seems, these writers emphasize emotional closeness rather than physical love. One has to wonder if this approach is an outgrowth of Christianity's traditional sex-negative stance, sprinkled with a bit of residual piety which assumes that Jesus couldn't have been interested in sexual relations in the same way ordinary men are.

But there are other strains of thought, both modern and ancient, which find the religious importance of a possible relationship precisely in the 'bridal chamber' or the wedding bed. A fourth century bishop of Amaseia, Asterius, reminds us of the widespread belief that "what is done by the two in the darkness is their salvation."

These writers often refer to a 'Sacrament of the Bridal Chamber.' The goal is not orgasm or ejaculation, we're told, and in fact that both are usually avoided. Some describe the goal as "ecstatic energy flow," and claim it can be much more pleasurable and "spiritually productive" than ordinary sex.

These writers imply that if Jesus and the Magdalene were lovers (or spouses) their sex lives would have followed these more spiritual and minimally orgasmic outlines. They almost seem to be describing the courtly love of the Arthurian legends—an intense devotion which had nothing at all to do with marriage. Probably they are saying that even if the relationship between Jesus and Mary were not marriage as we think of it, there was still a powerful spiritual relationship binding them closely. Usually these writers do not clearly express their opinion as to the possible marriage of Jesus and Mary, but then it doesn't seem to be the real aim of their concern. My guess is that they are attracted to the Jesus/Magdalene story line because it gives them 'celebrities' to hang their theories on, and no one can effectively challenge their ideas when the subjects are Mary and Jesus because no one really knows.

It isn't necessary for us to explore this more mystical slant put on the Jesus-Mary story by some modern writers. But it's useful to acknowledge that it's there because it illustrates the continuing power that the story, and the question marks the story contains, hold in the human imagination. And besides, they are essentially doing fiction and in that realm Dan Brown is a better read.

In reading the New Testament one can sense that Mary Magdalene is somehow a major player, and that is confirmed by other of the texts discovered since the New Testament was canonized. But there is also the sense of not getting the whole story—the frustration of always seeing her only through a screen, in scattered bits and truncated context. We are left guessing what her role really was. On the one hand why does this person appear in different situations, and on the other if she is named or alluded to why then is she not important enough to be explained—why is she still cloaked in a gauzy blur? Is the misogyny of the times enough to explain this mystery, or do the compliers of the gospel material have other motivation to keep her in the background? She becomes alluring in her shadowy place near Jesus—a tantalizing suggestion that there is a much larger story embedded here.

One recent book may deserve a special mention, however, because it's a long and largely scholarly attempt to answer the marriage of Jesus question directly and without equivocation. An Israeli-Canadian maker of documentary videos, Simcha Jacobovici, and a professor of religious studies at York University in Toronto, Barrie Wilson, authored "The Lost Gospel" (2014). The subtitle of their book sums up the conclusion of the book pretty well: "Decoding the Ancient Text that Reveals Jesus' Marriage to Mary the Magdalene." Like several other writers, these authors believe that the Magdalene was "intentionally" written out of the New Testament.

Jacobovici and Wilson found an ancient (estimated by them "at least 1,450 years old") manuscript in a dusty corner of the British Library, had it translated by experts from Syriac into English, and discovered its meaning "through an epiphany, a sudden blast of insight." To make a long story very short, they concluded that the text, ostensibly about Joseph, from the book of Genesis, and his Egyptian wife Aseneth, was really a coded story about Jesus and Mary Magdalene, which (if true) would authenticate the idea that they were married. In other words, the authors' work is a rather big leap of faith, or possibly sheer guesswork. Even so, it is germane to our current question and it is nicely written and contains a lot of valuable descriptive and interpretive text.

Their book also contains a postscript giving a detailed description and history of the now famous fragment disclosed in 2012 by Karen King which quotes Jesus as referring to "my wife," and which is increasingly accepted as legitimate after tests on the ink and paper for age. But legitimate or not, nothing much can be deduced from the fragment except that there were people of the period in Egypt who thought Jesus had a wife—the fragment tells us nothing more than that.

Karen King herself agrees with that assessment, and points out that other sources of about the same age say explicitly that Jesus did not have a wife. She says that this period, about 150 years or so after Jesus, was the first time the subject of his marital status had come up for Christians, and it was because of the raging question being debated by Christians at that time as to whether marriage was proper or not for adherents of the new religion.

Jacobovici was also co-author of an earlier book which also concluded that Jesus and Mary Magdalene were a couple; this time the other author was the well-respected James D. Tabor, chair of the Department of Religious Studies at the University of North Carolina in Charlotte. These authors remind us that Mary's first instinct on Easter morning was to touch the resurrected Jesus. In that first century Jewish culture for a woman to touch a man implies a familial connection, they say.

They conclude that we should assume that as a Jew of his time Jesus was married unless there is evidence to the contrary, and that married people at that time usually had children "as the First Commandment required." ['First' commandment here meaning the earliest commandment issued: Genesis 1:22; 1:28; and 35:11, 'be fruitful and multiply', not the first of Moses' ten.] They also point out that, had Jesus been unmarried, Paul would surely have used him as the primary example in urging celibacy on Paul's congregations.

It's interesting that most writers on this subject are careful to keep their own beliefs about Jesus' marital status private—which can be a bit frustrating to an average reader who plows through all the evidence and ideas they offer without the suggestion of a conclusion.

One group (sect) in Christian history doesn't frustrate us on that front at all, however. Their answer was an essential part of their identity—assuming we can be sure which Jesus they are talking about at a given time.

The Cathars of southern France during the twelfth and thirteenth centuries were dualists who believed there were two gods, one good and one evil, and two Christs, also one good and one evil. They saw the man who was crucified as evil and understood Mary Magdalene to be his concubine, whereas there was also a good Christ to whom Mary was a wife. Their marriage was thought to be the symbol of the creator's divine order. (The Cathars believed these were the true teachings of Jesus which had been brought to France by Mary herself; see the P.S. to this chapter).

While the Magdalene was being gradually edited out of the mainstream Christian writings which became our sacred canon, she thrived in Egypt, especially among the Gnostics. Among the works in the Nag Hammadi find, three featured Mary Magdalene to major degrees: the Dialogue of the

114

Saviour, the Gospel of Philip and the Gospel of Thomas, plus two Gnostic works acquired earlier, Pistis Sophia and the Gospel of Mary Magdalene. The Gospel of Philip, found at Nag Hammadi in 1945, is famous for the lines that can be interpreted to mean that Mary Magdalene was the wife or lover of Jesus.

● ISIS AND OSIRIS

A comparison between Jesus/Mary Magdalene and Osiris/Isis is made occasionally by writers contemplating this Biblical mystery couple. Some of them believe that Jesus and Mary Magdalene were intentionally playing out the role of Osiris and Isis.

Isis, the greatest goddess of Egypt, has shown up in many religious and cultural contexts outside her original home cult, as we've noted. She was born of an earth god and a sky goddess, and was the sister of Osiris, who also was her husband. Her basic legend tells the story of how she engineered the birth of her and Osiris' son Horus, the Sun God, after Osiris had been murdered.

To make a quick story of it, Osiris was killed by his jealous brother who then cut his body up into many pieces and scattered the pieces around Egypt in hidden places in an attempt to prevent Osiris' resurrection. Isis searched far and wide trying to re-assemble the pieces of her husband. She succeeded except for one missing piece, his penis, which had been thrown into the Nile and had been eaten by a fish. She had a new penis formed and joined to his body, and then mated with him successfully, becoming pregnant with Horus.

What the restored penis aspect of this story told people of old, or why it was even part of the story, I'd just be guessing. Today, however, it could be related to an almost literally same experience for some widows. Since the late 20th century many pregnancies have been achieved by dead men—some from frozen sperm saved back for, perhaps, just such a use, and others from sperm retrieved from the husband's body after his death. The old myths are somehow always reviving and revising themselves.

Scholars have noted the similarity of the gospel story of Mary Magdalene visiting the tomb of Jesus on Easter morning ("They have taken my Lord and I know not where they have laid him.") and the words of the priestess during the annual rites of Isis in Egypt ("Evil men have killed my beloved, and where his body is I know not").

Some believe that Jesus is equating himself with the dying corn gods that were prevalent in the belief systems of many people in his native Galilee. Indeed the whole Eucharistic discussion might suggest that, but it's far from certain whether Jesus himself thought in those terms about himself. He most likely would have been well aware of the mythology in any case, and thus able to apply it to his role if he wished.

● THE OTHER QUESTION: WAS IT A BOYFRIEND?

This chapter's focus is the mysterious yet towering Biblical figure of Mary Magdalene. But to consider this Mary is to venture almost automatically into all of those pesky questions about Jesus' sexuality or lack thereof. Mary was, after all, the only viable candidate in the gospels if Jesus had a female romantic interest, and she was painted as his nearly constant companion.

So far we have assumed that Jesus was "straight," which is logical given that most human males are, and evidently historically have been, heterosexual or basically heterosexual. We also know, however, that a homosexual minority has existed among humans as far back as historians can see, and that this minority has included very surprising figures (Alexander the Great, for example). So Jesus, simply by virtue of his celebrity status and his major role in the history of religion, is not thereby automatically rendered straight—the instincts and wishes of piety notwithstanding.

Based on reading the gospels alone, it would be equally justified to ask in place of "Did Jesus have a Girlfriend?" the flipside question, "Did Jesus have a Boyfriend?" Or even did he have both? Reading the New Testament gospels at face value makes this not only a legitimate question, but perhaps almost a necessary one. Jesus is portrayed as a man seemingly immune to feminine charms, without a wife or children (in a cultural context which almost demanded that adult men marry and have children), and with men scattered around the story whom he "loved" and who "loved" him back, or who were described as "beloved" by him.

There have long been folks, including serious scholars, who have wondered out loud about Jesus' sexual orientation. And to be fair, the Bible itself, as we have it, gives a certain amount of fuel to the question. All of the talk in John's gospel about a "beloved disciple" who is portrayed as male, for example. That's pretty easy to latch onto by those who want to raise the question, although as we've just noted it can get quite complicated quickly. Maybe this 'beloved disciple' was really Mary Magdalene herself, repainted as male by misogynist editors in order to get another female out of the Biblical spotlight. For the purposes of this chapter let's go with that explanation for now.

Then, as we've also noted, there are those who read the Bible at face value and see a young man named Lazarus whom we are told Jesus loved, and whom we are told loved Jesus. That does sound a lot like a boyfriend, doesn't it? While there's no need for us to consider Lazarus again (we've already concluded he was a code name for the young men initiated by Jesus), his name does (especially after the discovery of 'Secret Mark') add to the New Testament a hint of homosexual interest or activity by Jesus.

Re-reading the New Testament in light of a question like this reminds me again how easy it is to see and take away from the Bible whatever it is that one expects to find. The washing of the disciple's feet, for example, jumped out at me suddenly in a re-read as a possible foot fetish merely because I was looking for sexual indicators. It involved physical contact between or among males, and it shocked and even offended the disciples for whom it was an unwelcome gesture.

Of course we're used to the conventional explanations for a passage like this: Jesus is teaching his followers humility; the first shall be last and the last shall be first sort of thing. And the disciples were shocked not so much that someone was willing to wash their feet, but by who it was doing the washing—'it is I who should be washing *your* feet, Lord.' But who really can say where a vignette like this comes from? We not only don't know with certainty *why* the passage is there—we also can't be sure *if* it ever really took place as an event. Or, it could have been written into the record because of a later event or a ritual developed after the time of Jesus, and thus giving us no information about the man Jesus at all.

I'm not saying it was (nor do I think it was) the sign of a fetish, but I am saying that a well-intentioned and sober reader can find 'evidence' in the Bible for a wide variety of conclusions whether the evidence is really there or not. The Bible simply does not say that Jesus was NOT a foot-fetishist any more than it says that Jesus was NOT erotically attracted to other men. When something is not ruled out, it gets much easier to find evidence in favor of it.

As to our Chapter 2, the sheet boy in the garden (at least before Morton Smith discovered 'Secret Mark') was always a source of confusion for centuries of commentators, but it is interesting to note that almost all of them attributed some kind of eroticism to the scene. No one I can discover ever viewed the situation as sexually totally neutral or innocent (i.e. completely without any kind of sexual implication) although few did more than a slight wink before turning their heads in apparent embarrassment (or piety).

And most commentators along the way have adhered to Christianity's anti-sexual (or at least anti-eroticism) bias. They constantly painted the affection between Jesus and his "beloved disciple" as a "*spiritual* love" or a "*spiritual* friendship." This was done without pointing to any special evidence in that direction—only the apparent universal assumption that if Jesus were involved, this affection obviously (for whatever reason) could not have involved overt sexual expression.

Thus all of these commentators (from abbots to theologians to historians) tipped their hats to the pervasive Christian idea that once a couple was not consciously attempting to procreate, anything that smacked of sexual expression was extremely dangerous and impious territory. Several commentators along the way held out the relationship (which they always assume was merely "spiritual" love) between David and Jonathan as the Biblical standard to which Jesus and his "beloved disciple" needed to aspire and to be held. Anything more physical was anathema, and the subject was always dropped at that point with no effort to explore or explain why it should be, or needed to be, anathema. To challenge the iron-clad Christian negative attitude towards sex was a taboo which few were ready to challenge in the slightest—plus, if one dug too deeply or said too much, the pious would stop paying attention completely, so why bother?

The relationship between David and Jonathan is a strange template to apply to Jesus and his 'beloved disciple,' however. David and Jonathan were brothers-in-law and were negotiating the palace intrigue of a probably by then mad king.

Although David was married, the Bible makes a point of telling us only that his wife loved him, and gives no hint as to whether David returned her affection (and he needed her for career reasons—in order to succeed her father as king—whether he loved her as a wife or not). The Bible tells us that the king, Jonathan's father, described the relationship between his son with David as a matter of 'shame' and implied it would have been better had he not been born.

And finally the Bible tells us that the relationship between David and Jonathan did involve at least some physicality in that they "kissed" and "wept" with one another. After Jonathan was killed, David is recorded in the Bible as lamenting that Jonathan's "love to me was wonderful, passing the love of women," and thus voluntarily placing it in what would seem to be a sexual context. If the goal of using David and Jonathan as a pattern or template to describe Jesus and his 'beloved disciple' is to imply a platonic friendship rather than a romance, as so many commentators do, it may actually muddy the waters instead of clarifying them.

Lately modern commentators have grown a tad bolder. There is even an official document from a British Protestant group in the late 20th century which admits that Jesus "*may have*" had homosexual "inclinations." From there we've entered an era where so-called 'mainline' (larger Protestant) western churches are rapidly remodeling their sociological orientations in order to accept gay and lesbian members (along with their offerings, one can note), and some groups on the non-Roman side of things are actually ordaining "out" homosexual clergy.

This really says nothing about our evaluation of Jesus' own sexuality *per se*, but it does suggest that the long-held Christian anti-sexual bias may be beginning to yield to a more realistic and humane toleration of what it means to be human. It also means that modern Christians are beginning to accept some of the markers of the ancient priests and shamans of universal general religious mythology—to plug into mankind's larger religious history by accepting the ministrations of priestly figures earmarked by the gods for religious service (at least partially) by sexual ambiguity. The priest-figure in general human religion is a male/female, father/mother being set aside by divine intention.

Nor, of course, does it say anything at all about Jesus' relationship to Mary Magdalene. The more free we are to openly discuss issues which may be germane to that relationship, the farther we seem to be from arriving at any solid conclusions. The mystery woman of the New Testament still hides behind her veil.

There is probably little real value in deeply exploring the question of Jesus' sexual orientation to a fine point because the answer would not affect the religious structure of Christianity in one way or another at this late date—and also because the question immediately becomes a distraction from other questions we might come closer to being able to answer.

Obviously, however, if Jesus were perceived widely as having been sexually complicated it would have very strong implications for how the church should relate to sexual minorities. But true believers get so emotional and defensive at the mere suggestion that Jesus could have been anything beyond what they see as 'normal' that it's usually easier just to leave the possibility largely unexplored. It's sometimes not worth the effort if the jury has already made up its mind, and especially so when one knows in advance that there is no definitive evidence available—just a little smoke suggesting that there might have been some kind of probably minor fire at one point long in the past. Still, the gospels as we have them are not exactly a defense of Jesus as a standard-issue heterosexual man. In fact, they expend a lot of effort pointing out that Jesus was an exceptional man—not at all like other men.

From the viewpoint of the great mythology of general human religion, one would have to say that it would not be very surprising at all if the lead figure, the 'hero,' were homosexual or at least exhibited some homosexual characteristics. It was normal for religious heroes to be seen as summing up the total human experience within themselves, including both the masculine and the feminine simultaneously. And often enough homosexuality, or a combination masculine-feminine personality, was regarded as a priestly marker—as a sign that the shaman or hero was set aside by the gods for special duty. That did not quite make being "gay" part of the hero's job description *per se*, but it did suggest that in that particular line of work the "gay" orientation was almost expected and was considered an asset rather than a liability.

119

That idea quite obviously still has powerful echoes in today's ecclesiastical world if one follows the news, although the 'asset' aspect has probably disappeared among most observers and been replaced with disdain. It's easy to be shocked and/or saddened by the activities of some clergy or descriptions of hotbeds of clerical activity (such as the Vatican) which occasionally come to our attention through journalists these days. But the truth is that there's nothing much new under the sun—the priestly/shamanic vocation from general universal religion onward has usually and traditionally been marked by, shall we say, sexual ambiguity and fluidity.

And on a historical level, Jesus lived in a time when the Roman Empire ruled the known world. The Romans were fairly tolerant of sexual activity in a wide variety of guises. It's not unlikely that an adult man of the day would have had experiences which we today would instinctively label 'gay' as well as others we would call 'straight,' and probably he would not have seen or felt any particular contradiction in those various experiences. We can't legitimately use our 21st century categories or prejudices to define a man who lived thousands of years ago, even if we did know a lot more about his personal life than we know about the personal life of Jesus.

That said, however, if one believes in the doctrine of the Incarnation, one would need to believe that Jesus had some kind of sexuality or else he would not have been truly a human man. The only remaining question, therefore, is whether he gave his sexuality, whichever direction it inclined, any overt expression in his relationships.

Since I have complained that writers so often leave their readers without indicating where the available evidence leads them with regard to the relationship between Jesus and Mary Magdalene, perhaps I should state my own inclination on the subject. Of course, this is only an opinion—at best an educated guess—and an opinion is really all anyone can offer on the topic.

The most compelling evidence on this subject I see from the New Testament is found in the Easter stories. Mary Magdalene goes to the tomb, perhaps alone, to perform duties normally reserved for and preferably restricted to spouses. Furthermore, in the story fragment in which she encounters a risen Jesus, we are told that her first instinct was to reach out and touch him—another action which strongly suggests a spousal relationship (Jesus, however, refused the action we are told, giving rise to the now immortal Latin phrase *noli me tangere*). This fits the whole arc of the relationship between Mary and Jesus which we can deduce from the fragments allowed to remain in the canonical story. Another such strong indicator was the anointing of Jesus' feet with expensive oil and the wiping of them with her hair (assuming the story refers to Mary Magdalene, as

120

most scholars believe it does). And we should add to that Jesus' status as a rabbi who taught in synagogue, also a strong indication he was married. All of this would ring true if Jesus and Mary were married, and would ring discordantly if they were not.

Of the two most prominent elements in the New Testament pulling in the other direction (that Jesus might not have been married to a woman), both the "beloved disciple" of John's gospel and the initiation/Lazarus coded stories might point only in the direction of sexual orientation, assuming they say anything concrete at all. Orientation is not exactly the same question as marriage, and one does not guarantee the other in either direction—one could be married without being entirely heterosexual (even in the first century), and certainly one can be heterosexual without being married.

Furthermore, nakedness during initiation could be merely a hypnotic or teaching technique, or a long-standing custom which the participants accepted without really giving it much thought. While nakedness in our culture is often, perhaps usually, a suggestion of sexual activity or awareness, it hasn't always been so. Nakedness during much of the Christian era was seen as a symbol of innocence, or perhaps naivety. Therefore I don't see that spending a night with a naked stripling is necessarily significant evidence about where Jesus was on the sexual continuum, even if such events were a routine part of his ministry. In any case, I don't think these hints rise to the level of substance that we get from the Easter narratives, and therefore my guess comes down on the side of Jesus and Mary Magdalene having been a married couple (i.e. that at least one of the major strands of memory which influenced New Testament writers portrayed Jesus and Mary Magdalene as married).

● IS IT APPROPRIATE TO SPECULATE ON JESUS' SEXUALITY?

This is entirely a different question than "is there a basis for" doing so. Discussing Jesus and sexuality in the same breath upsets some believers— that's a given. The difficulty centers on an extremely murky question: *Which* Jesus are we discussing at a given time.

Let's say you set out to write a biography of an important man of a previous generation. Among many aspects of his life which you really could not leave out, even if you wanted to, is his sexuality. You could choose to write about it directly as one of many germane topics, or you could simply let it suggest itself indirectly through other aspects of his life story. If your subject had a wife and children, you would end up implying a lot about his sexuality even if you wanted to avoid any direct discussion of it. And if he did not have a wife or children, you would likewise have to report those details which your readers would assume were possible indications of the man's sexuality. In other words, you really could not avoid the topic of the subject's sexuality even if only by implication. The same is true in writing about Jesus.

Humans are sexual animals whether they like it or not, and sexuality is part of every person's story whether the person's biographer likes it or not.

So when one writes about Jesus it would seem that his sexuality would be a legitimate possible topic, and if one were attempting to write about him biographically, an almost unavoidable topic at least by implication. Yet there is something like a mixing oil and water tension at play when one puts Jesus and sex into the same sentence. Suddenly there is piety to deal with; the unspoken sense that surely Jesus was above such mundane concerns; that he was a better man than that (although at the same time that would make him necessarily less of a man than that). It's almost as if we see Jesus as having such a serious mission that it offends us a bit to imagine that he might expend any energy or allot any time to personal gratification, or even to simple enjoyment, or, for that matter, even to obeying the ancient command of the creator to "be fruitful and multiply."

This confusion is a little gift from something we affectionately call theology.

For centuries after the crucifixion (or after the Resurrection, if you prefer) learned men argued about just who this Jesus was, or is. So the same folks who gave you three Gods in one being (or one God in three persons) also gave you a Jesus who was "true man" at the same time that he was also "true God." And there was no recess from the situation (or 'condition'); he was not a man on Mondays and a God on Tuesdays, but both equally at all times and in all situations. One might expect that he could be viewed just as a man before the crucifixion, and then after the resurrection as a god—but no, theology (eventually) decided there was no distinction at any time. (This led, by the way, to some highly imaginative tales about Jesus as a child. At age three, let's say, he was, as a human, too immature to always be reasonable or considerate, but as a god he nevertheless had unlimited powers. Therefore we get tall tales of his employing his omnipotence as a device in playing with his little friends—of making birds molded of mud spring to life and fly off into the sky, for example. As a child, at least, he was, these stories imply, a bit of a show-off who could not restrain himself from one-upping his playmates.)

If one could write about only the Jesus who was "true man," the sexuality aspect would be a natural part of the story and could not really be challenged as to its legitimate place in the story. But probably the writer, and surely most of his readers, also have this "true God" lurking around in the backgrounds of their minds.

We walk around with this combo-Jesus in our heads. There is too much written about him in the New Testament gospels for us to think of him as *only* a God. He is pictured there as eating and drinking, as crying and loving, as having dusty feet at the end of the day.

But we can't quite conceptualize him as *only* a man either. The Creator opens the heavens and claims him (adopts him? Oh, sorry, that approach finally became a heresy) as his only son at his Baptism, and then closes the world down in darkness when that son is later crucified by politicians. So the theologians win, at least partially—there's a man in our Jesus, and a God as well, and neither of them will yield completely to the other.

If I write about Jesus as a man, I would honor him as truly human if I acknowledge his sexuality, even if that means speculating about its shape. But then the God part rears up and says, "How dare you!" And the writer has, in addition, readers to contend with—readers many of whom are likely to rise up and join the chorus: "How dare you!" How dare you imply that Jesus had a sexuality of any sort, let alone one possibly tainted with aspects that I can't personally condone!

Ultimately all of this brings us back to the generally sex-negative orientation Christianity has held traditionally. The Christian comfort zone is to downplay sexuality as somehow belonging to the baser, less noble, aspects of being human. Celibacy then becomes a major virtue, even if those officially committed to it don't always completely toe the line. The historian will most likely feel that it is, indeed, *appropriate* to try to understand Jesus' sexuality right along with all of the other aspects of his humanity. But the pious among us may never agree that it is *seemly* to do so.

● P.S. THE MAGDALENE IN FRANCE

Among the great beliefs which give New Testament characters a life and role beyond their Biblical stories is the persistent legend that Mary Magdalene, after the death of Jesus (or sometimes together with Jesus; his having escaped actual death on the cross), lived out the balance of her life in France. Many historians tend to disparage the notion, but millions of Frenchmen continue to hold the story dear and true.

The question of the Magdalene's late life in France is much written about and debated to this day. There's a group that adamantly says, no, it's nothing but a legend. There's another group who write that, yes, it's absolutely true and historical. And of course, there are some who flirt around the edges and hedge their bets.

Among those who think the legend grew from actual history there are some who point out that the stories are very old, and that their origins seem to fit a time-line consistent with that of the New Testament. They also contend that the bloodline of Jesus was present in the early days of the Frankish royal family (the Merovingian dynasty). They point to the many shrines, chapels, and churches in southern France which are dedicated to Mary Magdalene. Some say the legend includes the fascinating idea that Mary was a priestess in a pagan cult, probably an Egyptian Isis cult, before becoming part of the Jesus movement.

The legend contains, or at least implies, the idea that it was no longer safe for Mary to stay at home after losing her chief protector (husband? teacher?) Jesus. But the source of the danger is the surprise. It was not the political authorities who posed the problem. They had done their thing and now wanted to wash their hands of the whole Jesus episode; they certainly did not see a need to take on a mere woman who had, in their eyes, essentially been a powerless bystander.

So who "had it in" for Mary? Quite likely her old nemesis and rival for leadership of the Jesus people, St. Peter himself. Jesus was no longer around to arbitrate or protect her with his favor and love. So Mary had to flee Dodge. Another probable instance of a major Biblical character, this time St. Peter, not living up to our assumptions of his purity of heart or innocence of spirit.

The Cathars (mentioned earlier), especially, were the stalwarts for these beliefs about Mary in France and suffered because of them. Over a million people were massacred in the south of France for their 'heretical' belief in the role of Mary Magdalene as the wife of Jesus, we are told, and thus they learned the hard way to keep their beliefs secret. And these beliefs, they felt, were the teachings of Jesus which were brought to Europe by Jesus' partner, Mary Magdalene.

Of course, the French legends about Mary Magdalene are generally forthright in seeing her as wife and mother—sometimes in astonishing detail and specificity. For example, we are told that the first son of Jesus and Mary was given his father's name (so, "Jesus Jr."). Upon reaching majority age at sixteen, junior became Chief Nazarite, we're told, and so became entitled to wear the black robe of that office, as also worn by the priests of Isis, the universal Mother Goddess. Mary Magdalene has long been identified with Isis in a variety of ways, as we've learned, and some historians think Jesus himself may have been a Nazarite (an order of Israelite men dedicated to asceticism), so the story circles in on itself.

Their younger son was supposedly named Josephes and attended a druidic college. Where these ideas come from, if from anywhere outside sheer oral legend and ancient imagination, I've not been able to discern.

The child who is the key to the transfer of Jesus' bloodline to Europe, it is said, was a girl named Sarah, born in Egypt (where Mary, or perhaps both Mary and Jesus, had first sought protection after the crucifixion) before Joseph of Arimathea took Mary and her baby (and maybe Jesus himself) into exile in France. Sarah in Hebrew means 'queen' or 'princess.' Evidently there is still an annual festival and a shrine in the south of France honoring "Saint Sarah the Egyptian," also called Sara Kali, the 'Black Queen'. (No one seems to question how Jesus and Mary, both Israelites, could have a daughter who was black, or dark enough to be thought of as black. The "black" aspect seems to be simply a tangible link to Egypt, the stop-over point where they supposedly rested *en route* to France.) Some versions of this legend ascribe different relationships between Mary Magdalene and Sara Kali, such as Sara being Mary's servant instead of daughter.

Many of these legends, as you have probably already deduced, depend on the belief by some people of earlier times that Jesus survived the crucifixion by some means—they are not based on the idea of his resurrection, as in the Christian doctrine, but on the idea of Jesus never having actually died on a cross in the first place. These legends are very human stories, with any religious aspect being connected with Egyptian magic or mythology. Some suggest Pontius Pilot helped organize Jesus' survival of the crucifixion. Some say Jesus was given a drug to make him only appear to die so he could be revived later. Some say a substitute died for him on the cross. The Cathars said it was only the 'evil' Christ who died on the cross, while the 'good' Christ retired to France. Some say Jesus' own magic was enough to do the resurrection job, with a few other conspiracy theories showing up as well. In any case, there are still those who believe Jesus was able to accompany Mary Magdalene first to Egypt, and then after a period of recovery, on to France.

One fairly recent (1996) book, *The Tomb of God,* uses 513 pages to arrive at the conclusion that Jesus' final tomb is in Mount Cardou in France, near the famous tiny village of Rennes-le-Château. This little town itself was the scene of an intriguing later church episode involving an interpretation of the crucifixion. One of the stations of the cross in the village church, number 14, was discovered/thought to depict removing a living Jesus from the original tomb and thus buttressing the idea that Jesus survived the crucifixion.

In light of this aspect of the legend (that Jesus accompanied Mary to France) it is fascinating to note that it was the Magdalene who triggered the passionate folklore and shrines of southern France. There seems to be no major community memory or enthusiasm that Jesus (God himself, after all!) once may have graced those hills; just that the Magdalene had. This, I suspect, is testimony that Mary was in and of herself a major religious figure in her own day and that her reputation was not entirely dependent on her association with Jesus. It may also reflect her possible status, independent of her association with Jesus, as a priestess of Isis. And it may also be a remote echo of the system in which royal status descended through the female line, thus leaving Jesus a royal figure only because he was married to Mary.

This then brings us to the famous Black Virgins of France, of which the one at Chartres may be the best known. There may be as many as fifty Magdalenian centers in the south of France which also contain shrines to the Black Virgin. The greatest concentration of Black Madonna sites in France is centered on a range of hills dedicated to the Magdalene. The black virgins represented some kind of link back to Egypt and the worship of Isis but are otherwise poorly understood.

The areas in Burgundy and Provence associated with Mary Magdalene became great magnets for pilgrims, as one would expect given the era. Eventually she is said to have retired to a remote cave and lived out her life as a hermit for another thirty years.

While the stories of Mary Magdalene center in the south of France, it is a heritage honored and valued throughout the country. Just as young tourists skimming the surface, many of us have marveled at the great Parisian Church of the Magdalene in its very prominent location. It may have seemed a high honor for someone we took to be a relatively minor Biblical figure at the time we first saw the church, but now we can understand why she commanded this sort of veneration. (For some time I assumed that Proust's Madeleines, so tempting in the windows of Paris bakeries, were a tribute to Mary Magdalene as well—but it seems more likely their name came from the wife of the baker who invented them.)

As to a royal blood line, the idea that Jesus himself was the rightful successor to King David is somewhat confusing to begin with, in large measure because the later church insisted that Joseph was not his biological father. And yet Matthew traces Jesus' ancestors through the male line rather than through a matriarchal lineage as the Egyptian tradition had done and had passed along to the Hebrews—but then some say both Joseph and Mary were of the Davidic line in any case, so Jesus got there either way.

There is also the problem of the ancient tradition of the claiming of kingship through marriage to a daughter of the royal house, in the way that King David himself had claimed kingship by marriage to the daughter of King Saul, and as Egyptian tradition had apparently imposed on Judaism. If Jesus was unmarried, a conclusion we may be pointed towards by the canonical Biblical sources, his claim to David's throne would therefore have been further weakened or even eliminated. Could it be that any claim Jesus had to being of royal lineage was actually through his wife Mary Magdalene? (It should be noted that there are scholars who think all claims of Jesus' Davidic descent are merely fictions of the early church, rather than fact. There are also scholars who feel David and his 'kingdom' are vastly overrated in the Bible and therefore that being a descendant of David would not have been much of a big deal in any case.)

As we've noted, many serious historians discount the European legends of early apostles and saints setting up shop on the continent—Joseph of Arimathea in Britain, Mary Magdalene in France, and the apostle James in Spain, for example. However, the *conviction* that Mary Magdalene lived in France is an indelible part of the French cultural memory, as could be said of Glastonbury's attachment to Joseph of Arimathea and Spain's to its patron James as well. So, in that sense she did come to France, and belongs to France in a special way. Part of human reality is what we sincerely believe to be true, even if its historicity is dubious.

There is not much left in our Bible about the personal relationship between Jesus and Mary Magdalene. Scholars assume a lot of material was edited out for various reasons. What's left, however, does paint a picture of a very close personal (as well as 'professional') relationship. For the most part we're left with conjecture after that. Circumstantial evidence in the New Testament is consistent with Jesus and Mary Magdalene relating to each other as man and wife, so such a relationship is certainly not ruled out.

The idea of an asexual or a celibate Jesus contributes nothing helpful in any direction as we read the canonical Bible, although there are extra-Biblical traditions and lore which it might bolster. But that's in the realm of religion, and the question of his marital status or parental status is in the historical realm (assuming Jesus was an actual person, of course), and probably cannot be known with any certainty by this point in time. Ultimately the Bible as we now have it will never tell us conclusively whether Jesus and Mary were husband and wife. The closest we can get to an answer is to keep trying to figure out how and why the Biblical authors were trying to paint the relationship as they did. As always with the Bible, one can still mine potentially interesting stuff between the lines, although of course one can also go far astray that way.

As to veneration, it's pretty clear that Mary the mother, *Theotokos*, has already been enshrined by most of Christianity as the divine feminine principle of the religion, the chief female, so that role is taken, albeit somewhat unofficially.

It's a role that could well have belonged to the Magdalene in the earliest church, and then have fallen victim to the prejudices (both cultural and theological) of the groups who ended up writing and forming the Christian canon. In any case it is clear that the Magdalene played a major role in early Christianity as Jesus' closest disciple. Adding "wife" to that is not such a great leap. Quite a few idolized professors along the way have married their top female student.

Why *are* we interested in whether Jesus and Mary Magdalene were married? Probably mostly because we see Jesus as a celebrity. Like any famous person, he draws our curiosity. Why *should* we care if Jesus was married? Probably we shouldn't care by this point.

The four Evangelists gave us their accounts of Jesus without specifically getting into the question, at least in the edited versions we have. However readers of their day may have understood things they wrote in different ways than we can because of the accepted and prevailing cultural and religious assumptions of their day.

Jesus apparently did not have much to say about marriage, unless the Evangelists are not telling us everything—it appears he talked about divorce, but not much about any other issue connected directly to marriage. And the institution of marriage itself has done quite well through the ages without any known supportive words from Jesus (except his teachings against divorce, and those teachings have not prevented untold divorces among Christians, and even among Christian clergy). Any theological issues which might hang on Jesus' word in the matter have been hashed through over the ages, and nothing is left hanging (so far as I know) which depends on whether Jesus himself married.

So probably there's not much left, aside from mild curiosity and a certain disappointment, that our fan magazine (the gospels) didn't tell us what we'd like to know. Besides, we've got Dan Brown, and his version is sufficiently entertaining.

Speaking of Mary in France, however, re-introduces the "other" Mary from the opening of this chapter. Mary the mother, in her later role as the great virgin goddess, showed a particular affinity for France just as had the Magdalene, apparently. During the 19th century alone she is believed by the French faithful to have appeared at least twenty-two times in that country, including three apparitions which deeply color the cult of the virgin to this day: Paris (1830), LaSalette (1846), and most famously Lourdes (1858). We're left almost asking yet again, was there something in the water in France? At least there seems to have been something in France which attracted the two main women in Jesus' life; the two Marys.

Both Marys' associations with France have their skeptics, of course. Historians, at least many of them, are skeptical that the Magdalene ever reached France. And a good many observers are skeptical that the Marian appearances were anything beyond optical illusions or pure phantasies. Nonetheless France managed to claim a piece of the Jesus legend for itself—if he didn't retire there himself, at least the two women closest to him put their imprimaturs on the country in significant ways.

● NOTE ON MARY'S DESIGNATION AS THE MAGDALENE:

The basic assumption of most people, scholars and ordinary Christians alike, is that "Mary of Magdala" is a reference to her hometown. This would be consistent with the way other Biblical characters are designated—"Jesus of Nazareth", for example, although there's no real evidence that Jesus ever actually lived in Nazareth. So Mary became 'Mary Magdalene' because of Magdala, the theory would have it.

Scholars, however, have found that there does not seem to be a geographical place historians are confident was this town called Magdala. Several places around the Sea of Galilee have been proposed, but none of them fit the bill very securely from a linguistic perspective. Magdala, linguistically, however means "tower." So if the word stuck to Mary, maybe it was used as a description, or nickname, rather than as a geographical reference—Mary *the* Magdala instead of Mary *of* Magdala.

The Magdalene in that case would have been being described as a tower; one presumes as a 'tower of strength' or at least in a similar honorific way. One ancient town on the coast of the Sea of Galilee evidently once had a tall lighthouse for the guidance of ships into its harbor. It has been proposed that this was the tower in Mary's designation—'Mary the Beacon', in other words. The implication to some is that Mary could have been a beacon to Jesus as well as a student and disciple to Jesus; a full partner in his life, his mystical understanding, and his ministry. ⌘

7.

Son of God or Sun of God?

If I asked you to name the geographical center of Christianity today you might well think of Vatican City in modern Rome. Even for non-Catholics, Rome provides a sort of center of gravity for the religion—a symbol, at least, of authority and government (and orthodoxy) for the Christian church. To visit St. Peter's Basilica is to thrill to the accumulated power and majesty of one of humanity's major religions and historical forces. Doctrinal differences and fine points aside, St. Peter's Basilica holds a certain 'home base' comfort for all Christians. Is this, then, a place one would expect to find such starkly "pagan" images as the signs of the Zodiac?

Glance back from Michelangelo's masterpiece basilica into the great colonnaded square you've just crossed. There, in the center, stands the most improbable of objects—an actual ancient Egyptian solar obelisk. It points to the sun, the main god of ancient Egypt. It contains a sun dial and the signs of the Zodiac. The arms of the square reach out to surround and embrace this object of religious devotion and instruction from millennia past, baptizing and adopting the Zodiac and Egypt's Sun God as Christian symbols for today.

As you continue your tour of Rome you will happen upon another hill and be surprised by another ancient obelisk from Egypt standing proudly in broad daylight. This one is in the entrance square of another Roman church of more than local importance—the Cathedral of St. John Lateran, seat of the bishop of Rome. Both of the Pope's great churches, in the Vatican and at his own cathedral, are host to a full-fledged obelisk from Ancient Egypt bearing tangible witness to Christianity's link with Egyptian religion and worship of the sun.

The most enduring and universal religious symbol of all time may be the sun. It finds some kind of place in almost any religion one can think of, ancient or modern. So too in Christianity. I'd say, perhaps with a bit of a vengeance. So, surprise! Christianity can be regarded as a Sun God religion right up there with the best of the ancient near eastern religions.

130

● CHARIOT OF FIRE

As an ancient man of the Mediterranean area felt the warmth of the mid-day sun on his back and glanced down at his vivid shadow, he could visualize the Sun God above traveling the sky in his fiery golden chariot led by magnificent white horses. If he were an Egyptian, his Sun God would instead be floating through the sky in a fiery boat (the ancient Egyptians thought the sky was composed of water).

The man probably knew his Sun God by a different name (Ra, Horus, Apollo, Helios, Mithras. Sol Invictus) than did his counterpart in a neighboring kingdom, but they were fellows in what seemed the obvious conclusion that the sun must be a very powerful god. The sun made life on earth possible, and itself held on to life despite being banished nightly to the realm of death. These ancient people bequeathed to younger religions, including Christianity, probably the most unifying religious idea in human history—worship of the sun.

These ancient people looked also with wonder, awe and accumulating wisdom at the night sky. The sun in his fiery chariot, or his night time boat, was now traversing the underworld, fighting off death and gaining strength to be reborn at dawn.

But the great celestial map was clearly visible at night. Astronomy began as astrology—a serious attempt to understand what could be seen with the naked eye in the night sky, and to organize it so as to calculate and fathom the changing seasons. Again, these early astrologers/astronomers bequeathed to following generations a quasi-religious system we call the Zodiac, which plays a role (sometimes coded) even in the Bible and then in Christianity. ("The heavens are telling the glory of God; and the firmament proclaims his handiwork...In them he has set a tent for the sun...Its rising is from the end of the heavens, and its circuit to the end of them." Psalm 19: 1-6). We even identify and symbolize the very writers who tell us what little we know about Jesus (the four evangelists, or gospel writers) by way of four zodiacal signs.

Archaeologists have found early Christian tombs marked with both of the earliest iconographic symbols of Jesus, that of the Good Shepherd and that of a chariot of fire which identifies him with the sun. When the Jesus message started to spread in and through the Roman Empire, the Romans saw Jesus himself as a solar being, a Sun God, the Hebrew version of Mithras. Christians are close cousins to the devotees of Adonis and Osiris, Dionysus and Mithras, although they're often unaware of these family connections.

A friend, a Roman Catholic bishop, tells me that deep under St. Peter's Basilica in an ancient burial ground can be seen Sun God imagery applied to Jesus and images of Jesus as Apollo, one of the Sun Gods of antiquity.

131

All of Christianity's symbols, rites, and everything Christians profess in creeds can be found in the religious literature of Palestine, Persia, or Egypt, scholars tell us. The canonized scriptures of Christianity and Judaism have Egyptian origins, they say, with the Sun God becoming Jesus and the twelve rays of light that streamed from the central radiance becoming the twelve 'fishermen'—the main disciples, or 'Apostles'.

There is essentially no limit to features of the Sun God myth to be found in Christianity some scholars say. We are told that the earliest Christian community offered prayers addressed to 'Our Lord, the Sun.'

One scholar claims to have found one hundred and eighty points of similarity, parallelism, and identity between the Egyptian Sun God Horus and Jesus as portrayed in the Gospels. Tertullian, Justin Martyr, and other early Christian church fathers have noted that the leaders of the Christian movement confessed that many of their doctrines, rites, creeds, and symbols were identical with their ancient Egyptian counterparts.

It is fairly easy to find scholars who share the conviction that the scriptures of Judaism and Christianity were basically Egyptian formulations. One wrote that the Gospels "were spiritual allegories and ceremonial dramas that had escaped from the [Egyptian] Mysteries," the same mysteries into which young men were being initiated in Chapter 2. Another agrees that "the historical core of the bible accounts, for both the Old and New Testaments, came from Egypt"—Egypt, where the Sun God and the king were the heart of cultic practice. Pharaoh played the crucial role in the daily ritual; he was the main officiant, the sun priest.

One of these scholars calls ancient Egypt the "mother religion" of Christianity, and laments that Christians are made relatively familiar with their Hebrew roots, but not their Egyptian roots.

The early Christians promoted syncretism (fused religious symbols) between Jesus and the other Sun Gods in order to attract peoples from the Roman Empire into the Christian tent. Eventually it became illegal in the Roman Empire for anyone except Jesus to be depicted with the ancient Sun God symbolism, which included the zodiac—not even Caesar himself.

Some thinkers have decided that Christianity was flat out a purloined worship of the sun, as Thomas Paine, one of America's 'founding fathers,' does in his famous pronouncement: "The Christian religion is a parody on the worship of the sun, in which they put a man called Christ in the place of the sun, and pay him the adoration originally payed [sic] to the sun."

The identification of Jesus with the sun has deep Biblical roots. The early church saw Jesus as the incarnation of divine wisdom, or Sophia, (herself most likely a derivation of Isis) who says of herself "Alone I have made the circuit of the sky and traversed the depths of the abyss." (Sirach 24:5) This is a pretty clear reference to the Egyptian Sun God who was understood to sail across the sky by day in his fiery boat, and then to cross the underworld by night until he could again rise from the depths at sunrise.

It's quite possible, too, that the idea of Jesus' descent into hell during his three days in the tomb, as Christians declare to be true in their creeds, grew out of the Egyptian understanding of the sun crossing the underworld each night in his barge, surviving challenges and death, and gaining strength to be reborn at dawn.

Gospel references to Jesus as a Sun God are, like Jesus' teaching itself, veiled. They are couched in symbolism and the language of allegory. One oblique such reference can be found, for example, in the crucifixion episode (Matthew 27:45). As Jesus hung on the cross near death, the world was plunged into darkness. I've heard many attempts to turn this reference into literal truth, such as proposing an eclipse of the sun must have taken place just at that moment, even though an eclipse never lasts for hours. But we, as always, need to remember that the evangelists are not attempting to relate history; they are trying to shape a teaching narrative about religion. The period of darkness at the end of the crucifixion is an allegory which connects Jesus with the Egyptian Sun God Horus, whose travail also produced such a darkness. The message is: the killing of Jesus extinguished the sun, i.e. Jesus was a Sun God, the sun of god.

Sometimes these gospel references to Jesus as a Sun God are a little less oblique, however, as in John 8:12, "I am the light of the world; he who follows me will not walk in darkness." Less oblique, but still veiled. (Of course, as in all matters Biblical, there are numerous other interpretations to this or any other passage.)

When we were small children singing "Jesus wants me for a Sunbeam" in Sunday School, little did we know that we were flirting with some of the most ancient roots of Christianity. Little were we prepared yet to luxuriate in the Christian realm of the sun and his zodiac. St. Francis of Assisi, in his famous Hymn to the sun refers to "my lord Brother Sun" and says the sun shares the "likeness" of God. And he praises "Sister Moon and the stars," another Zodiacal reference.

Maybe you've been surprised to overhear a clergy person refer to the altar area as the "east end" when the church is obviously oriented in a different geographical direction. Or maybe you've wondered why so many churches are actually built on an east-west axis. The answer is simply that the sun rises in the east, and this orientation of our ecclesiastical buildings, whether actual or just "liturgical" (symbolic), is a remnant of a religious past in which the sun played a definitive role. If you ask a clergy person about this orientation to the east, you will probably be told that the sunrise is a symbol of Jesus' resurrection. Whatever may be the current quick explanation, notice that it still links Jesus with the sun—a mysterious remnant of ancient Christianity still hiding in our midst today. The original idea was to align each new church to due east on the day of the saint to whom the church was dedicated.

This 'facing east' concern has Egyptian antecedents, just one example being that mummified bodies were laid on their sides toward the rising sun to help facilitate their resurrection. Sunrise was the daily promise of rebirth and renewal. This is a universal religious concept for humanity. The Buddha was facing east when he achieved illumination.

It is also a pretty tame guess that the steeples we often continue to build onto our churches are echoes of the obelisks of Egypt which pointed to the sun (i.e. to God).

In the same way we note that Christians adopted Sunday (Sun Day) as their main day of worship, the "Lord's day," rather than the Jewish Sabbath (Saturday). And despite a complicated system for dating each year, Easter always falls on a Sunday.

Many years ago on a church youth exchange trip to Europe, I met another boy who taught me much about the mystical aspects of Christianity. One day out of the blue he said to me something like, "If I weren't a Christian, I believe I'd be worshiping the sun." The comment has long intrigued me, especially since he ended up as a respected professor at both theological seminaries I attended (although after my time at these schools, alas). But of course, as a Christian he was religiously already intimately connected with sun worship whether he was aware of it at the time or not.

Why are there suggestively potential Zodiacal numbers as part of the New Testament? For example, why twelve main disciples or apostles? Every Sun God figure of ancient times had twelve companions. The number twelve carried religious freight in a number of ancient cultures. In ancient Greece there were twelve Olympiad deities, and the 'Feast of the Divine Twelve' was celebrated. There are twelve signs in the Zodiac.

We know from the New Testament itself that Jesus' followers had to number more than twelve if for no other reasons than that there were also females to be added in, and several additions to the group were made along the way and noted in New Testament writings. The Bible tells us it was Jesus himself who decided to pull a *special* twelve disciples out from the many, in order to establish an inner core—the Sun God needed his twelve. The most logical reason for use of the number twelve is that there are twelve signs of the Zodiac, and twelve stages (months) of the solar year. Jesus traveled around with his twelve, just as the sun travels around with its twelve.

One could take the view that twelve special disciples were singled out because there were twelve tribes of Israel, and it's true that Jesus himself

134

made a connection of that sort when he later indicated (Matthew 19:28) that the twelve would "sit on twelve thrones, judging the twelve tribes of Israel." But that interpretation would probably put the cart before the horse because the twelve tribes idea most likely came from the Zodiac to begin with.

In Genesis 15:5 God tells Abraham that his descendants will be like the stars of heaven. That doesn't just mean that Abraham's descendants will be as numerous as the stars. It means they will be ordered as are the stars. The descendants will be ordered into twelve tribes, just as the stars are ordered in the twelve constellations of the Zodiac. (It is interesting to note that ancient Egyptian pharaohs were thought to become stars in the firmament after death; possibly giving us another hint to the origins of this promise by God to Abraham.)

As tourists (modern day pilgrims?) we can find the Zodiac embedded in many of the churches we have grown to admire—San Miniato al Monte in Florence, being a good example

Hieroglyphic records exist of the hymn sung in the Egyptian litany of hours—twelve each night and twelve each day, just as in a clock today. There are twelve cycles of the moon within one sun cycle, and this monthly procession affected religious views and expression just as did the twelve processional stages of the zodiac. It was the ancient Egyptians who gave us the calendar we use today. They divided the year into twelve months, they fixed the year at 365 days, and they fixed the day with twelve hours and the night of twelve hours. This was all from the work of ancient Egyptian astronomers, and intimately tied to and expressed by the Zodiac.

● CROSS OF THE ZODIAC

Ancient religion placed a serious emphasis on the Zodiac. It felt that the drama of mankind's spiritual life had been written in the sky before it took place on earth. Eventually astrology became taboo in Christian thinking, but only after the Zodiac was enshrined as a symbolic drama which helped define her chief protagonist, Jesus.

The use of a halo in religious art is so common as to be taken for granted. It's origin is most likely the sun disc which became a distinctive feature of ancient Egyptian religion (especially under the Pharaoh Akhenaten, Chapter 8). The halo was, and is, used to designate figures of religious importance or great holiness, i.e. "saints." For the figure of Jesus, however, something more was needed than the simple halo used for others of religious distinction, because he had been named an incarnate god. So his halo became the cross of the Zodiac (explained in the following paragraph), which then designates him as the sun, or the source of life, and thus God (in distinction from the other figures with a simple halo who were merely 'holy').

135

Thus one of the most widespread symbols tying together Christianity and the Zodiac is the representation of Jesus (often as Pantokrator, sometimes spelled Pantocrator) with a halo having four equal internal spokes. This comes from an older symbol of two concentric circles divided by such an equilateral cross into quarters like a pie, and centered on a smaller circle, or disc, in the very center. The center represents the sun, while around it are the twelve signs of the zodiac divided into the four seasons. When Jesus is placed in the center, in place of the sun, we have the Zodiacal halo image ("And his face shone like the sun," Matthew 17:2).

Perhaps the best known such image is in the great church (later mosque, then museum, now mosque again) of Hagia Sophia in Constantinople (now Istanbul). But that's not an easy reach for most of us as tourists. We need a more accessible place for this exploration. Venice, so long at the cross roads of east and west, is a good European place to find a lot of iconography suggesting the influence of sun worship on Christianity.

Numerous examples of Jesus depicted on the cross of the Zodiac can be found at St. Mark's Basilica in Venice, on mosaics both inside and outside. One of the most interesting to me is a rendering of Jesus as an infant in Mary's lap, in which the baby has a grand Zodiac halo, and the mother a merely standard one. In a culture so enamored of the Virgin, this is a dramatic reminder of who's ultimately God in the image.

Venice may offer a better set of examples at the old cathedral in Torcello, where mosaics of eastern design show at least four obvious halos in the Zodiac Cross pattern. And, as would be expected, the Greek Orthodox Church in Venice has a wonderful apse icon of Christ in glory (with Zodiacal cross) as well as an instructive museum of icons next door (which contains a sixteenth century icon showing the Virgin and child surrounded by a complete cycle of Zodiac signs).

The Correr Museum in Venice contains a seventeenth century icon of the Holy Trinity showing God the Father and God the Son (both, along with the dove representing the Holy Spirit, with halos containing the cross of the Zodiac because they are religiously one, and thus have the same relationship to the sun) holding between them a blue sphere representing the world and surrounded by a horizontal band with signs of the Zodiac (Libra, Capricorn, Cancer, and Pisces can easily be made out in the gold leaf).

In the Scuola Grande Dei Carmini there is a gilded altar piece which illustrates nicely an alternative way to accomplish much the same thing iconographically. In front of a large sun burst sit the virgin and child surrounded by a circle of twelve stars, clearly representing the Zodiac.

A little further south along the Adriatic in Justinian's western capital Ravenna, lies a treasure trove of mosaic art and within it Christian iconography from an earlier and purely eastern perspective. The church of St. Vitale there is probably most famous for the mosaic portraits of Justinian and his empress St. Theodora, but inside the church one's eye is drawn to the dominating figures of Christ, all of which bear as a halo the Zodiacal cross. The great arch leading from the apse into the body of the church is surmounted by a Christ Pantokrator and on each side leading to the floor are images of six of the twelve apostles (twelve signs of the Zodiac) plus an honorary portrait of one of St. Vitale's supposed two sons (we know almost nothing of Vitale, let alone whether he had sons).

In the other direction, a bit north of Venice in Padova (Padua), the cathedral baptistery shows a dramatic fourteenth century Pantokrator Christ top and center, complete with a cross of the Zodiac halo as well as numerous other Zodiacal crosses on the Jesus depictions in the frescos there.

The baptistery's most telling fresco, however, is another fourteenth century painting called 'creation of the world,' showing Jesus with his sun halo lifting his hand in a gesture of creation and blessing. He is standing, supported by angels, on a complete Zodiac cycle (all twelve signs in their counter-clock-wise rotation), which surrounds the world. His feet are resting on the Pisces sign, the age of which began at the general assumed time of his earthly birth, and facing ahead to the sign of the next age, or house, that of Aquarius, beginning more or less now (the length of an age can vary in a range of about 2,150 to 2,500 years). It would appear he spoke of the Aquarian age, in code, to his disciples in telling them to prepare for their Passover meal together by finding a man in the city carrying water (a job reserved for women at that time) and to follow him into his 'house.'

There is in the floor mosaic of a synagogue in Hammat Tiberias in Galilee, a perfect pattern of the Zodiac ring, with each of the twelve signs identified in Hebrew, and in the center ring a depiction of the sun itself, as a man with a halo from which emanate the rays of the sun (in this case seven visible rays). Substitute Jesus in the center ring with his Cross of the Zodiac halo and the image would have been perfectly at home in most churches of the day (fourth century CE) and beyond.

During Bronze Age Egypt the reigning Pharaoh was seen as the son of the father (the sun) who did the sun's work on earth—he was therefore a god, and in effect the sun incarnate. This idea surfaced again in the Bible as a description and depiction of Jesus. "The sun of righteousness shall rise, with healing in its wings," Malachi 4:2, is a clear Egyptian religious image among others in the Bible.

The Egyptian influence on Israel's religious perspective must have been pervasive in many ways, not only in the matter of the sun as god. When Moses handed down the Jewish law (ten commandments) from Mt. Sinai, it rather obviously looked a lot like the Egyptian Book of the Dead, as many scholars have noted—"I have not killed," became "Thou shall not kill," etc. And the Egyptian incantation to the Pharoah/God Ahmen (Amun, Amen) found its way too into the prayers of the Judeo-Christian tradition as "Amen." So the notion of religious themes and ideas moving with the Israelites out of Egypt and home to Palestine should not be understood to be anything surprising. Far more than just the sun as a symbol or model for Jesus came out of Egypt—it was the source of many stones which were integrated into Christianity's foundation.

Sun imagery is widely seen in Europe's ancient cathedrals, and Chartres Cathedral in France is another ideal place to look. A façade relief shows Jesus in a Vesica Pisces (an architectural shape similar to two joined parentheses marks usually containing a human figure) surrounded by four zodiac figures—Aquarius (which Christians adopted as a symbol for the Evangelist Matthew), Leo (Mark), Taurus (Luke), and Aquila (John). It was typical during a period in Christian art for the Christ to be portrayed inside a Vesica Pisces along with these four zodiac signs. Surrounding his head would be a halo resembling the Sun. The symbolism here suggests that the Christian doctrine of the End Times is actually about the rebirth of the sun, which heralds in a new age.

Of special interest at Chartres also is the famous Black Madonna, probably representing the Egyptian mother goddess Isis, and an ambulatory stained glass window containing the full twelve signs of the Zodiac. In Rome at Michelangelo's Church of St. Mary of Angels and Martyrs in the ancient baths of Diocletian, Pope Innocent XII ordered a full Zodiacal line to be incorporated into the floor to trace the sun through its yearly cycle; the placement inside a church bearing further testimony of the accepted association between the sun and the Christ of Christianity.

There are ripples of the Zodiac sprinkled around the New Testament. Why specifically twelve Apostles, for example? Luke 6:13 tells us that Jesus intentionally pulled twelve men out of his wider circle of followers and gave them that added distinction. Luke then spends a fair amount of space detailing just who these twelve specifically honored men were. The point of the story would seem to be *who* was chosen from the many. But the probability is that the real point is the *number*—there needed to be twelve. Even the respected American theologian E. P. Sanders, noted for not going out on limbs, wrote that Jesus was using the number twelve symbolically.

Later, when there were only eleven of these apostles left (because Judas had died after betraying Jesus) Peter announced that it was imperative that the full dozen be filled out again. Lots were drawn between two candidates and a replacement for Judas was appointed (Acts 1:12-26). Again, the real message seems to be that there must be twelve; the emphasis was on the number. Although later Christians might rail against astrology, it is obvious that the Zodiac was a very significant factor in early Christian thought and formation. And it is also obvious that there could be only twelve apostles. Paul's later claim to be an apostle on equal footing with those in Jerusalem was dead on arrival.

● ARE CHRISTIANS STILL SUN WORSHIPERS?

Students of religion in our day are still discovering the Egyptian roots of Christianity we've been discussing. You'll recognize one of them because the student who wrote the essay has become an icon of contemporary American culture: Martin Luther King, Jr. In a college essay in 1950 he wrote, "The Egyptian mysteries of Isis and Osiris exerted considerable influence upon early Christianity." His weighty essay also pointed out that such themes as the descent into hell, and even the crucifixion itself, had roots in the pagan religions which preceded Christianity.

Religious traditions filter down from generation to generation without many questions ever being entertained about what is actually being claimed and stated. Few 21st century Christians, I'd guess, have given even the briefest thought to the sun as a religious aspect, or symbol, despite the enormous role it has played in human religion generally, and Christianity specifically.

Are Christians today still sun worshippers? It is safe to say that there's a lot of residue of Egyptian sun worship still in our midst, but it's doubtful many religious people today recognize it even though they use the symbols and sing the words. They have long-since stopped giving much consideration to the religious symbols or the words they use across the board. If religious people today actually did consider the words they recite in ritual and liturgy, would more of them begin remaining silent during recitation of the ancient creeds? My guess is yes, because what we say there is literally far-fetched by today's perspective.

At an Anglican Evensong I recently attended, the congregation lustily sang one of those beloved hymns with the lovely tune and mysterious, poetic text. But I was stunned to re-read the words they were so enthusiastically singing: "Ancient of days, pavilioned in splendor, and girded with praise. Whose robe is the light, whose canopy space. His chariots of wrath the deep thunder clouds form, and dark is his path on the wings of the storm." This quite obvious sun worship imagery didn't even bother to name the Jesus these folks thought they were singing about—it just referred to "King." Could it have been sung with equal nonchalance by a congregation in ancient Egypt?

Were we singing about the Jesus who had inherited all of this sun imagery—Jesus the "sun" of the early Christians? Were we singing about Jesus the Christ, resplendent in his cosmic glory and outshining the sun (St. Paul's "Lord")? Were we actually honoring Pharaoh, the son of the sun, and therefore the sun on earth? The singing congregation, to the extent its members gave much thought to the situation, surely believed they were singing about the familiar Jesus of our imagining. But, if so, they were using sun worship imagery—Jesus the "sun" of god.

Hymnody may, indeed, be a good place to look for some of the deep roots of Christianity to which we've grown oblivious over the years. An eighteenth century hymn by John Keble, for example, praises the "Sun of my soul, Thou Savior dear, it is not night if Thou be near." This ventures not only as far as directly labeling Jesus as the sun, but on to the Sun God of Egypt making his daily pilgrimage between day/heaven and night/hell.

Son of God or Sun of God?

In one of their most widely used and most beloved hymns, Christians sing of "Watchers and Holy Ones," without any clue they are wading into the most esoteric reaches of Biblical and mythological traditions—traditions of which their clergy would possibly be as ignorant as they, and which the scholars of their faith would likely refute resolutely. "Watchers" in the Bible are portrayed as "angels" who started to inter-breed with humans. Some think the Biblical record here is actually referring to aliens from space who left their genetic material behind in humans, as well as traces of their superior culture and knowledge which humans could not have acquired on their own. But none of this is the type of thing going through the minds of worshippers singing a familiar old hymn. The roots of the concept may reach back to very ancient Egypt where some of the lesser divinities' titles are translated as "Watchers."

Are Christians still sun worshippers? They, like humans everywhere have linked the return of the sun in spring with hope and new life, emotions which are components of religion from as long ago as we can fathom. Somewhere deep inside which we no longer see in the mirror, probably yes, we're still attached to the sun in a way which could fairly be termed as 'religious.'

Of course there are people who are uncomfortable with some of these images and symbols. They maintain that Christians do not, or did not, actually believe what their symbols seemed to proclaim. Most of us could easily agree that it is the function of symbols to suggest and illuminate, rather than to equate. They were, after all, teachers in an age of illiteracy.

The famous early Christian Ichthys (Ichthus) symbol of a simply drawn fish was used as a code of affiliation, not as a statement that Christians were fish, or worshipped fish, or that Jesus was really a fish. It was a play on words, a visual anagram.

So too, some would say, the sun is a mere symbol for Jesus which no one really took seriously, and certainly did not take literally. I agree that it was never intended to be taken literally, of course. But the question is not one of literal vs. figurative interpretation. The question is whether people believe, or still believe, what the symbol was intended to say. Speaking of Christians today, the skeptics' stance may be correct. We have become pretty lazy and hazy in our interpretation of Christianity across the board these days. And we have generally forgotten the origins of Christianity which gave rise to the symbolism of Jesus as 'Sun of God.' Today's Christians are probably indeed religious orphans, having long lost the heritage of their religion's two chief parents, Judaism and the religion of ancient Egypt. ⌘

Zodiac clock in St. Mark's Square, Venice

8.

The Bible and Egyptian Royalty

It's possible that your Bible contains a long story about an ancient Egyptian pharaoh that is completely hidden in its pages. And not just any old pharaoh, but the husband of the beautiful Nefertiti, and the father of the now famous King Tut. What's more, it's even possible this pharaoh wrote the story himself and thus may be the author of a good bit of our Old Testament.

Note, however, that I said 'possible,' which is a step or two shy of 'probable.' We need to approach this story (or possible story) indirectly, however.

● MAGIC/MOSES/MONOTHEISM

Magic is a word which for most people today probably conjures either light entertainment or something dark and evil—in either case something decidedly not 'Christian.' Yet magic played a significant role in Christianity's origins, from ancient Egypt onward into the New Testament and maybe even beyond. You can't read the Old Testament without encountering magic, and the New Testament is full of Jesus *doing* magic (although the word used would be 'miracles' or something similar).

Magic today conveys a somewhat negative impression, whereas deep in the history of mankind's religions it was usually a force for good; a tool used to bring about helpful results such as protection from evil. In the early period of Christianity magic was simply a natural inheritance from previous religious thinking. Only later, as the young religion developed, did magic begin to acquire a negative connotation, culminating in its practice becoming regarded as somehow sinful.

Religious magic, in the simplest terms, is using specific formulaic words and actions in an effort to conform outside reality to the will of the magician. Unlike in our own times, magic in the ancient Near East was most decidedly not done for entertainment; it was done to achieve a result. Magic and religion were virtually indistinguishable in ancient Egypt, we are told by scholars. Magic was a tool used for serious purposes, not a game used for fun.

143

Illusion was not the point, as it usually is today. However if people thought they saw or experienced something which had no factual basis it might actually be helpful so long as it contributed to the goal at hand. Evidence has been found by archeologists that at least some of the speaking oracle statues in ancient Egyptian temples utilized illusion. The statue would be mounted on a hollow pedestal with a speaking tube which went down into a secret chamber underground where a priest could then speak for, and as, the oracle. So evidently trickery was just fine as long as it served the right purpose (rather like some politics today).

Still, the point of magic in ancient society and religion was not deception. Magic was about power and the ability to make things happen. No less an authority than James Frazer tells us in *The Golden Bough* that magic is always and everywhere lying just below the surface of religion. And he says that did not end with ancient Egypt, but that belief in the mix of religion and magic is still alive today. In modern Europe he describes a Mass of the Holy Spirit by which Catholic priests in France are believed by some to be able to *force* God to grant whatever is asked, and he calls this belief an exact counterpart of attitudes about magicians in ancient Egypt. Magic was a tool, and could accomplish certain tasks. It could possibly even place an obligation on the gods to cooperate with the will of the magician, whether they especially wanted to do so or not.

Other writers too have noted that magic in ancient Egyptian religion was thought to work by compelling the desired result, rather than merely requesting it or pleading for it. Magic was the stick, not the carrot. Magic was viewed then as science is viewed today. It was a tool which could be utilized to achieve things. And, again, there was no real distinction between magic and religion. Magic was man's connection to supposed immutable truths and powers which had existed from the very foundation of the universe. Magic was everywhere. Magicians were on the royal payroll in ancient Egypt and were thought even to be useful in diplomatic relations with foreign governments.

Moses is the key figure in our discussion at this point. Some have said he was himself Egyptian, or half Egyptian, although the Bible in general terms seems to indicate both parents were Hebrew (aside from one verse which says flatly that he was an Egyptian). In any case, he was raised as an Egyptian (despite his own mother being his wet nurse, according to Genesis). Being raised in an Egyptian royal household he was surely knowledgeable in the ways of Egyptian religion and magic.

The New Testament says he "was instructed in all the wisdom of the Egyptians," Acts 7:22. This would necessarily mean, then, that he had been initiated into the mysteries in the Egyptian way, as we discussed in Chapter 2. The Moses we meet in the Old Testament is full of many ambiguities, and even the Bible in one specific spot, as noted above, agrees that he was an Egyptian rather than a Hebrew (Exodus 2:19). Maybe he was even a member of the Egyptian royal family, with the Biblical story of Hebrew parents and being found in a basket in the Nile merely a set-up to better fit into the coming story of the Exodus. In any case, the Biblical ambiguity as to his nationality is merely a prelude to a long story full of possible contradictions and surprising possibilities.

As with Jesus of the New Testament, and like many other characters of the Old Testament (Abraham, David, Solomon), there is no real historical evidence outside of the Bible itself to prove Moses' actual existence as a real human. Finding the historical Moses is complicated by the Biblical stories being so old, and by their probable existence as oral folklore for so many generations before being written down. That's part of the problem with Jesus too, although on a much, much smaller scale. With the Jesus stories it was essentially just a gap of two or three generations before the first written record. But it was a gap of a great many generations in the case of Moses. The bottom line is that, like Jesus, we have only murky and unverifiable details about Moses despite the amount of space and the importance he commands in the Bible.

Moses, as we've noted, was probably (inevitably?) an initiate of the Egyptian Mysteries. Some describe him as having reached the level of an adept, i.e. an initiate who emerges as a master of what he has learned and is proficient at utilizing these mysteries into which the elite young men were initiated.

And here's the big punchline for this chapter—Moses is even regarded by some sober scholars to have been the pharaoh Akhenaten himself. Or if not Akhenaten, at least a high official in Akhenaten's court, perhaps his high priest.

It was Akhenaten who tried to install monotheism into Egyptian religion, and the memory of whom the Egyptians tried to erase after his death or departure (more about this idea below). Some (including Sigmund Freud), on the other hand, have thought Moses may have been an officer in the court of Akhenaten, having grown up in the pharaoh's household. There are some who see him as Senenmut, a shadowy figure, astronomer and astrologist, much trusted by the royal family, who then disappears from history leaving his elaborate tomb unused. Monotheism, Moses' great religious contribution in addition to religious law, according to the Bible, was surfacing as an idea and practice at this time in Egypt, just prior to the reign of Akhenaten.

Another idea which we'll look at later is that Moses was an Egyptian priest, and possibly the chief priest of Akhenaten's religious cult. In that case, it is posited, the Exodus could have resulted from a rift between

Akhenaten's successors who returned to traditional religious polytheistic practices and those still loyal to Akhenaten who clung to his monotheistic ideal.

Digging some plausible identity for this Moses figure out of the depths of time is hardly an easy task. Scholars think it may have taken over a thousand years after his presumed lifetime for the first written record bearing his name to have been executed—a very long time for memories to fade and errors to creep into the oral history. But most new scholarship on Moses centers on or around the Amarna period of Egypt—around the "heretic" pharaoh Akhenaten ("heretic" to the Egyptians because he closed down the worship of so many of their favorite gods).

Whatever his position and status, the Bible tells us in Exodus 11:3 that Moses was "very great in the land of Egypt, in the sight of Pharaoh's servants and in the sight of the people." Oddly enough, that phrasing leaves open most possibilities, including even the idea that Moses himself could have been pharaoh, although the rest of the text would refute that notion if only one author's material is represented. Whoever Moses was, he eventually became an exalted figure in three major world religions, the so-called Abrahamic religions of Islam, Judaism, and Christianity. He is evidently the most often mentioned prophet in the Koran, showing up by name more than twenty-seven times more often than does Muhammad himself it is said (I haven't read enough of the Koran myself to verify this claim).

It is interesting to note that the great patriarch Abraham is also seen by some as the Pharaoh Akhenaten, just as is Moses by others. We're not standing on the firm ground of established history here, we're flirting with the 'could be' and 'might be' fringes of history despite the existence of some supportive evidence.

Whomever Moses was, or was not, he's cemented in as a key figure in the Judeo-Christian tradition. The tension as to whether our Biblical narrative is built on real characters or on mythological stereotypes did not wait for Jesus; it began long before we even had a written "Old Testament." It began with Moses.

● AKHENATEN AND THE ATEN

Not all that many decades ago few people had heard of a pharaoh named Akhenaten. Now he's all the rage. Book after book has been written about him and he seems to have emerged as perhaps the most visible of Egypt's pre-ptolemaic pharaohs. Most rulers gain fame and historical reputation from military exploits or for being ruthless tyrants or benevolent near-saints. Akhenaten, however, accomplished his celebrity by the most unusual of means—proposing, and trying to enforce, an abstract religious idea; an idea almost everyone except the pharaoh himself absolutely hated.

The Bible and Egyptian Royalty

Before the reign of Pharaoh Akhenaten humans were animists who saw spirits inhabiting and animating absolutely everything. They were thus polytheists, believers in many gods. Every city and village in ancient Egypt had its own chief god and a small army of lesser gods. The ancient Egyptians may have been the most polytheistic people the world has ever known.

Akhenaten tried to change that. He took a minor Egyptian Sun God, the Aten, and installed it not only as the new chief Sun God, but as the only god allowed for Egyptians to worship. He proceeded to try to erase the previous gods, closing their shrines and temples and dismissing their priesthoods (perhaps partially because the priesthoods had grown too powerful for his taste). He moved the capital to a new city, Amarna, which he built in the desert as part of the effort to alter Egyptian religion. Eventually this revolutionary religious idea would find expression in the religions of Judaism, Christianity, and Islam, all three claiming to be monotheistic as well as all three claiming to be descended from Abraham.

But at the time none of this was in the slightest popular with the Egyptian people, who later would try to erase Akhenaten from history in the same way he tried to erase their hoard of familiar gods. Historians have varied quite a bit in their efforts to assess this pharaoh. Some see him as a great religious visionary, some as a revolutionary, some as a genius. Others see him as "unbalanced" and "self-obsessive," an "iconoclastic freak" or a "recluse with a single fixation," and a "fanatic" or a "radical." And the list goes on: "madman," "narcissist," "sociopath," "ruthless egocentric." That he was controversial and enigmatic, and that his reign had far reaching consequences, all agree.

Now we can begin to get to the reason an Egyptian pharaoh has a starring role in the questions of 'who was Moses?' and 'what was the Exodus?', as well as some understanding of why Jesus eventually came to be seen as a Sun God.

Is the fall of Akhenaten (and thus, ultimately, of Egyptian monotheism) possibly the trigger for the Exodus?

It is thought by some that Moses, as a faithful and believing minister to Akhenaten, gathered a group of followers in the delta and left Egypt with them in order to continue the phenomenon of monotheistic religion after the reign of Akhenaten. Some feel, however, that there may be a difference between Akhenaten's monotheism (all gods were actually the same god but could be known in various places by various names) and the monotheism Moses established (the one god can only be known through his name and works as experienced by the Israelite tribes). In any case, monotheism is another example of a religious concept or practice which originated in Egypt and was carried home by the Israelites and Moses, at least according

147

to Biblical traditions (and thence obviously spread on to Christianity in due course).

Akhenaten's religion was illustrated in iconography as shafts of sunlight beaming down to earth, each sunbeam ending with a human hand. This iconography also gave the most prominent usage yet to the ankh. An ankh was basically a slightly elongated "O" sitting on top of a "T." Human figures in Egyptian hieroglyphs often carried an ankh by its top circle. In yet another connection between Christianity and ancient Egypt, early Christians utilized the ankh as a primary religious symbol and as a means of mutual recognition. For them, the top circle represented the sun (Jesus was seen as a Sun God, after all) and the bottom "T" represented the cross upon which their Jesus was crucified. The ankh had existed in Egyptian iconography previously, but Akhenaten raised it to its most prominent level.

Some scholars feel the Essenes had a community in Egypt, that Jesus was an Essene who spent time at the Egyptian community during the 'silent' or 'missing' years before his public ministry, and therefore that Jesus was familiar with the history and geography of Akhenaten and his milieu. The Essenes, as a result of this Egyptian community, would have a special interest in Pharaoh Akhenaten, and therefore that the earliest supporters of Jesus would also have had a similar interest and continuing allegiance to Akhenaten. The idea that Jesus spent all or a large part of his pre-ministry, or 'hidden' years, in Egypt is a widely shared theory among scholars, and a possibility or even a probability when working from coded Biblical texts.

An amateur Egyptologist well known to us for other reasons, Sigmund Freud, reasoned similarly: If Moses was an Egyptian and if he communicated his own religion to the Jews, it would have been Akhenaten's religion, that of the Aten.

So if we find it credible that Moses brought the monotheism of Akhenaten to the promised land, then it is also likely that the subject of that monotheism—sun worship—came along for the ride. Despite ample overt sun references in our Old Testament, it is not particularly easy to trace this influence, largely, perhaps, because we don't know specifically what to look for.

To summarize so far: The Aten was a pure manifestation of the sun; a simple disc (and probably the origin of the artistic halo used later by Christians). It had been in the Egyptian family of gods for a long time, but in a minor capacity. The pharaoh Amenhotep III raised the Aten to the top of the hierarchy of Egyptian gods, perhaps partially for political reasons involving tensions with the priesthood. But it was under his son, the next pharaoh Amenhotep IV that the Aten cult reached its zenith. This Pharaoh changed his name to Akhenaten, declared Aten was the sole creator God and closed the temples dedicated to the other sun gods, now seen as rivals to the Aten. Akhenaten then moved the capital to a new site, named Amarna, dedicated to the Aten.

Unlike the many Egyptian gods of the past which could be satisfactorily represented by specific animals or objects, the Aten was an abstraction. It was the giver and source of all life. It was represented in iconography by ephemeral sunbeams rather than tangible animals.

The basics of the story advance: When Akhenaten died (or left the throne for whatever reason) he was succeeded by his queen (and sister) whom he had named as his co-regent, the now famous Nefertiti. The real end of his reign, however, came at her death. Their son, the young Pharaoh Tutankhamun (the now famous 'King Tut'), abandoned Amarna and returned the capital to Thebes. He presided over the return of the Egyptian religious hierarchy to the old order—Akhenaten was now considered a heretic and all references to him and the Aten in the record were erased. His capital city was officially abandoned and left to be rediscovered beneath the desert sands centuries later.

The reason for this backlash against Akhenaten and his only god had not only to do with a distaste for monotheism, it was also a backlash for the changes in Egyptian daily life Akhenaten created. Akhenaten not only undermined an important segment of the national economy by his deposing all the old gods and closing their temples, but he also eliminated major aspects of the social lives of the people. The old temples of the minor gods and their precincts were schools which produced scribes, doctors and artists, and offices where the services of these professionals could be accessed by ordinary people, most of whom were illiterate. Few Egyptians mourned Akhenaten when he either died or abdicated and fled Dodge. They were only too happy to get back to the comfortable gods of yesterday.

• WAS MOSES REALLY A JEW?

There is an alternate version of Akhenaten's late life story which is accepted and promoted by some. In this version it was indeed the baby floated down the Nile in a reed basket for his own safety who grew up to become the Pharaoh Akhenaten. He did not die in office, but was forced to abdicate because of his wildly unpopular monotheism and was then sent into exile out of Egypt. He took with him his royal scepter with the bronze serpent on top. He was followed by a large group of retainers who still regarded him as the rightful Pharaoh, or 'Mose' or 'Mosis.' Among the retainers fleeing with Akhenaten/Moses were the family of Jacob (now called Israel), the Israelites. The important Biblical figure of Moses, in other words, was actually the deposed Pharaoh Ahkenaten. (Another version, this one promoted by Freud, holds that Moses was the brother of Akhenaten.)

This story, while beguiling, would seem to have met a big roadblock when later royal tomb builders think they discovered the tomb (but *not* the

149

mummy, it is said) of Akhenaten, the "Great Criminal," and in a zealous frenzy removed his names from the tomb, removed the golden face mask, and mutilated his lower face so that he would not be able to breathe or speak in the next world (say others who believe the mummy *was* discovered). Akhenaten's presumed sarcophagus was protected on each corner by renderings of his queen, Nefertiti, with outstretched arms. The failure of Akhenaten's monotheism was likely hastened by the jealous reactions of the priests of the many demoted gods.

It is important to note, however, that a number of sober historians relate that no evidence was found in the tomb to indicate it had ever been used— and thus the possibility that the end of Akhenaten's reign came from his being exiled from Egypt, rather than dying in office, remains viable. Which in turn would preserve the option that he could have been in fact the Moses who led the exodus. The ancient Egyptians normally constructed the tombs of their pharaohs while the king was still alive and filled them with items which would be needed and used only at his death. Thus Akhenaten's tomb, as found, could have indicated he was never buried there and had left office before his death to lead his followers into exile while still bearing his royal staff of office with its bronze snake.

Actually there is still a good deal of scholarly confusion about Akhenaten's death and burial, and even about whether his intended tomb has or has not yet been discovered. Part of the haziness on this score has to do with the constant tomb robbing by Egyptian locals for so many centuries in search of saleable treasure, which left so many tombs stripped of features which scholars could use to identify the royal personages for whom they were intended. Scholars feel that many important personages, including Akhenaten, may ultimately not have been buried in the places originally intended for them, rendering the tomb markings not only unhelpful but confusing.

The inconclusiveness of the evidence surrounding the end of the Amarna period could thus be seen to provide back-up to the theory that Moses could have actually been Akhenaten because no remains have ever been conclusively identified as his. Probably the better way to state this is to say that, while no hard evidence has been found to support this theory, neither has any hard evidence been found to contradict it.

Thus, we have no proof that Moses could *not* have been Akhenaten. The fantastic idea still lives in the land of the possible.

*To summarize: The sun was the **main** god of Egypt for centuries, then for the brief reign of one king it was the **only** god of Egypt, and then for centuries to follow it was again the **main** god of Egypt. Some Egyptologists believe that the Aten religion actually began during the reigns of Akhenaten's father or grandfather and may have survived,*

*inside the royal family, a bit after Akhenaten, but that in any case it was Akhenaten
who made it the state religion and caused the violent reaction of the populace.*

We started the previous chapter with the question of whether Jesus was
worshiped as a Sun God. Now we are presented with a prior question. Was
the 'one' God of Israel actually the Aten, the Sun God of Akhenaten?

If Moses himself was actually Akhenaten, the question would seem to be
a very serious one. Even if Moses was not Akhenaten, and merely one of
Akhenaten's lieutenants, the Aten would have traveled with him out of
Egypt as the seed idea for Hebrew monotheism (and the Judeo-Christian
association of the sun with god).

In either case, from a religious perspective, Christians are the religious
grandchildren of Egypt.

● NOTE ON THE GENDER OF GOD IN ANCIENT EGYPT

One footnote to the story of Akhenaten which carries some religious
weight, is the problem of the gender of god, especially important if there is
only one god (thus eliminating the idea of a male god and a Goddess
working together). So, in monotheism, is god male or female? And in turn,
this raises the same question also about the pharaoh because he was the son
of god (the sun) and thus the sun's incarnation on earth.

Artists had to struggle with the way they represented the pharaoh, and
we often find Akhenaten portrayed unlike the usual, physically powerful
images of past pharaohs. Akhenaten was portrayed as androgynous with a
slender upper body, delicate features, and round nearly female appearing
breasts. By long tradition depictions of a pharaoh were supposed to make
him look like Charles Atlas on the beach. He's supposed to be a hunk, an
ideal specimen of manhood. Instead, in this case, Akhenaten was made to
look like the 97 pound weakling getting sand kicked in his face. And some
Egyptologists think this may even have been voluntary on Akhenaten's
part!

Remember that the sun had been regarded as female, or at least both
male and female. Now a pharaoh claimed to be the actual son of this sun
on earth, and thus himself a god rather than merely representing god on
earth. That could have been a special challenge to artists charged with
depicting the king, and might have tempted them to introduce some of the
feminine aspects of the depictions of Akhenaten which now puzzle
historians.

Some less sober observers think that the strange appearances of
Akhenaten and Nefertiti owe to their being at least partly alien—aliens
somehow get involved in many of these explanations of ancient Egyptian
phenomena, perhaps because (pardon me) they are so alien to our own

ways of perceiving and explaining what we see. The alien theory probably owes a lot to the elongated shape of the heads of this pharaoh and his wife and son in art, but again more sober minds attribute this strange shape to the ancient practice of head-binding (similar to Chinese foot-binding) infants intentionally for the purpose, especially among the upper classes.

Of course, the practice of incest within the royal family probably had an effect on the appearance of the kings and their offspring as well. (The pharaohs essentially had to marry their sisters for legal reasons, because the line of inheritance was matriarchal.)

Some historians think this new art form was intentionally instituted by Akhenaten to make a theological statement. A discovery of what some archeologists feel is possibly his mummy revealed a corpse which was not deformed. In other words, the king had been using art to make religious assertions rather than biological ones. Ancient gods were often seen as combining male and female, father and mother. When a pharaoh declared himself the actual son of god (son of the sun) on earth, he became both father and mother to his people as well.

The proposal that Moses was actually an Egyptian pharaoh echoes similar theories about other Hebrew patriarchs, so tightly bound are the ancient Egyptians and the ancient forerunners of Judaism—and so ancient and riddled with folk lore and mythology is the Bible. Writers have toyed with the idea, as just one example, that the great king David of Judaism was simply a retold story of one of the Egyptian pharaohs. (And among historians who prefer to see David as an historical character in his own right, many now believe he was a relatively insignificant local chieftain in Judea, south of Jerusalem. David gets a substantial demotion from being the great king we learned about in Sunday School. And Jesus gets a demotion in his 'royal' role as Son of David. But don't tell Dan Brown.)

The idea that aliens provided the ancient Egyptians with the sophistication and knowledge to outshine other civilizations of the future (for example by building the pyramids at Giza which were nearly perfect mathematical representations of the earth) may hark back to the Biblical story of Noah and his Ark. Scholars tell us that the Noah's Ark story is part of a universal myth of mankind which recalls an ancient widespread devastation by water, and constituted a great disruption in the evolution of mankind's growing technological sophistication. (This approach sees Noah and his ark as one of the many legends arising out of the Younger Dryas period from which civilized humanity had to re-emerge after the event.)

When mankind again collectively gathered its wits after the disruption, it was the equivalent of starting over from scratch in most areas of knowledge, including technology. People looked around and beheld such wonders from the past as the Giza pyramids, realized that they did not currently possess the technology to construct them, and speculated on how such marvels could have come into existence. Part of the speculation attributed the superior knowledge of the distant past to gods from other realms who must have intervened to give secret knowledge to ancestors from that distant past. Of course, the story is much more involved than this and it hinges on when the Giza pyramids were actually built, which is a matter of on-going scholarly debate. But the human instinct to credit "the gods" with whatever people can't readily figure out for themselves is spotlighted by these efforts to understand how distant ancestors could be smarter than the current generation. To a large extent we're still trying to figure that out with regard to ancient Egypt and those Giza pyramids even today. ⌘

9.

The Levites and Circumcision / the Exodus

Central to Judaism as monotheism is, it is not sufficient just to point out that this one concept was inherited from Egypt—there's much more than that which deserves mention. Take, for example, the mark which has become so identified with Judaism in the popular mind, that of male circumcision. It was a known practice in ancient Egypt. The ancient Greek historian Herodotus writing of his travels in Egypt observed that the Egyptians "circumcise themselves for the sake of cleanliness."

Is it possible that the Egyptian origin of male circumcision was known and acknowledged even by the early Christians who wrote the gospels? John 7:22 offers an intriguing viewpoint. In any case, the two major markers by which most people know Judaism—monotheism and male circumcision—both had their origins in Egypt (along with the prohibition of eating pork and other less major religious markers).

It has been pointed out that all references to circumcision in the Biblical book of Exodus come from Levite sources. One (at least) major scholar believes that it is only the Levitical priesthood that made the Exodus from Egypt. He also points out (as have other scholars) that the priests of Israel had Egyptian names (including Moses) while no one else in Israel did. We are also told that the word 'Levites' is based on a Hebrew root meaning "to be joined to."

According to this well-argued theory, the Exodus was not a mass event involving the whole of Israel, but a much smaller event in which only the Levites (Egyptian priests) left. They, of course, under the leadership of Moses and Aaron, then became the priestly class of Israel—arriving without land of their own in Israel and managing to set themselves up as the nation's priests deserving of a tithe to live from. This would mean that much of the religious structure of Judaism, not only monotheism and circumcision but the whole structure of its priesthood, came directly from Egypt where these priests were active before the Exodus.

In due course Judaism embedded the Levites into Israel's long story by calling one of Jacob's twelve sons "Levi." The Egyptian Exodus priests thus came to be regarded as one of the twelve Jewish (Hebrew) tribes.

Reading the Biblical account of the Exodus yields references to the "Sons of Levi" which seem to bolster this interpretation of the story. In Deuteronomy, God tells Moses' people "you shall be to me a kingdom of priests, a holy nation."

Circumcision as a commandment for Israel comes only from the Levites, the main proponent (Richard Elliott Friedman) of this theory notes. And it is only in the Levite sources that circumcision remains a continuing concern, he tells us.

Even though the Exodus may have involved only the Levites, it became an integral part of Israel's memory and eventually involved everyone on a mythic and religious level. The story was told over and over for three thousand or so years, and is still told to this day at Passover. It came to be a core element in the community's history, regardless of its historicity, and regardless of its applicability to the genetic background of every person who valued the story.

It is interesting to note that the subject of the Exodus, which most of us remember as a fairly simple and straight forward story from the Bible, gives scholars fits today. For historians, including historians of religion, the Exodus memory is far from simple or straightforward, and some think maybe not even related to actual events. At very least it stands as a reminder of the essential role played in organized religion by group memory and how such group memory comes into formation.

This is why so many historians of religion speak of the "myth" of the Exodus, by which they are saying that the Exodus is difficult to pin down as history. But it has acquired mythic proportions in the culture of Judaism and, although mostly hidden, perhaps in the cultural memory of Egypt as well. (And obviously it remained a pivotal memory for Christianity, in turn, also.) The story as folklore, in other words, has acquired a mythical and religious importance which is larger than the import of the quasi-historical elements that make up the story.

We think of the Exodus as a Jewish story, and to some extent as a Christian story. But it is also, not so surprisingly, an Egyptian story—although hidden, coded, and recalled dimly from a variety of perspectives. Probably the most widely known of these versions of the story from the Egyptian side is the tale of the lepers, which a prominent Egyptologist has termed "a case of distorted and dislodged memory."

In the Egyptian version, the Jews are shown as lepers, as impure people, atheists, misanthropes, iconoclasts, vandals, and sacrilegious criminals, this Egyptologist writes. Such a group, naturally, had to be expelled for the sake of the health and well-being of the country. Thus it is reasoned, so many ancient historians, and especially Flavius Josephus, "conflated" the story of the lepers with the account of the Jewish Exodus from Egypt. Many historians identify Moses as an Egyptian priest. Some see the story of baby Moses placed in the bulrushes to be found by an Egyptian princess as a way of giving Moses a Jewish/Hebrew ethnic connection when in actuality there may not have been one at all.

Remember too, in this regard that leprosy was used by Moses in his confrontation with Pharaoh by putting his hand inside his clothes and then revealing it to be leprous—and then repeating the action to again reveal it as clean. This seems to be utilized in the text as description of another magic trick, but it may instead have originally been employed as a demonstration of Moses' royal status because just such a ritual was part of the celebration of royal Jubilees.

It seems odd that Leprosy was used for this purpose, but it does introduce the disease into the Exodus story in the Bible. Leprosy is used in a similar way in the Biblical story of the children of Israel wandering in the wilderness, thus supporting the notion that the disease had some role in Israel during the Exodus period. Actually, the trick of the appearing and disappearing leprous hand had a role in pharaonic ritual, as mentioned, so it wasn't without a context in the story. An historian from the time of the Exodus was Hecataeus, a Greek living in Egypt. He placed the exodus of the Jews led by Moses in the context of the expulsion of the Hyksos.

The Bible also gives us a prelude to the Exodus story by telling us how the Israelites came to be in Egypt in the first place. It is the well-known story of Joseph, but a number of historians don't see it as actual history. One calls it a "novella created sometime during the seventh or sixth century B.C." And others suggest the same may be true for the entire Exodus story, saying it could simply have been just a story concocted, like *Gilgamesh*. There are also modern scholars who suggest that the Exodus story is a mythical rendering of a successful peasants' revolt against Egypt and its allies in Canaan. Almost all agree that the story of the Exodus should not be believed to be historically accurate as it is laid out in the Bible.

In light of this discussion a re-read of the New Testament book of Hebrews can be interesting, discussing as it does priesthood within Judaism and the support of priests by a tithe from the people. And John 8:33 and Acts 13:17 give an interesting commentary on the standard Exodus slavery assumption.

● MOSES THE MAGICIAN

It is safe to say that Moses (assuming he existed as a man) was hardly naïve about Egyptian magic (especially if he grew up at court and himself became pharaoh or an official of pharaoh—some kind of connection with the

Egyptian royal court seems likely from the Biblical text rather than just being a fanciful idea). Although the Bible attributes his knowledge and practice of magic to the direct teaching and assistance of God, i.e. the god of Israel, it is also difficult to read the Bible without feeling that Moses, the man, could probably handle a good deal of magic without additional instruction from God.

Exodus chapter 4 paints a picture of God teaching magic to Moses, thereby implanting an Egyptian religious idea into Israel's religious milieu. That such magic was an integral part of Egyptian life and religion is attested when pharaoh called in his "sorcerers" and had his "magicians" mimic "by their secret arts" the feats which God had taught to Moses. That Moses' magic proves superior to Egyptian magic as the story unfolds only illustrates that the student has trumped the Egyptian master, and this aspect of Egyptian religion is now firmly entrenched in the Jewish experience. Or, it illustrates that Moses was already deeply steeped in the ways of Egyptian magic because of his royal or governmental status. In any case, the Moses of the Bible was a master magician.

The magic given to Moses involved, probably among many other aspects, turning serpents into rods, and back again. A twentieth century writer offers some personal experience with Egyptian snake charmers which can color in many details of this type of magic used with "incantations and adjurations." The author himself took some instruction in this art, and reports that the serpents were as still as a fixed rod during the proceeding. And later he was taught to apply a paper talisman which rendered a snake motionless—perfectly rigid. (The concept of scriptural words written on paper having inherent power and thus being able to serve as a talisman or amulet shows up in Islam, another of the Abrahamic religions, along with the idea that the Koran as an object can have or wield effective magical power. It also shows up in Judaism. See Chapter 11.)

The Egyptian god Heka ("magic") was often pictured in ancient Egypt as holding two crossed snakes, both as stiff as rods, further suggesting that the rigid snake magic was not a rare aspect of the ancient Egyptian mythology on magic, but was perhaps fairly common.

This idea of the rigid serpent has been proposed as an explanation for Moses' and Aaron's magic before pharaoh by Henry Ridgely Evans, author of one of the earliest known histories of magic. The rod, he proposed, was not really a rod but a hypnotized serpent, stiff as a pole and looking like a pole. It then awoke from its trance when it hit the ground, and started to slither, obviously now recognizable as a snake. But the Judeo-Christian tradition considered Aaron's performance to be a genuine miracle because it had the assistance of the Hebrew God, so that meant the Egyptian magicians who duplicated the feat were the only ones who were seen in the

Biblical account as having utilized the dark forces of magic. It appears likely, however, that the scene merely offered two opposing sets of Egyptian magicians battling it out in what for both of them were familiar strategies.

A variation on the snake magic which appears frequently in Egyptian lore is the making of a wax crocodile which then turns into the real animal. At least one scholar maintains that Aaron's staff actually turned into a crocodile, and that "serpent" was a mistranslation.

Just as a point of interest, it can be noted that various religions throughout history have utilized snakes without harm to the participants (at least most of the time) even without any known preparation such as hypnotism. The Hopi Indian priests of America, even perhaps to this day, have a rain dance ritual in which they dance with wild (and poisonous) snakes held in their mouths. We are told that these snakes hang, both head and tail, limp and docile because the frenzied and trance-inducing antics of the dancers have created a sense of brotherhood between animal and man. Similar ceremonies are said to take place still throughout the modern world, and even in some Christian sects.

One of the weirder Biblical themes to come down to us is that Moses couldn't shake the snake habit once he was initiated into that magic. In Second Kings we find the Israelites long after Moses still worshipping the image of a serpent which Moses had set up in bronze. Much later Jesus tells Nicodemus that "As Moses lifted up the serpent in the wilderness, so the son of man must be lifted up." So the serpent on the pole became Christ on the cross. The Gospel of Mark foresaw the day when those who practiced Christianity wouldn't be able to resist the old ways: They will pick up snakes with their hands. The influence of Egypt and its magic continues into Christianity.

It should be noted again that a staff with a bronze serpent atop was the symbol of pharaoh's authority, which has bolstered the case for those who believe Moses was Akhenaten—he simply took the staff with him into exile. Perhaps this entire snake magic episode should not be seen as a discussion of magic *per se* at all, but rather as part of the buried evidence linking Moses with the Pharaoh Akhenaten. Egyptologists point out that the rituals of the serpent-rod and the withered hand, both described as magic in the Bible, were aspects of the ceremony of the rejuvenation of the Egyptian kings. Thus some Biblical passages could well be describing rituals associated with pharaohs, but describing them out of context and applying them to Moses (assuming Moses was not himself a pharaoh).

In any case, "Below, behind, beneath, and around all the other religious practices of the ancient world lay the often hidden domain of magic," James J. O'Donnell writes.

It was magic, too, which let the Israelites escape from Egypt, at least according to the Bible. God told Moses to lift up his hand over the sea to part the waters so that his people could cross on dry (relatively, at least) land, and then by the same motion from Moses let the waters close in on the pursuing Egyptian army when Israel was safely on the other shore. Few scholars, if any, think of this as we've seen in a scene out of the movies. It's more likely, they think, that the 'escape route' being remembered was a marshy area of the Nile delta and that the pursuing Egyptian chariots simply got bogged down in the mud.

This was not strange or unknown magic in any case. There are stories from ancient Egypt that the lector priests (those priests who could read the ancient books of magic) could part water at will in a similar way. One of the most famous of these stories involved a pharaoh taking a recreational cruise on a lake when one of his rowing virgins lost a piece of jewelry overboard and stopped rowing. The pharaoh, perhaps amused, had to call in his magicians to part the waters so the ornament could be recovered. "The rolling back of the water to get at the dry bottom, and the flood of water to drown enemies, are both known in Egyptian folklore," one Egyptologist confirms. So the Biblical Exodus story was not making up stories of new magic, but simply reflecting known elements of existing Egyptian magic.

The lector priests were those who read the liturgy, and therefore were literate and learned. "I am an excellent lector priest, exceedingly knowledgeable in secret spells and all magic," was found among the tomb curses intended to protect against intruders. The term 'lector priests' was also used to indicate someone efficient in working magic, such as reattaching severed heads back onto their bodies.

● IS THERE A BOTTOM LINE?

This whole Moses/Exodus/Egypt/Akenhaten discussion is a lot to try to absorb. There are many possible interpretations and variations on the historicity, or the lack thereof, of the story and so many scholars offer so many different ideas.

Some elements do begin to stand out from the Biblical story as possibly plausible historical truth: 1) Moses was most likely Egyptian, and even the Bible asserts that clearly at one point. 2) He had some kind of significant connection to pharaoh's household and some kind of apparently political or governmental authority. 3) He was proficient in Egyptian magic. 4) He was probably involved with whatever gave rise to the story of the Exodus, although it was probably not a big event involving throngs of people. 5) He somehow had a leading role in the establishment of the Hebrew people in the "promised land." 6) His memory in Hebrew oral, and then eventually written, religious history is strongly associated with law and priesthood.

None of these points is too far out on a limb to be impossible as history, although all of it still involves some level of fitting together a variety of bits and clues which at times can seem contradictory. But after these six elements are considered, Moses becomes much more difficult to pin down as a probable figure of history.

Equating Pharaoh Akhenaten with the Biblical Moses is an interesting and enticing idea to say the least. And while it sounds exotic, it is not without significant evidential elements. But it is nonetheless a huge step made with only circumstantial evidence, although that evidence is intriguing and tempting.

Then next, linking Akhenaten and Moses in some significant, but lesser, way is an infinitely smaller and safer step—the concept of monotheism alone does that job, given that Moses was an Egyptian (or at least raised as an Egyptian) and Egyptians were addicted to polytheism (except for the royal court during the reign of Akhenaten). In fact, it is not much of a leap at all judging solely from the Biblical text which says plainly that Moses was some sort of Egyptian big-wig.

Finally, the suggestion that Moses and his brother were Egyptian priests begins to look almost like a tiny baby step, and maybe even simply a logical conclusion when working from the Biblical texts.

One thing emerges clearly, however. We need Egypt to explain Israel, especially on the level of religion. Egypt is essential to the Jewish story and to any understanding of Judaism the religion, or the history of the Hebrew people as set out in the Bible.

Then, Judaism is essential to any understanding of Christianity the religion. Not every Egyptian influence on Christianity necessarily came via Judaism. Some may be traceable directly through Jesus. But again Egypt is a tangible part of the story even if that part of the story has been somewhat ignored for a very long time.

So we end up with a triangle, another religious trinity: Judaism, Christianity, and Egyptian religion. Three traditions each with its own story, but irrevocably linked with each other. Three traditions essential to any kind of overall understanding of the current dominant religious ethos of the western world. Three religious stories which tangle themselves into each other and which need each other in order to be interpreted with any degree of integrity.

The interlacing between Egypt and the Hebrew people, and Judaism as a religion and as an ethnic culture, was far more complex and subtle, far more extensive and direct, than we could ever have guessed from the Biblical narrative as presented and interpreted to us by preachers and Sunday School teachers from childhood. We then were offered an Egypt which was the enemy; the cruel oppressor of "God's chosen people." Hidden from us was the Egypt which had formed the most basic tenants of the Judeo-Christian tradition. Hidden from us was the true origin of our own Christian religion.

One of the most intriguing insights I gained from working with the material in this book is a new appreciation for the importance and power of the 'story' in formation of the group's sense of community—in this case a religious community, but the phenomenon is broader than religion. Like most Christians I knew that the Exodus was Judaism's great story and I had some appreciation for that story's centrality in the religion. I really started to become alert to its true significance, though, when I realized that this great Jewish unifying story might not actually (historically) belong to the Jewish people, or at least not to all of them.

Not only is the story itself probably an amalgam of bits and pieces from various times and experiences, both Egyptian and non-Egyptian, but it may tell only about one segment of the Hebrew people—the priestly clan which became the tribe of the Levites. So there could have been many thousands of people through the years who claimed this story as their own even though the actual people of the Exodus were not their blood ancestors at all. The story of a few became the story of the many; a story which bound together disparate people into one ethnic group and one religious identity. A mere story can be powerful indeed, and can have ample real world consequences.

As to picturing Moses as a man, we run into a certain irony compared to our effort to picture Jesus as a man. With Jesus the Bible gives us *too little* biographical material to work with effectively. With Moses, on the other hand, the Bible offers almost *too much* biographical material to melt down into a single storyline—too many options to trace and evaluate in trying to focus on one man's biography.

For starters, the Bible seems to, at different places, disagree with itself on whether he was an Egyptian or a Hebrew. And it tells us he was a big-shot in the land of Egypt who had connections with the royal household (the stuff of potential solid biography), but then leaves everything open-ended so that a reader can go off with any number of different ideas.

It also gives us a side story wherein Moses acquires a wife and a son while on the lam from committing a murder in Egypt—almost a mini-novel within the greater story. A number of scholars don't accept the reality of the wife, or reject other aspects of the various Biblical accounts. But no matter how one looks at it, the Bible does give us an ample amount of potentially biographical material about Moses, while being skimpy about biographical material about Jesus—a case of way too much for Moses, and then not nearly enough for Jesus.

Of course, as we've noted, part of the difficulty of attaching biographical detail to Jesus was that by the time the gospel writers began work, their task was not writing about a mere human, but about a god, or at least at that point a fledgling god. The writings we have about Moses never reached that fever pitch and therefore never posed the same problems. Various strands of the Moses story may flirt with the idea that he was an Egyptian royal, but never that he was a god (although if actually a pharaoh he would have been seen as a god, at least while on the throne). The Moses story is more anchored in humanity than the overall Jesus story. Although some scholars have questioned the actual existence of both, of the two it seems that perhaps it is the Moses story which more resolutely points to a historical human figure—albeit a very complex figure with a many faceted storyline. ⌘

10.

Christmas

Trying to brighten the gloom of winter by festivities to mark the shortest day and longest night have been part of the human experience far longer than just in the Christian era, and in most "pagan" religions that preceded Christianity. Obviously none of them used the term "Christmas," although many of them utilized themes we now associate with Christmas such as gift-giving and candle-light. For most of these religions the main focus was actually a couple or so days after the solstice, as it is with Christianity. The day of renewed hope and encouragement was the day the sun could be perceived as lengthening daylight again.

Lots of us can remember learning early-on that Christmas was supposed to be much more than Santa Claus, decorated indoor trees, piles of gifts, and frosted cookies. Of course it was definitely those things as well, and had been celebrated as a special day by humans long before Christianity entered the picture. Much of our celebration of this day, so magical in our childish eyes, was carried over from ancient pagan custom, despite our civilization having fairly recently stuck on the 'Christ' title. That was probably true even of those enchanting "Christmas trees." Protestants liked to say the idea first occurred to Martin Luther, but the likelihood is that lots of children long before Christianity enjoyed decorated trees brought inside to celebrate the winter solstice.

But our parents and teachers were careful to make sure that we also focused on the day as "Jesus' birthday." They would have spoken with greater accuracy if they had called the day "the birthday of the gods." The day was not exclusive to Christianity, and the birthday was not exclusive to Jesus, as we then assumed, but was actually shared on a religious level with a great many ancient people—ironically people we would have termed "pagans;" people with whom we would have thought we had nothing at all in common.

As we grew in years we heard complaints from various sources about rampant commercialism which was "driving Christ out of Christmas." We were too young to understand that Christ was never in Christmas to begin

163

with, except for the name given to December 25 by our particular Johnny-come-lately religion.

Of course scholars, even if they depend only on the Biblical account, don't believe Jesus was born on a December 25th—otherwise, for just the one example usually given, the Biblical description of shepherds and their lambs visiting the manager could not be accurate; lambing season was still well ahead by December.

December 25th was picked for a reason other than that of historical accuracy, and it is safe to say that no one alive today has the foggiest idea of what day the man Jesus may have actually been born. It's a bit like the Queen's birthday in England. There's a day in the calendar which is the actual anniversary of her birth, although most people probably don't remember what day that is, and then there's a different official day in the calendar set aside for the public celebration of her birthday.

Certainly a major part of the reason for the date we celebrate as the birthday of Jesus was because several other gods were believed to have been born on that date, and being in such company made Jesus look good, elevated his status, and bolstered the claim of his being divine.

And the reason behind this, the reason so many gods stood in line to be born on that particular day, was because the sun, seen from the northern hemisphere, rose from its lowest point of descent on that date and began once again to ascend in the sky—it was thus seen as an apt birthday for a god who was himself the sun, or the son of the sun—the son of the god who is the sun. December 25 was first seen as the birthday of the sun, if you will; the day it begins to rise in the sky again after reaching its nadir followed by a three day perceived hiatus.

Historians say the Roman emperor Constantine the Great deliberately pursued a policy of uniting Christ-worship with sun-worship, using December 25 which was already an important Sun God festival. This was easily facilitated because Christians already used the sun as a Christ symbol. Thus, some say December 25 was basically a date chosen to win over pagan sun worshipers to the new religion. The dates of Christmas and Easter are determined by the winter solstice and the vernal equinox. They are major dates in the sun's annual cycle and had been celebrated long before the time of Jesus as symbolizing the birth and death of the Christ principle in the life of humankind. The dates of Christianity's two major feast days are therefore determined by the sun's position in the sky.

St. Ignatius, writing to the Ephesians some time after Paul's letter to them in the New Testament, also related the appearance of Jesus in the world to the sun and Zodiac: "How, then, did he appear in time? A star, brighter than all other stars, shone in the sky, and its brightness was ineffable and the novelty of it caused astonishment. And the rest of the stars, along with the sun and moon, formed a choir about the star."

Even the New Testament gets in on this astrological association by reporting that wise men from the east (the magi, or magicians, who were probably Zoroastrian priests) knew of Jesus' birth and tracked him down by means of a star. That story, if it has any historical validity, probably doesn't belong in the birth narratives where we find it, but a lot of Christmas pageants and manger scenes would suffer if we took a more historical view.

Later astronomers have looked for astrological explanations for the "Star of Bethlehem" and one of the most probable involves the three stars in Orion's belt, which were known as the "Three Kings of Orion." Just after the winter solstice these Three Kings align to point to Sirius, the brightest star in the sky. There are myriad connections between the bible and the sun, moon and stars that again point us back to ancient Egypt—the three great pyramids at Giza are now thought by (probably) most observers to be a mirror pattern on the earth of these three stars in Orion's belt. Why the pyramids were thus aligned, or for that matter why they were even built, we don't really know yet. But all roads seeking to explain Christian origins seem to lead back to Egypt. Some think the explanation for the star may be as simple as just that, referring to the Gospel of Matthew, which many scholars believe may have been composed in Alexandria, Egypt. This might help explain the story of the star of Bethlehem as signaling the birth of Jesus because of the fixation the Egyptians had with Sirius as a star symbolizing the birth of a significant being.

Like Jesus, the sun was understood in ancient Egypt to have undergone death, entombment for three days, and resurrection. Or is it better phrased as like the sun in ancient Egypt, Jesus was understood thusly?

As it nears the end of December the sun reaches its lowest point on the northern hemisphere horizon, and then seems to rest there without any discernable ascent for three days. People of the time saw this as the 'death' of the sun, its entombment for three days, and then its resurrection on about December 25 as it again started to ascend in its orbit in a way visible to the naked human eye. The historical question is then, was the later understanding of Jesus in part modeled on the way the sun was understood, or was Jesus actually being equated with the sun by his early followers. As we've seen, there is a viewpoint out there that Jesus is a fiction created by sun worshippers, and if one digs there is a surprising amount of associations and "evidence" that can be read as pointing in that direction.

When the sun reached its nadir on about December 22 it began pivoting around on the "hinge" of the solstice, symbolically seen as seven days. Therefore on December 25 it began its return toward the full light of summer. In one of the oldest known Christian 'Christmas carols,' from the fifth century, there is a revealing phrase: *a solis natus cardine*: "born from the hinge of the sun."

There are allusions in the gospels to the old solar mysteries and the ritual slaying and resurrection of their god-kings which point unmistakably to what the evangelists saw as the symbolic nature of Jesus' death. His death too, as in the pagan tradition, was intended to illustrate the supreme initiation and translation of a god-king from human to divine solar status. As you will recall from earlier in our discussion of ancient Egypt, it was believed that the pharaoh after death became a star, or was reunited with our own star, the sun.

● OUT OF EGYPT HAVE I CALLED MY SON

This may be one of the most pregnant sentences in the New Testament. Yet its ocean of probable meaning has been evaporated down to a puddle of intentionally murky innuendo. There would seem to be a parallel with Mary Magdalene, a towering figure in the New Testament plot who was (evidently) intentionally obscured in the Biblical telling to the point of now seeming insignificance at first glance. Egypt is at extreme least an equally towering figure in the New Testament story, and (again evidently) the subject of a similar editorial effort to obscure its true significance.

Scholars tell us it is impossible to understand Jesus without understanding the Jewish experience and memory from Egypt, whether that was an entirely historical experience in all its details or not. Long before the Exodus, there were Egyptian traditions and concepts leaking into Judaism. And it is probably equally impossible to understand how Jesus was painted in the New Testament without both acknowledging Egypt's primacy in his religious formation and knowing something about Egypt's ancient religious character.

We don't know how much of this the gospel writer Matthew understood (we don't even know who he was). But we do know that the Egyptian connection had come down to him in oral history with sufficient clarity and strength to require that he note, at minimum, that Egypt had played a significant role and needed to be acknowledged.

Matthew's proclamation, "Out of Egypt have I called my son," can take on many layers of possible meaning, not only mystical but stretching to the historical. Some worry about this phrase's origin in the Old Testament book of Hosea—was it history (just retelling the story of the Exodus) or was it prophecy (thus referring to Jesus having been in Egypt)? In either case, it is clear that Matthew has tied it to the wider Christmas story, and thus in his gospel it is a reference to Jesus even if the words he is using were previously used to refer to Israel as a whole.

Did Matthew think that this obscure quotation from a minor prophet was so important that it needed to be incorporated into the story he was telling (which he did)? Or did he need something to hang his hat on, an excuse in effect, in order to say something entirely different that he himself felt needed to be said? Did he portray God as, in effect, making a new proclamation connecting Jesus with Egypt, and thus explaining in short hand much about the teaching and magic of Jesus?

We are so leery of the fundamentalist tendency to read the Bible as literal word-for-word truth, and so accustomed to hearing our preachers and teachers pointing out the Bible's use of allegory, that we have become conditioned to ignore the obvious—anything which sounds a bit strange or challenging must be merely myth or parable, we tend to assume.

So the question here is not what Hosea meant, but what Matthew meant. He gave us a declarative sentence in the New Testament which specifically refers to Jesus, and which then received the imprimatur of those who pulled together the official Biblical canon. Therefore, we can safely and honestly say that the gospel of Matthew quotes God as saying about Jesus, "Out of Egypt have I called my Son."

Is this then a comment on geography? Is it a commentary on theology? Is it a comment on history? Is it a validation of the stories about Jesus in Egypt during his 'lost years'? Is it merely Matthew telling us how learned in Scripture he is, or how highly in regard he holds Hosea?

Maybe this is an instance in which something in the Bible is staring us in the face, but we can't recognize it because we assume it has to be mythological. Could this actually be a simple explanation for the shape of the religious milieu Jesus brings with him? Could it be that Jesus' was so tied to Egypt for his own education and religious formation that the Egyptian connection could not escape mention by the evangelists even decades down the road from Jesus when the evangelists were writing.

There are plenty of scholars who believe that Jesus' association with Egypt is intentionally played down in the gospels. A few even believe that Jesus was born in Egypt. Regardless of where he was born, he probably spent his youth in Egypt, many feel. They remind us of the many associations between Egyptian texts and the Old and New Testaments which have been traced, and the probability that some biblical elements were derived from Egyptian beliefs. Egyptian wisdom instructions may have directly influenced biblical texts, and some parallels have been drawn between these instructions and expressions in the books of Proverbs, Ecclesiastes, Song of Solomon, Psalms, and Job.

Not only was ancient Egypt the source of so many of the concepts that built Christianity initially, but Egypt then played a major role in the further development of these concepts through the patristic writers living and working there (in Alexandria) and through the initial development of Christian monasticism. 'Out of Egypt have I called my son' may make sense from many different angles. It may also be a hint about things we simply do not understand yet.

● OTHER ASPECTS OF EGYPTIAN INFLUENCE

So many key elements of Christianity originating in ancient Egypt seem to be part of its basic structure, for example the concepts of a last judgment, life after death, and original sin. The idea of original sin was first encountered in the Egyptian "Coffin Texts", which are described as a modern name for the body of spells or recitations painted on wooden coffins.

Not all of Christianity's ties to Egypt are such weighty matters of theology or belief, however. Some are just everyday bits of more-or-less innocent superstition, or even fun. Go into most religious shops, such as the gift shop or 'bookstore' of a big European cathedral and you will find an ample offering of medals and objects to wear as necklaces, such as St. Christopher medals for just one example. These have their origin in the amulets produced in ancient Egypt, and worn by Egyptians of that day with probably the same mix of devotion, superstition, and simple decoration which motivates modern people to wear the updated versions.

Amulets in ancient Egypt were believed to provide magical protection by merely being carried or worn. This applied not only to the living, but also to the dead who were routinely buried wearing amulets. These beliefs involved much more than hoping for good luck; their effect was thought to be real in an everyday sense. Amulets, it was felt, could attract good forces to the wearer, or could repel evil and danger.

In art, it is widely felt that representations of the goddess Isis suckling her child Horus are the impetus for the ubiquitous Christian images of the Virgin nursing, or even just holding, the baby Jesus. And in the liturgical practice of Christianity, the celebrant relies on something called "rubrics," which are essentially instructions printed in red to distinguish them from the text that is to be actually read aloud or sung—it turns out the ancient Egyptians invented these as well, by writing headings in red, or from Latin rubrum, "the red."

In the area of food, the Jewish prohibition of pork almost certainly had its origin in ancient Egypt as well. "The Egyptians consider the pig to be an impure animal, and therefore if a man in passing by a pig should touch him [even] only with his garments, he forthwith goes to the river and plunges in," wrote Herodotus.

Nor was every Egyptian influence on the Hebrews of a particularly religious nature. Some scholars believe that the written Hebrew language itself grew out of Egyptian hieroglyphics (and that Moses wrote the Torah in Egyptian hieroglyphics, creating a nightmare for the transcribers who followed). And among the familiar Judeo-Christian words which scholars tell us had their origin in ancient Egypt is "Zion," the place of sanctuary.

● HOLY NAME

The Christian celebration and veneration of the "Holy Name" of Jesus arises from Egyptian roots, as does so much of Christianity's lore. It also grew out of the Egyptian sense of magic at a time when religion and magic were inextricably bound together.

It was believed by ancient Egyptians that a being's name carried the essence of the being. Therefore to know a person's (or a god's) name was to have some power and influence over that person, and thus that to know the name of a god, and to address the god by his name, gave the petitioner an advantage denied to others. The chief Egyptian God, Amun, for example, was held to be so holy and powerful that only his mother could know his true name.

This concept has left many traces not only in Christianity, but also in the magic of more primitive religions in which to know the name of someone was equivalent to having a piece of clothing or a personal item of the person whom the magician was trying to affect (a la voodoo). One's name carried one's essence. It was a code for access to the person's core being. Thus Christians came to believe that the name of Jesus carried intrinsic power and had religious value and potency just as had the names of the ancient gods of Egypt.

The carry-over from ancient Egypt to Christianity is obvious at this point. Acts 4:7 clearly equates the (holy) name of Jesus with power. "There is no other name under heaven...by which we must be saved." Acts 4:12 and 4: 17-18. Paul, Christianity's dominant voice, agrees that "every one who calls upon the name of the Lord will be saved" (Romans 10:13).The Egyptian concept of the sacredness of the god's name started making an impact on Judaism very early-on as we can see from Exodus 3:13-14. Judaism grew to embrace the concept that its own God's name should not even be spoken—that the name of God was too holy to be spoken.

When Jesus set about teaching his disciples how to pray (by teaching them the "Lord's Prayer") the very first concern he expressed was that the *name* of God should be acknowledged and honored: "Hallowed be Thy Name."

Protestant Christians might seem immune from the 'Holy Name' echoes, as opposed to Catholics for whom they are definitely a big thing, with Holy Name having its own feast day and being itself the name of many prominent churches, cathedrals, and schools as well as the stuff of personal devotional practices.

But if we look even just at church hymnody the echoes jump out strongly and quickly even for Protestants. A 19th century hymn known to most mainline Protestants begins "At the Name of Jesus every knee shall bow." And another from the 18th century commands "All Hail the Power of Jesus' Name!" And still another, "Holy God, we praise thy Name."

This strain of Christian hymnody has developed from deep roots and even a tie to the Zodiac—a 7th century hymn (thought by some to have been written by the great Bishop Ambrose of Milan), *Conditor Alme Siderum* translated usually as "Creator of the Stars of Night," sets the tone for hymns that follow: "At thy great Name, exalted now, All knees in lowly homage bow."

Early Christians, we are told, maintained that Jesus was a 'name above all names.' Origen, the early church father, even apparently boasted that the name of Jesus possessed more *magical efficacy* than those of the pagan divinities. For a quick look at gospel echoes of this theme see John 16:23, 17:11, and 17:26.

In a discussion about Egyptian art, Barbara Mertz illustrates the role of the 'name' in Egyptian thinking in a way which is fairly easy to understand. Egyptian artists, she says, really were not generally attempting to make an exact likeness of the subject. The important aspect was the *name* of the subject (usually the king) which was then inscribed onto the statue. The work of art truly became a depiction of the king only after the king's name had been inscribed on it.

When later pharaohs came along, the name on major sculpture pieces was often merely changed from that of the old monarch to that of the new one. The face or body did not have to be altered because the essence of the new king was not in his appearance, but in his name. Once the name was changed, however, the essence of the new king had been transferred to the statue and it represented him just as faithfully as it had represented the previous king. Mertz calls a name used in this way a "magic spell."

This kind of thinking seeped into Judaism and Christianity as well from these Egyptian roots. It even formed part of the Mosaic law as a plank in the 'Ten Commandments' thus coming, reportedly, directly from Yahweh. Therefore we have the tradition of "Holy Name," devotion paid to it, and the prohibition of the use of god's name taken "in vain." Judaism, as noted, did not even allow god's name to be spoken. The name, after all, captured the essence of the name's bearer and thus was too precious for everyday or casual conversation.

Christians fretted about swearing—not only by using god's name, but even with sounds which might be a simplification of the name of a god. I remember well from Confirmation class being lectured that a true Christian would not even say something like "Gee Whiz" because the 'Gee' sound might be a short form of "Jesus" or at least suggest that to the hearer. The mild sounding "Geeze" was especially bad and to be avoided at all costs.

Christmas

(Christians may have escaped living under the Mosaic Law, as Jesus apparently wanted for his followers, but they certainly did not escape living under some complicated rules and regulations.)

Even as a child, and as a religiously absorbed one at that, I was rather skeptical that making "gee" sounds could be an affront to God or was a violation of religious taboo. And I never bought into the idea that saying "Gee Whiz" could be worthy of some kind of divine retribution. But seen now from an adult vantage it was impressive business nonetheless—it was remarkable that the ancient Egyptian reverence for, and fear of, using the name of the chief god had filtered all the way down to a small town in Iowa in the middle of the 20th century. The memory and concept had by then become askew and a bit trivialized, but it had survived in basic terms all that far down the road and was still being taught to awed (and bewildered) children.

For the ancients, to say the name of god was to touch the very essence of their god, or to call upon it for one's own merely human purposes. This even caused some reported concern in the New Testament stories of miracles performed by Jesus: was he healing in the name of God his Heavenly Father, or in the name of the chief of demons? Either way, apparently, the power being utilized was derived from the *name* being evoked.

● NOTE ON THE SCHOOL-YARD NAME FOR JESUS:

It's likely that this ancient perception of the nature of names still has some faint echoes in our time. If we feel someone is damaging our reputation, we might say "Don't drag my *name* through the mud," or "I'm protective of my good *name*." Even in our entertainment arts a character can wax eloquent about a name: "I just met a girl named Maria, and suddenly that *name* will never be the same to me…say it soft, and it's almost like praying."

But for the most part now that we're in the 21st century it's not likely too many people fret about the magical or mystical power of names anymore, although we still want respect shown to the names of people we love or hold in honor, including our religious heroes. With that release from magical thinking, although still not wanting to offend, I hope it's okay to mention the version of Jesus' name every school boy has heard, and probably used—Jesus H. Christ. It shows up even in our secular culture in the writings of America's great chronicler Mark Twain. And many an adult has reflected back on grade school and wondered where in the world the "H" came from and what in the world it could mean.

Scholars can explain a lot of reasons it could have crept into usage because of name fragments, symbols, and cyphers applied to Jesus in various languages of his time, and they are probably correct. Still, to inject a lighter touch into this heady discussion, I'd like to share one imaginative

171

explanation. The Lord's Prayer as we memorized it begins, "Our Father who art in Heaven, hallowed be thy name." Evidently unsophisticated folks along the way thought the phrase was really "Harold be thy name." And thus, it is said, we inherited Jesus Harold Christ.

By the way, the name we translate as "Jesus" was evidently a very popular name for males in the time of the New Testament gospels, so there were most likely a lot of characters named Jesus walking around in Palestine during the period. And they are with us still, as you know if you live in an area of any significant Hispanic population. Permit me one more favorite story and then I promise to drop the subject.

The city in which I live has a distinguished old liberal arts college whose campus is dominated by a lovely Gothic Revival style chapel. The chapel in past years was usually left unlocked because it's used by students all day for a variety of purposes including practicing on its great pipe organ. Students, being students, can be absent-minded about details such as closing doors, which during a New England winter poses a problem. The Campus Safety department employee assigned to the chapel for many years was a friendly Hispanic guy known to many of the students who frequented the building. One winter evening exiting students found a note taped to the chapel door: "Please remember to close the door." [signed] –Jesus. ⌘

11.

Can an Object be Holy?

Could it be that one of the least understood and enigmatic Biblical characters is the Bible itself?

Evidently there are still a good many Christians who think the book had only one author, and the author was not even a person, but God himself. In fairness to them, their preachers have yelled about "the Word of God" incessantly, possibly while waving a book in the air *a la* Elmer Gantry and pronouncing all kinds of things the book does not really say in the first place.

So let's note up front that Christianity does not teach that the Bible, either as a whole or in part, was directly dictated by God as we are told Moses received the ten commandments. Nor does Christianity teach that the Bible came directly from Heaven engraved on golden tablets as Joseph Smith convinced his followers was true of the Book of Mormon. Yet Christians in large measure still act as if they believe that the Bible is somehow the literal "word" of God: without error, inviolate, historically accurate, and representative of the highest aspirations and behavior that could possibly be ascribed to, or for, humankind.

Unfortunately the Bible doesn't always live up to that standard. It was never dictated by a divine being, and it contains a lot of material which is historical nonsense and theological junk. It also contains long ribbons of human communal memory which have likely been contaminated along the way, sometimes unintentionally but in some cases perhaps even intentionally. However we've been trained to expect that if it's in the Bible, it must be right, true, and good. It is, after all, the Word of God we were taught. This idea leads literalists off the deep end and convinces many people that God himself is favorable to some of mankind's worst foibles— one example frequently cited is the belief that God endorses slavery (Gen. 17:12-13). Just because something can be said to be "in the Bible" may give it very little religious or theological weight or accuracy.

A colleague of the late American theologian W. Norman Pittenger once related to me a little anecdote from Pittenger's time in England where he was an honorary Fellow at King's College, Cambridge. At Evensong one day the prescribed scripture lesson was one of those dubious passages. The reading concluded with the tradition of lifting the book and the proclamation: "The Word of the Lord." Pittenger, without attempting to lower his voice, responded: "It most certainly is **not!**"

Some of the problem may be that the book is usually called the "Holy" Bible. Another part of the problem is that it is so often, as I've said, called the "Word of God."

The Bible is not referred to as 'holy' because of some special property of the paper and binding and ink. It is labeled 'holy' because it speaks of concepts and mythology which many people regard as holy, or believe can lead to holiness if strictly followed. It is not the object itself which is holy, but the import of its contents—the Biblical 'story,' loosely defined.

Likewise, to call the Bible the "Word of God" is not to refer to the words printed on its pages—its collection of nouns, verbs, adverbs and adjectives. Again, those who use the phrase are trying to refer to the overall import of its contents. They are, to be simple about it, trying to say that the collective ideas, history, mythology, and concepts in the Bible are pointing to the Divine.

The collection of material modern Christians refer to as the Bible was written over a vast amount of time, by probably hundreds of people or more, especially if one counts all the scribes adding bits along the way (inadvertently or not) before invention of the printing press. Parts of it were appropriated almost verbatim from other religious sources, as we've noted in earlier chapters. The Old Testament borrows religious ideas and sometimes actual passages from ancient Egypt.

The New Testament part of the Christian Bible, as we've also said previously, was written for the most part by Paul and followers of Paul. God had little direct hand in the process, unless perhaps one believes that God was actually speaking to Paul during Paul's hallucinogenic fits (or 'visions' if you prefer). And the ideas Paul put forward were also in large measure derivative; an amalgam of mostly Greek religion and mythology, as well as ancient Egyptian religious elements that had reached him largely through Judaism.

That there were many authors involved is part of the fascination of Christian history. Near the beginning of the new religion there were many writings regarded as scripture. Each congregation in various geographical settings might have treasured scriptures used in teaching and liturgy which another congregation a few miles down the road may never have heard, or heard of. In the long run there were a great many written candidates for inclusion in a Christian Bible. Sorting all of that out over time so that a "canon" of scripture (an authorized Bible that most Christians could accept as authentic) could emerge was a major part of the early Christian story. Even today scholars of Christianity find new insights in freshly discovered material which appears to be much like some of the canonical Biblical material, but was either passed over for inclusion or was as yet unknown when the canon was agreed upon.

An over-riding reality of all Biblical material is that the motivation of the authors was religious. They were attempting to tell a religious story and build foundations for the nature of their own religion. Very few of them, if any, were really attempting to be historians. Even if they listed generations and years, the object was to bolster or make a religious, rather than historical, statement. The few who may have thought they were contributing historical detail, such as genealogies, were dependent on material passed down to them which may have been contaminated or was based on poor scholarship or pure imagination.

Scholars also point out that some of those who appear as Biblical authors are probably several people rolled into one name—an Old Testament book like Genesis, usually ascribed to Moses, probably contains material from many sources. A good illustration of that being that many scholars believe there are two different versions of the creation-Eden story sitting next to each other there (the break between Gen.2:3 and Gen. 2:4 is fairly obvious, for example, with mankind being created both before and again following it). And in the New Testament, we have no idea who Matthew, Mark, Luke, and John were, or even if those were their real names.

So no matter how 'holy' one may consider the Bible to be, the book itself is intended only as a vehicle. It is, like any book, intended to convey information and ideas. It is not intended to be some kind of Christian Golden Calf, holy in and of itself, and to be worshiped as an object. The book itself, as an object, does not convey holiness.

When I became pastor of a German Lutheran parish in New York City many years ago, I noticed that the gilded stand on the altar held a handsome copy of the Bible, whereas the lectern from which the Bible was actually read during liturgies was empty. So I moved the Bible from the altar to the lectern and replaced it on the altar with an equally handsome altar service book, needed there during liturgies.

Within a day I was confronted by the long-time church cleaning woman, who out of frustration shouted at me, "Pastor, the next thing I know you'll be throwing *Jesus* out of this church."

The Bible on the altar, the physical book, had become, for her, an object of worship in and of itself. And probably she, and others, felt it was in and of itself a holy object which lent holiness to the altar. Even more telling, the Bible on the altar had most likely never been read from during services in

175

the first place. Until my arrival, all services in the church had been conducted in German. The altar Bible was in English. The Bible on the altar was merely a totem begging reverence and somehow conferring 'holiness.' It was an object begging veneration for itself, but otherwise without any practical purpose.

I'm not without sympathy for the disillusionment which can be caused when symbols no longer hold their perceived value. From childhood I remember witnessing a group of adults change the paraments (decorative cloth hangings on the altar, pulpit, and lectern) in our church at the beginning of a new liturgical season when these hangings changed color. They simply pulled the "altar" out from the "east" wall (it was actually the north wall) and removed the color set to be used for the new season, and then put back inside of it the retiring color set. And there was I, a wide-eyed church mouse of a kid who had just learned that the holy focal point of the church was actually a hollow storage box.

This kind of unthinking, or magical thinking, reverence is not all that unusual in Christianity. A Swedish priest once told me about a parish church in that country where for generations people entering the church bowed to a blank wall in the narthex. No one knew why they bowed to the wall, but the custom was firmly established and no one felt safe in breaking the pattern.

Eventually it was discovered that before the Lutheran Reformation, the wall had contained a small niche holding a statue of the Virgin Mary. Shortly after the state church turned Lutheran, the statue and its niche had been removed. Yet devout Christians kept doing what their ancestors had been doing for so many generations; they kept bowing at the same point of entry even though the icon was no longer present.

In our scientifically sophisticated age it might seem that superstition must be losing its hold on people, and that religiously inclined people must be gaining in rationality. Don't bet on it. There is a Catholic priest in my area who buys highway billboards to proclaim his religious devotion in public (which Jesus, of course, counseled against doing, i.e. wearing one's piety on one's sleeve for all to see), and occasionally purchases an insert in the local newspaper. A recent newspaper delivery included a cardboard sheet about the size of a giant postcard which was paid for by this guy. On one side was depicted a white man with long flowing hair, a long flowing gown, and bare feet—the stereotypical image unfortunately almost universally now associated with the Jesus of Christianity. On the back were instructions to post the card "on your front door to protect you and your family." Another line says "by means of this image I (Jesus, one presumes) shall be granting many graces to souls." The idea seems an apparent take-off on the Passover theme, but that is the only remote connection to

Biblical religion I can detect. Basically it's just raw superstition and magical thinking, just as alive today among fairly educated Americans as it ever was in the primitive reaches of pre-history.

One of the three Abrahamic religions, Islam, can illustrate this phenomenon well for us, and help us decide whether we really want to invest our scriptures (and books of scripture) with quasi-magical properties.

Islamic writers tell us that to merely open the book, the Koran, is to place oneself in direct encounter with energies that offer possibilities beyond mere comprehension. Actually reading the book, they imply, may be nice but being read is hardly the only way for the book to shed its power (and magic) on the individual.

The Koran can be thought of as a magical book because it shares in the divine power of which it speaks, we are told. We are told by Islamic scholars that the Koran is more than simply an archive of statements and meanings needing comprehension and intellectual study. They say the Koran is widely regarded as a "point of access to transcendent forces and an abundance of beneficent energies," which can be harnessed through relationships to its words other than the mere reading of them. The words *mean* things, but they also *do* things.

Magic has thereby now been introduced and invested in the book and its words. New magic is now part of the picture, as I fear it is also for many Bible-centered Christian groups today.

Evidently Muhammad's companions used recitation of the opening lines of the Koran to heal people suffering from ailments such as "scorpion stings, snakebites, and madness." Evidently it was felt that mere narrations of these words have "special healing properties." The idea is hardly new, and even Jesus used words in a similar way. However, today's Christians need to decide whether reliance on magic should be left in the past, as best as possible, or whether we should create new magic around our 'holy' book.

Muhammad is said to have recited portions of the Koran into his hands, and then rubbed his hands over his body to impart their power. This was said to be a technology of protection, capable of functioning in ways other than simply as a text to be read and understood. Through the exhalation of God's speech into his hands, the Prophet was thought to be able to redirect the flows of baraka [sometimes spelled barakah] upon himself through embodied contact.

We are also told of the widespread use of the wearing of verses from the Koran as necklaces to serve as amulets. And that some healing practices involved the drinking of water affected by encounter with the Koran. Sometimes the ill were given water to drink into which ink had dissolved from Koran verses written out for the purpose. As to wearing a passage of scripture on one's body, we've seen that approach in ultra-orthodox parts of Judaism as well.

The rituals of Christianity may seem to exalt the Bible into some kind of holy object in and of itself. Some groups raise the book aloft before or after reading it in liturgy; some groups kiss the book during liturgy. But there is no legitimate tradition in Christianity which sees the paper and ink of the book as a means of grace, or invests it with quasi-magic. "The Word," in even Protestant usage, does not refer to a physical object or to the combination of words it contains. Idolatry of the book is an easy trap for today's Christians to fall into, but also an easy idolatry to avoid by simply taking the time to study what the book has to say. What the book conveys is the whole point of the exercise, not the touching or adoring of the object itself—not just living in proximity to it for some kind of protection.

We must remember that the Bible, too, can be used to justify almost any action or prejudice or hatred the reader wants to find there, and of course that Christianity is no more innocent of blood and suffering than is Islam or many other religions. The point is that the world does *not* need more blindly naïve religious zealots of any faith—it *does* need more people who can look rationally at their inherited or adopted religions and who understand something of the origin and process involved with that religion's scriptures.

Our politicians have noticed our tendency to idolize the book itself, and a vivid example of this came not all that long ago. During the national upheaval of both a deadly pandemic and a string of mass demonstrations against racial injustice, U.S. President Donald Trump evidently felt the need to re-establish his authority and credibility and chose as a vehicle being photographed outside a church holding up a Bible. He did not open the Bible, he did not quote from it, he merely waved it in front of the camera. He even held it upside-down until an aide corrected him.

The message seemed clear—the book itself held great powers of potency and somehow his merely holding it was supposed to prove that he was on the right side of things and that anyone opposing his interpretation of events was on the wrong side of the ledger. It was just a book; many sheets of paper with words printed on them. But the president evidently felt that merely by holding it and associating himself with it he was demonstrating the rightness, and righteousness, of his position.

That's magical thinking at least, and idolatry at worst. It's idolatry of the book.

If you overheard a couple at the next restaurant table discussing a "good book," you'd probably hope to catch the book's name so you could see for yourself. It might provide a nice read. But if just one other word, "the," were added, you would immediately know with certainty which book they were discussing. The Bible is "the good book" in the minds of millions and in the language we all share.

But the Bible has no monopoly on "good," and not all that is in the Bible is good by any means. Just being written in those pages does not Baptize an idea, a character, an attempt to write history, or a false memory. And a lot of the Bible's content is rather dubious on a scale of bad to good.

Perhaps the problem is that if something is labeled "good" or "holy" we tend to take it literally; we believe that it lives up to its name automatically—at least if organized religion (sometimes actually 'religion for profit') keeps insisting on the adjective. Television evangelists used to ask their viewers to hold a Bible while watching, as though it could magically connect the preacher with the hearer. Some of them loved to sell Bibles to their TV flocks—send in your money and we'll send you a Bible blessed by the evangelist (although the words inside it will be the same words available at your local five and dime store for considerably less money).

It's probably very safe to assume that almost all of the viewers ordering "blessed" Bibles from TV evangelists already had at least one in their homes. The motivation for acquiring another Bible was therefore not to find out what it contained; the motivation was simply the acquisition of another copy because each new copy somehow magnified the holiness attached. The proliferation of Bibles in American households is, I think, another clue about the quasi-magical way we think about this book.

The Bible is the best-selling book of all time, we're told. Although there are no statistics on its actual readership, it seems not a far-fetched guess that the Bible may be at one and the same time the best-selling book and the least-read book. We tend to acquire Bibles well beyond any readership need. Bibles are a common gift for rites of passage occasions, even though the recipient probably already has a copy or two. And then there are Bibles given and purchased with no expectation whatsoever that they will be read—they are to be the 'family Bible' used to record births, marriages, and deaths. Somehow these tender statistics are more precious if preserved in a Bible than in some other kind of journal, it would appear.

In short, we seem to feel there is value in simply owning Bibles, and maybe the more the better. We invest their mere presence in our homes with a value beyond the information or inspiration they could convey if we actually read them. We would not use the word 'magic' to describe this attitude, but I can't think of a more descriptive word unless it's 'superstition.'

Without actually counting, I'd have to admit my home has at least four or five Bibles in it. Of course, unlike most people I was a religion professional which is a partial explanation because of being given Bibles at various stages of ordination, or because of my own curiosity when new translations appeared. One copy rests almost in tatters, having been used as a note pad in many university and seminary classes over the years, and now serving both as text and commentary on the text. (Some good Christians would probably be scandalized by the mere idea of making notes in a bible.) But other of my Bibles stay put, never read and never consulted, yet secure in their place. They serve no real function beyond being souvenirs of past events. So perhaps I'm also guilty of feeling some value in merely *having* Bibles or hesitating to let go of excess copies. It's an easy disease to catch.

It might be nice to have a book which contained nothing but good. A book which was absolutely without error of any kind; a book which could be completely trusted in every detail.

But we don't have such a book. What we have as the book endorsed (canonized) by official Christianity is a book that was pulled together from multiple sources in an attempt to codify the history and folklore of a long rooted ethnic group (the Jews), and then to quickly give a pulpit to Paul and his disciples, which pulpit has been labeled the New Testament.

The attempt was not the problem; the motivation was likely as pure as the driven snow. The result, however, is full of problems because the words were written by humans. Humans have memories which are prone to confusion and mistakes, especially when they are trying to remember or reconstruct events which took place over vast periods of time—events which have been handed down in a long chain of oral folklore and religious mythology.

So we end up with a book which is confusing and sometimes confused, despite "good" intentions. It is full of some beautiful poetry and inspiring sentiments. It tells of people doing good things. But it also tells of people doing bad things. It is also full of false history and fantastic ideas. It is to some extent a conduit of human folklore which can be found in every culture, such as a great flood covering the whole earth—a 'memory' of humans in general which is not historical, at least not in all the details of the Biblical account. It is a 'religious' or folkloric memory, but it is neither specifically Jewish nor Christian.

If some people can find peace or encouragement or solace in its pages, that is all to the good. If some people are inspired by it to live lives which are more positive and more constructive, and less judgmental of others than would otherwise be the case, then I say Bravo/Brava! But let's not fall into foolishness. We should all be able to agree, at minimum, that the object itself is just a book. The paper and ink are not holy, or even necessarily 'good' paper and ink if the purchase price was low enough. As to what the words in this book convey, you need to be your own judge.

Most people who call themselves "Christians" got there by default. Even those who are the loudest, proudest, and most enthusiastic about doing so. They fell into Christianity because of family tradition, most likely, egged on by living in a culture where Christianity is generally considered the norm and given lip service at every turn. How much advance theological or historical thought do you suppose the guy who has a cross tattooed on his chest gave to that decision? Most likely he was just claiming membership in a tribe. The Bible may be the official handbook of the tribe, but it is just that—nothing more. ⌘

12.

Amen

Even though this is the final chapter, the 'Amen' here does not mean 'goodbye.'

As a kid attending Sunday School I was taught that it meant "it is finished." No, it doesn't mean that here, and it didn't mean that then either in my opinion. The more optimistic explainers suggested it meant "let it be so," but they were wrong too I believe. Some think the word comes from roots in the Hebrew language, and there's a good deal of "yea, verily," "yes, indeed," kind of explanation floating around out there, even in weighty sounding dictionaries.

Another childhood memory was of my dad reluctantly filling his role as the patriarch at family dinners. He was a second generation German-American and it fell to him to offer a prayer at the beginning of the meal. He never departed from script; he never improvised in the slightest. And when he had finished his recitation of the formula he had been taught, he capped it off with a rather unenthusiastic "A-mun."

I always was a touch startled by his pronunciation because in church one was constantly surrounded by a chorus of "A-men," over and over. I never counted, but it wouldn't surprise me if the good Christians of the day said "Amen" more frequently even than "God" or "Jesus," at least in public liturgical worship.

So I wrote off my father's quirky sounding pronunciation as either a trace of German accent inherited from his childhood, or maybe just sloppiness, or even his manifest lack of enthusiasm. I certainly never questioned it. The poor guy was clearly ill at ease with his religious role in family life, and I saw no point in dwelling on it further.

It turns out, however, that he may have been percipient. If his pronunciation was heard as "Ah-mun," he could have been a religious historian without realizing it. And it's quite possible his pronunciation had indeed drifted down from a more targeted attempt by past generations.

'Amen' is actually a persistent carry-over from ancient Egypt. It is a punctuation added by Egypt's religious descendants to all kinds of pronouncements and prayers through the ages. A stamp of authenticity and worship which speaks aloud the name of Egypt's chief god, Amun (later Amun-Ra). It is as much a little capsule prayer on its own as a punctuation mark to a longer prayer. (My opinion here is not unanimously held, but those who link the word linguistically to Hebrew may forget that even the Hebrew language itself may well have grown out of that of ancient Egypt, as did so much of Hebrew religion.)

Is it a big surprise that the name of a "pagan" god should have been carried through all these centuries into, and then by, Christianity? Not if one looks even casually at Christianity's roots. Even the New Testament acknowledges Egyptian involvement (perhaps reluctantly), and hints at much more than it acknowledges. You've heard of Israel in Egypt (at least if you love classical music). What we've paid too little attention to is Egypt in Israel, and by extension Egypt in Christianity. One Egyptologist-historian entitled one of his books in a way which summarizes the situation nicely: *Christianity, an ancient Egyptian religion.*

● EGYPTIAN RELIGIOUS INFLUENCE WE CAN RECOGNIZE TODAY

Here are a few Egyptian Influences on, and contributions to, the Judeo-Christian tradition and theology (some of which preceded Egyptian religion but were likely transferred to Christianity through Egyptian influence). Some get to the theological heart of religious beliefs; others may seem minor or even trivial similarities. But all form a religious context in which the Judeo-Christian tradition can be easily seen as a successor to that of ancient Egypt:

-----A-----

♦Afterlife, belief in. Death could not hold the hero/king captive, and therefore will hopefully not hold the rest of us captive either.

♦Altars for sacrifice, actual or ritual.

♦"Amen" (sometimes spelled "Amun") from the name of the Egyptian chief Sun God Amun-Ra, and used as a kind of religious punctuation mark.

♦Amulets (think St. Christopher medals, or a Rosary worn as an amulet, or even a tattooed cross; intended to plead for protection or assistance from a particular god or saint).

◆Ancestor worship (muted a little in Christianity, but think "saints" and praying to them).

◆Ankh as a primary religious symbol (used for years into Christianity before yielding to the crucifixion cross; Christians originally thought the round part on top was a symbol of the sun).

◆Anointment of the Messianic figure (with fat from the sacred crocodile in the case of Pharaoh!).

◆Astrology, finding religious significance in the stars ('Star of Bethlehem' at Jesus' birth for example).

-----B-----

◆Baptism, as both initiation and purification.

◆Bread and wine, gift of Osiris, cultic use in Egypt as also later in Christianity.

◆Birthday of a God, or, gods have birthdays like everyone else.

-----C-----

◆Cantors (cult singers; temple/church musicians).

◆Circumcision of males, as related to religion (and also simply as a medical practice).

◆Coffins and sarcophagi, use of for the dead (as opposed to direct burial in earth or sand).

◆Creation by the god(s), with dry land emerging from watery chaos.

◆Creation myths, multiples of.

◆Creation by divine dictum/fiat ("and God said, let there be...;" the Egyptian god Ptah conjured up life and created it by merely speaking his thoughts, as did the God of Genesis).

◆Cross as ubiquitous religious symbol (in Egypt the Ankh, seen as a combination of sun & cross symbol and widely used by early Christians as previously noted).

Amen

◆Curses on enemies or unbelievers (ancient Egyptians wrote the curse on a pottery bowl and then smashed the pottery to destroy the enemy).

-----D-----

◆Darkness over the land at a god's loss or endangerment (sting of Horus; crucifixion of Jesus).

◆Death, obsession with (Paul centered Christian theology around the death of Jesus).

◆December 25 as birthday of god (both Osiris and Jesus, plus quite a few other 'gods').

◆Decent into Hell (sun descends into underworld at each nightfall; Jesus, a Sun God, descends into hell prior to resurrection).

◆Deification of mortal beings (for Christianity, read creating/declaring mortals as saints with many godlike powers).

◆Delegation of religious authority/responsibility (Pharaoh was high priest but had delegate priests to act for him; Bishop is chief vicar of God but has priests to act for him).

◆Demons (as cause of illnesses, etc.).

◆Direction (location) of heaven (up/ascend) and hell (down/descend).

◆Divine Right of Kings, the monarch has divine authority which is bestowed and backed by God.

◆Duality of gods, good/evil (Jesus/Satan, Horus/Seth, etc.).

-----E-----

◆East, orientation to because of rising sun; relating to enlightenment and resurrection.

◆Eternal life, promise of.

◆Eucharist (God feeding his people with his own body; became Christianity's main worship ritual).

◆Evil, personification of (figures to represent evil forces, such as Seth in ancient Egypt; the Devil, Satan, Lucifer, Judas, etc. for Christianity).

◆Exorcism, casting out of evil and illness by recitation of words which have magical power.

-----F-----

◆Feast days of religious import.

◆Fire as punishment for the wicked after death; Hell in eternal flames.

◆Flood, to destroy sinful humanity (a staple of ancient mythology even before and aside from Egypt and Noah's ark).

◆Flowers at funerals (Egyptians used 'flowers of life' to decorate coffins).

◆Forgiveness of sins, as related to religion.

◆Funerals as religious services; need for ritual, liturgy, prayers, spells, in addition to proper burial.

-----G-----

◆Goddesses (female) as well as gods (male); Isis to Wisdom/Sophia and onward to Blessed Mary Ever Virgin.

-----H-----

◆ "Healing in its wings" (winged sun disc).

◆Heart, Sacred; as seat of emotions and intellect for ancient Egyptians; Sacred Heart of Jesus (ancient Egyptians believed people thought with their hearts and didn't know what function to assign to brains).

◆Heaven (Egyptian concept of an "afterworld" in the sky with all of life's pleasantries leading to Christian concept of a place, also 'in the sky,' of reward for the religiously pious).

◆Hell (Egyptian "underworld" concept of the realm of the dead leading to Christian usage as a place of punishment of the dead).

◆Heresy and Orthodoxy as religious concepts.

◆Hermetic philosophy.

◆Hierarchical organization of priesthood (in Christianity: Deacon, Priest, Bishop).

◆Holy Name (name carrying the essence of a person or god; secret name was source of power of the Sun God; Isis gained equivalent power to Ra by learning his secret name).

◆Holiness as a status or concept.

◆Houses of god on earth (temples/churches).

◆Hymns, to and about gods, written and used in liturgy.

-----|-----

◆Iconography, symbolic representations of god(s).

◆Immortality (of the soul).

◆Incarnation (god becomes Pharaoh and/or god becomes Jesus).

◆Incense, use of in ritual.

◆Infallibility, religious (Popes, like Egyptian kings, can define and shape religion by dictum).

◆Initiation (probably transferred intact to Christianity from Egypt, then later being diluted to simple baptism for those not to be fully initiated).

◆Inner sanctum of a temple, which only the high priest is allowed to enter, carried forward in temple era Judaism ("holy of holies").

-----J-----

◆Jubilee Year(s) carrying special benefits such as indulgences for the common populous.

-----K-----

◆Kings, divine right of (ruler as god or representative of god on earth).

-----L-----

◆Last Judgement by the god(s).

◆Limbo (purgatory), as a status between the achievement of Heaven or Hell.

◆Litany as a prayer structure.

◆Liturgy, as ritualization of concepts and the collective experiences and memories of a people.

-----M-----

◆Magic as a religious tool (Jesus as magician and miracle worker; 'faith healing' etc.).

◆Male preference in offspring.

◆Matriarchal descent, as now found in Judaism and as referenced in the Bible.

◆Meal for survivors and mourners following a funeral.

◆Minor gods, plethora of ('pick a saint, any saint').

◆Miters, worn by Egyptian kings and later by Christian bishops.

◆Monasticism and monasteries (the first Christian monasteries were in Egypt).

◆Monotheism as a concept (but in Egypt only during the period of pharaoh Akenhaten).

◆Morning and evening daily religious services (leading in Christianity to the several monastic "hours" of prayer, but even among Protestants still in evidence largely as Morning Prayer and Evensong).

◆"Mother of God" (in Egypt Hathor, then Isis as mother of Horus, sometimes termed "Great Cosmic Mother;" in Christianity the Virgin Mary as understood gradually after the life of Jesus).

◆Mystical aspects to religious thought, and religious mysticism.

Amen

-----N-----

◆Name, Holy (the name of a god as expression of his essence and power).

◆Non-religious use of religious buildings and facilities (even governmental functions such as tax collection in ancient Egypt or voting stations in modern America).

-----O-----

◆Oath taking in the name(s) of god(s) (".....so help me God").

◆Obelisks/Steeples, pointing to god/sun.

◆Offerings from attendees at liturgical events; possessions or money to help fund the cult.

◆Oratories (places to hear the gods speak, or spoken for).

◆Original Sin.

-----P-----

◆Pictures as well as text in religious scrolls, carried forward by Illuminated manuscripts copied by Christian monks.

◆Pilgrimages to holy sites.

◆Polytheism (if one counts in Christianity the Trinity, "veneration" and prayers to the Virgin, the Saints, etc.).

◆Pork, prohibition of, in diet (in Judaism and Egyptian religion as well as in the third Abrahamic religion, Islam).

◆Prayers to the god(s), prescribed formulas and the recitation thereof privately or liturgically (originating from incantations).

◆Presentation, of a days-old child to religious elders in the temple (in Judaism and Egyptian religion).

◆Priests and Priesthood as religious practitioners on behalf of the people.

◆Processions, religious, often carrying aloft a statue of the Egyptian god, or the Christian saint.

◆Purification rituals (applies to Jewish inheritance from Egypt probably more than to that of later Christianity).

-----Q-----

◆ "Queen of Heaven" (Isis for the Egyptians, Mary for the Christians).

-----R-----

◆Recitation of ritual words (prayers) at time of burial of the dead.

◆Records, kept in temples/churches (baptism/confirmation/weddings etc.).

◆Reenactment of important religious events, with audiences (the Osiris mysteries at Abdju; for Christianity think Passion Plays and Stations of the Cross).

◆Resurrection from death (at least for Gods and 'Sons of God;' Pharaohs were Sons of God). Ultimately, both in Egypt and in Christianity, It came to be thought that everyone could get in on the act.

◆Rites of Passage, celebration of (Confirmation, Baptism, Bar Mitzvahs, Bat Mitzvahs, etc.).

◆Role assignments, division of labor, to gods (in Christianity three persons of Trinity, and Saints, with various areas of work, influence, and power).

◆Rubrics, written instructions for the performance of liturgy.

-----S-----

◆Sacrifices *to* the gods.

◆Sacrifices *by* the gods to benefit the people.

◆Saints: mortals (non-gods) who are prayed to and around whom cults develop, with statues, shrines.

◆Scepters as sign of religious authority, often shaped as a crook (brass snake scepter for Pharaoh, croziers for Christian bishops).

◆Schools, use of temple or churches as.

◆Serpent(s) as religious symbols and in religious ceremonies.

◆Shrines dedicated to a specific god (or saint); sometimes set up at home for family use.

◆Soul, which survives death of its body.

◆Statues of religious figures.

◆Sun, as religious symbol for the chief god (Pharaoh/Jesus).

◆Sun, worship of and use in general religious iconography.

◆Sunday, set aside for special rituals.

◆Superstition(s) as source for some religious beliefs or protective rituals/talismans.

-----T-----

◆Theological debates among various religious ideas.

◆Three, number with religious implications and value (3x3 signaled completeness to ancient Egyptians).

◆Tolerance of other religions, especially during the Ptolemaic period [sorry, this was added tongue-in-cheek; Christians never figured out how to be religiously tolerant despite the good example from Egypt].

◆Trinity of deities (Trinitarianism as a religious concept; Trios of Gods).

-----U-----

◆Unction, religious anointing.

-----V-----

◆Various gods for various needs and purposes in Egypt; various saints for various needs and purposes in Christianity.

◆Vestments, distinctive clothing for priests while functioning liturgically.

◆Vigils, religious, anticipating and getting a jump on a major holy day.

◆Virgin and Child iconography (Isis suckling Horus as an ubiquitous Egyptian art form, to Mary holding, sometimes suckling, Jesus ubiquitous as a Christian art form).

◆Virtue rather than vice; afterlife reward or punishment determined by actions during life.

◆Votive objects.

-----W-----

◆Water, Holy ("holy water;" descending from Nile River water used for religious purposes to Jordan River water for baptism, on to blessed water for baptism or personal piety; water that carries religious blessing and/or meaning).

◆Wisdom literature as part of religious tradition (parts of which in the Bible were taken verbatim from ancient Egypt).

◆Words having powers to heal, damn, etc. when recited in prescribed ritual ways (pronouncement of absolution by a priest, for example).

-----Z-----

◆Zion (place of sanctuary or refuge).

◆Zodiac, seeing religious meaning in and use of in religious iconography (12 apostles, for example; 'Star of Bethlehem,' etc.).

● A SUMMATION OF OUR STORY

This has been a long and complex story. It's not easy to imagine it in a linear simplicity, and there are a great many remaining questions unanswered by history and scholarship. Nevertheless, here is a very simple summary of the religious story and characters we've been considering.

Religion may well have been the first invention of mankind. The sun may well have been the first consensus god. Probably it was the first symbol for god in any case. Humans were totally dependent on the sun for life, and they recognized that fact early-on. The sun fed people thereby making life on earth possible. So food and the gods were intimately associated, and the leaders, priests, and shamans took up the responsibility of feeding the people with their own bodies, symbolically mostly but sometimes literally.

Much later, but still lost in the mists of time, a great civilization took root in Egypt. This civilization was centered in religion because at that stage of the human experience religion included all fields of knowledge—it was science which began as magic, it was astronomy which began as astrology, it was agriculture which conferred the gifts of the gods, it was architecture which gave praise to the gods, it was everything. These Egyptians had many gods, but the sun was their chief god. Eventually they understood their chief leaders to be sons of the sun. When the leaders (kings) died, they were believed to become a new star in the sky, a brother to the sun.

This great religion and culture was the envy of neighboring peoples because of its concentration of useful knowledge, because of its summation of human wisdom, and because of its sophistication. The Egyptians devised a way to pass the kernel of this wisdom (enlightenment) on to succeeding generations by initiating young men into the "mysteries," a drama that let the initiate experience directly the conquest of death and the deeper meanings of life.

One of the great ethno-religious sagas of mankind belongs to Judaism. The raw bones of it say that God made a promise to an ancient man, Abraham, whose descendants then, over time, became slaves in Egypt. One of them was adopted by an Egyptian princess and grew up in a Pharaoh's household. This man, aided by magic, won freedom for the enslaved masses and led them out of Egypt to the land God had promised to them. The great liberator's name was Moses. He brought with him out of Egypt an obsession with monotheism and a pharaoh's signature staff with a brass snake at the top. Christians, and then Muslims, would also claim this story as part of their own religious heritage.

Scholars of history and religion feel that the story has problems as a whole unit, but that elements of it could be historically true while other elements could not be true as history. The Moses figure was very likely not one of the Hebrews himself despite their claims, but he was most likely an Egyptian. He was probably from the royal family or was a high ranking priest in royal employ. The group he led out of Egypt was not a gigantic swarm of thousands of slaves, *a la* Cecil B. DeMille, but could have been a smaller group of Moses' associates, such as fellow priests. He and his brother might be the founders of the Hebrew priestly class called Levites. He might even have been a particular exiled pharaoh himself (Akhenaten), judging at least partially from his religious orientation to monotheism and his staff of authority (the pharaoh's brass staff bearing the brass snake).

The Hebrews, known collectively as Israel, might not even have been ethnically tied together as descendants of Abraham. They could have been in large part simply descendants of people who already lived in the "Promised land" and did not have to actually arrive there as a result of an exodus from Egypt. In any case, the Exodus story eventually bound them together with a shared sense of ethnicity. The children of Israel accepted it as their own story and gave it religious weight, whether it was actually their own blood ancestors who crossed the waters from Egypt or not. This was encouraged by a religious clan of priests called Levites who may well have immigrated from Egypt, but who in any case held the Israelites to monotheism and some other Egyptian ideas and customs (circumcision of males, for example). This religious heritage eventually filtered into a new religion which came to be called Christianity, named after the Greek idea of a cosmic Christ figure.

Christianity carried on much of the religious heritage from Egypt which Judaism contributed to it, plus perhaps some additional Egyptian religious heritage acquired directly (perhaps through the personal experience and training of Jesus). It was built, in theory, around a man named Jesus who is said to have lived about two thousand years ago in the 'promised land' of the Jews. He may have thought he was a long-expected political and religious figure called Messiah (translated into Greek as "Christ"). If so, he had a lot of company. In any case, his followers began to think along those lines, especially after his death at the hands of local representatives of the occupying Romans.

Not a lot is known about this Jesus in a biographical, historical, sense. A lot of potentially biographical detail in the Christian scriptures is obscured because the writers overlaid it with existing religious symbols, allegory, and mythology. In addition, the earliest New Testament gospel material was written some decades after Jesus by men who were not his living contemporaries and thus had no first-hand knowledge of their subject. It is strongly hinted in these scriptures that Jesus carried on Egyptian religious traditions, was adept at Egyptian magic, and that a significant part of his ministry involved initiating young men into the "mysteries" as the ancient Egyptians had done.

Jesus' contemporaries probably thought of him first as a magician, as his near contemporary Apollonius also had been seen. Ultimately the portrait of Jesus painted by the New Testament gospel writers is so overlaid with allegory, mythology, and symbols from ancient religions that some serious observers have suggested that maybe that's all there was—maybe this Jesus was nothing more than a collection of religious ideas and images rolled into a story (or an old story repeated anew). At least, these observers say, if Jesus was an actual man at a specific point in history, it is nearly impossible at this stage to see anything but the religious icon he has become. Still, scholars continue to look for the man behind the façade of mythology and allegory hoping to discover new insights.

Christianity came to believe that Jesus was both a human and a god at the same time. It came to believe that although as a human he died, as a god he lived on. It came to believe that he nourished his followers (church) with his own body and blood, following in some of the oldest religious traditions known to mankind. It saw Jesus himself as the sun, or a son of the sun, and it associated him with the Zodiac. It also came to believe that Jesus shared being God with two non-human peers, and that he was therefore part of a trio of gods. At the same time, however, Christianity claimed, and continues to claim, that it is 'monotheistic,' and thus a religious descendant of the 'heretic' Egyptian pharaoh Akhenaten.

Ironically, while Christianity initially sprang from a Jewish sect we can call the "Jesus movement," it quickly replaced the Jewish concept of Messiah (a political and religious figure, but not a heavenly figure) with a Greek concept of Christ, a universal savior. The man responsible for this shift was Paul, and thus he is considered by scholars to be the founder of what today we know as 'Christianity.' Ironically again, this Paul split in bitter disagreement with the leaders of the Jesus movement in Jerusalem, and thus he became an enemy of Jesus' brother, James, and of Jesus' chief disciple, Peter. Even so, Peter came to be regarded as the first chief bishop (Pope) of the western (Roman) version of the new religion he and Paul had fought over—despite Paul having won the ideological battle and the new religion therefore now no longer reflecting Peter's view or direct experience of Jesus.

Christianity's Jesus had become god on the installment plan, one could say. The experience of his contemporaries was that he was a miracle worker, or a magician, which were the same thing in that context. Soon their perception of him was that he was a wisdom teacher, or even the incarnation of the ancient Biblical goddess Sophia. Then he was executed and a new perception arose among his inner circle—that death had not held him; that he lived still. That led to all kinds of debate and posturing for years, but gradually a new perception was gaining the upper hand: Jesus was, and had been all along, himself God. Although he had to share that designation with at least two other co-gods, and his probably primary title became Son of God.

Egyptian religious traditions, symbols, allegories, and mythology were in surprising measure preserved and practiced in Christianity. They were also developed further, and sometimes somewhat altered. Initiation into the "mysteries" (now called only "Baptism") survived strongly in Christianity although its shape changed significantly with circumstances and distance from its origins. Most Christians today do not realize they are religious descendants of ancient Egypt. (At this point I will resist the urge to add: "Amen.")

● NOTE ON THE EVOLUTION OF PRAYER

"Amen" ties together western Christian styles of prayer to an extent, in that both Protestants and Catholics use the term to cap off their prayers both private and liturgical. Yet the conception of what prayer is, the philosophy of prayer as it were, and how to go about it has diverged markedly between these two arms of western Christianity over time.

Protestants seem to approach prayer, certainly in public but normally in private prayer as well, largely as talking with God—almost as a conversation in which the human tries to reason with the god, or as an opportunity to point out circumstances we want to be sure God takes into account, or even as an attempt to instruct God. This is especially true in public prayer: "Lord, we are gathered here today to dedicate / honor / install / remember /????..." We start right off orienting God to the occasion at hand, not wanting to risk any confusion in the matter. The assumption is, I guess, that God needs to be brought up to speed before the meeting begins.

A public prayer by a Protestant clergyperson calls for a good measure of improvisation, and becomes a mixture of petition, stage setting, and a mini-sermon. Protestants like to remind God of events leading up to the occasion, and to spell out not only what they may be requesting, but why it would be helpful and probably beneficial to many. Rarely will a Protestant use a set text or a formula as a public prayer, and even in private most Protestants rarely use formula beyond repetition of a few memorized favorites, such as 'The Lord's Prayer,' 'Come, Lord Jesus, be Our Guest...,' and 'Now I lay me down to Sleep...'

For Protestants, prayer in public is directed to the audience (congregation) as much as to God. It's a little sermon as much as a prayer. It tries to be sure all parties fully understand what's at stake, both God and the humans in attendance.

Prayer in this (Protestant) context could be described fairly as a performance.

For Catholics, on the other hand, prayer is still grounded in formula, even much of the time at public events. Prayer is not conceptualized as a conversation with God, but as getting God's attention and thus hopefully triggering the anticipated reaction by demonstrating piety through the repetition of long-cherished and long-tested formulae. Prayer for the Catholic is a religious function and a religious device. We're all familiar with the stereotype of the individual leaving confession and being instructed to "say five Hail Marys, seven Our Fathers...." In other words don't improvise; use the tried and true words which have proven successful for generations. Prayer in the Catholic tradition is not just to ask for something, it is to perform something of inherent religious worth—it is a religious action. Prayer can be an act of penance or an act of praise and homage, and either can be accomplished with formula, and indeed accomplished *best* with formula.

Prayer in this (Catholic) context could fairly be described as an act of magical intention (expecting a result from the repetition of a set formula), or an incantation.

A priest friend of mine once was in charge of a challenging organizational matter in his diocese and I watched on television some of the commission meetings he chaired because the challenge intrigued me. Not too surprisingly he called for prayer to begin each session. He began, "Let's open with prayer." Surprisingly, at least tome, it was then it was off to the races: "Hail Mary...Our Father..." Everyone, including me, knew the words in advance, and the opening prayers gave no hint at all about the topics to be discussed after the prayers, as certainly would have been the case if a Protestant clergyperson were the chairman. The prayers were thought to have accomplished their intended purpose without the need to instruct God on why the meeting was taking place. It seems the Catholics gave God credit for probably being able to figure out why the meeting was taking place.

It was easy for me to imagine how a Protestant clergyperson would have handled the same situation: "Dear Lord, we gather to ponder what is good for your church during these trying times, and we ask that you send down your Holy Spirit to guide us as we deliberate...." Protestants, leaving little to chance, like to set the stage for God in case He hasn't been paying close attention of late. Their public prayers tend to begin by bringing God up to date on the subject at hand. Prayer is not so much an act of piety and obedience as it is for Catholics, but an action of attempted dialogue with the Almighty. That said, however, prayer for the Protestant Christian is still a required religious activity just as it is for the Catholic Christian.

Praying by rote could be characterized as the general Catholic approach, whereas praying by dialogue (or sometimes maybe by monologue) could be characterized as the Protestant approach. Christianity's earliest roots reach back to one of these approaches, that of using formulae, but not very much to the other (although it should be noted that the gospel account of Jesus praying in the garden has much more in common with the dialogue approach).

So, do we say that Protestants have strayed from the most ancient conception of prayer, or that Catholics have remained the most faithful to it? Did Protestants refine the art of prayer in ways which make it easier for God to understand? Or do Protestants end up praying (talking) as much to themselves as to God? In any case, if one wants to get a feel for what prayer was like in ancient Egypt, one would need to look to the Catholic side of contemporary western Christianity. It was pretty much a matter of formula and rote back in those long ago days by the Nile, and that approach has lived on in the biggest swath of contemporary Christianity.

Looking back on my own clergy days and recalling the difficulties of needing to offer public prayers at various community occasions, I'm a little jealous of my Roman clergy friends. How much more secure it would have felt to have the option just to launch into a formula which everyone in the room would have already known and treasured; "Our Father...." But no, the expectation was that I deliver a little speech which summed up the occasion but at the same time was crafted as a prayer to a god everyone in the room could imagine as the particular god worshiped in his particular church (denomination). ⌘

Mosaics in the Basilica of San Vitale, Ravenna

198

A Postscript:
Will Christianity Survive the Age of Aquarius?

We grew up thinking Christianity was about Jesus. Now we are beginning to learn that his role could have been almost accidental—that he was a vehicle for carrying an ancient religion into yet another era. Jesus was a vehicle for returning the relative simplicity of monotheistic Judaism back into echoes of the ancient mystery religions of Greece and Egypt by way of Paul's Christ-religion. He was a vehicle for the religious ideas, hopes, prejudices, and dreams of other people.

The Biblical figure we know as Jesus of Nazareth has been painted with almost every sign and image of divinity available to those who wrote about him in our scriptures. He was said to have been born of a virgin; fathered by the spirit of God as had been said of several god-men before him. He had, or was said to have, superhuman powers to do all kinds of miracles, even to heal the sick and raise the dead, as was said also of his near contemporary Apollonius of Tyana. He was compared to the sun itself. His arrival was said to have been expected for ages by holy men of the deep past. Then he was said by his closest disciples to have arisen from death himself and ascended into 'Heaven' in full sight of his chief followers. And that's just skimming the surface. Some of his contemporaries flirted with the idea that he was the long-awaited Messiah (in Greek "Christ") of Judaism. The self-appointed apostle Paul, his greatest publicist, claimed he was in fact the *cosmic* Christ, the savior of the entire human race. His image was now stretched from that of a simple rabbi teaching and preaching in his native countryside to his having been creator of all that exists.

But all of those attributions of godly traits, powers, and identities raise a question. Especially when there are few obvious biographical details offered about this Jesus, and when secular historians of the period draw a blank on him, or mostly ignore him. Even those who try to describe him in the New Testament had never met him, the first written 'gospel' having been composed a handful of decades after the crucifixion. By that time the coating of religious expectations had already started to crystalize around him, and the gospel writers were less interested in his biography than his status on the human/divine scale. And their depictions of him almost always harkened back to the history and scriptures of Judaism or to ancient Egypt. We're left with an epistemological problem. How do we begin to know such a figure?

Was he just a human being, but one to whom his followers ascribed all the godly attributes and markers they could come up with? Or was he just a collection of those attributes and myths rolled into a fictional god-man; a sort of one-stop history of divinity?

199

In other words, was he just a story? Perhaps even a story written well before the time of his assumed life—certainly many elements of the divine-man story were firmly in place long before Jesus could have conducted his ministry in Galilee. Is he to be seen through the eyes of faith, or through the lens of provable (or at least plausible) history? Was he a man, or was he a hybrid god-man? Or was he just an idea, a concept of what some thought a Messiah should be? Was he a one-figure summarization of religious mythology? Or could he have been an ancient figure dredged up into an attempt at contemporary retelling.

It turns out that the biggest mystery man in the New Testament, and maybe in the entire Bible, is this Jesus himself. Another Biblical character we don't really know despite being so familiar with his name since childhood—or at least with one of his names.

It also turns out that there is another major character in the Bible we never took seriously enough, and didn't understand. That character is Egypt, as in the famous Handel oratorio 'Israel in Egypt'. Maybe it should really be reversed: Egypt in Israel, and thereby Egypt in Christianity.

Jesus began his ministry at the dawn of a new age. During that age of Pisces, the church that grew out of his teaching (and then in huge measure out of the ideas of his self-appointed apostle, Paul) became one of the largest and most powerful institutions on earth, taken collectively, reaching and changing both individual lives and entire cultures. (Not to mention inspiring glorious art and music, a few wars, and a lot of executions and suffering along the way as well.)

Now we are at the dawn (or early stages) of the next age, the astrological age of Aquarius. Jesus had been depicted as standing squarely on the Zodiacal sign of Pisces, and poised next to stand on Aquarius. Jesus had promised his disciples to be with them through the age of Pisces (Matthew 28:20), but he made only one direct reference to the age to follow (Mark 14:13), and that reference carried no similar promise.

(In the above reference to Mark I have followed those who read the 'man carrying a jar of water' as a reference to the Age of Aquarius. Not everyone makes that connection, it needs to be pointed out. John Bergsma, for example, sees this simply as a reference to an Essene man who, contrary to the Jewish custom of leaving such work to women, would have hauled the water himself.)

What will be the religious shape of the new age upon which we are embarking, or have recently embarked upon? Christianity began as an obscure Jewish sect. Roman Empire politics eventually turned it into a major world religion. It survived the age of Pisces in relatively good shape. Does it have another astrological age left in it? At the end of Aquarius Christianity would be fully twice as old as it is now. That's a long time for a

Postscript

particular religion to hold sway over vast numbers of people. Even the religious history we sum up as "ancient Egypt" had a heyday of only about three thousand years according to most observers.

This far into Aquarius it appears that the Christian church may be fading almost in reverse parallel to its rise during Pisces. Attendance is alarmingly diminishing in most mainline churches, and in whole countries where Christianity had for centuries been part of the national identity. The Christian message to a frustrating extent has been taken over by preachers who use it as a means to personal wealth, and who lure an audience by assuring them that the point of Christianity is to live as high on the hog as possible. Traditional church buildings are sitting abandoned or repurposed throughout our landscapes. Parishes with long and strong histories are being closed or merged. Seminaries are starved for new students and bishops are starved for clergy. Younger people seek truth from other sources, and church pews are warmed by mostly older folks when they are warmed at all.

The president of Union Theological Seminary, Dr. Serene Jones, was quoted recently in The New York Times as saying, "Christianity is at something of a turning point...The structures of religion as we know it have come up bankrupt and are collapsing."

Will Christianity survive the age of Aquarius? Or will it become just a fascinating episode in the history of mankind's spiritual search, left to be studied by scholars and historians but not affecting the actual lives of our descendants? Will Christianity eventually give rise to a successor religion, as ancient Egypt eventually gave rise to Christianity itself? These questions are just more of the mysteries of our church unfolding gradually to our eyes.

On the grand scale of time, even the great religions of mankind are mortal. The view from the cusp of the next age may bear little resemblance to our view here at the end of Pisces and the beginning of Aquarius. Still, what we have seen and experienced will somehow inform the future of religion for the humans who follow us. We are all, past, present, and future, bound up in a great swirl of searching which ultimately binds us together as co-religionists despite the different views and expressions of any moment, or any set of doctrines, along the way. In other words, we're humans, and humans have always experienced some sort of religious (or at least spiritual or mystical) component to life.

Each new generation seeks its own way, and tests out whether the ways of parents and grandparents are still relevant. Not just the religious beliefs of their ancestors, but even the sense of community and purpose for which their fathers and mothers depended on organized religion. Each new generation inevitably launches a new evaluation of our religious assumptions, and each new generation has to take into account new scientific and technological advances which color our view of the universe.

While we can't make any sure-fired predictions about the church at the end of this age we are just beginning, there is at least one general observation which does not seem much of a reach. If Christianity is still around at the end of Aquarius in a form we could recognize, it's a good bet that women will be, and will have been, playing a major role both as clergy and laity, and the church will be imbued with the feminine sensibilities and qualities so long denied her. Hagia Sophia, and maybe Mary Magdalene, will finally triumph.

Recently at dinner with a friend who is a Roman Catholic bishop in one of the nation's most prominent dioceses, I was surprised at the quickness and ease with which he agreed with me on this subject. He mentioned that he is already able to see an increasingly intensifying concern and devotion from women in the face of a general decline in church loyalty and participation.

To state it as simply as possible, I see Pisces as the age of men in the church, and I see Aquarius as the age of women in the church. After all, ancient Egypt, to which Christianity owes so much, allowed women to be priests—and the pendulum is now swinging back in that direction. And with the change from masculine domination to feminine domination (because that's what we're actually talking about here) will come change—perhaps subtle, perhaps obvious to a long-enough lived observer, but change in religious and theological perception and application in any case. It's begun already.

But the question is bigger than that.

In her best-selling book A History of God, Karen Armstrong (in an intriguingly titled chapter "Does God Have a Future?") states what so many recent Christian thinkers have struggled with: "Maybe God really is an idea of the past." It's happened before, after all. James J. O'Donnell closes his book "Pagans" with a sentence which sums up the demise of the pre-Christian era: "The gods were no longer needed."

There are those who see the future of religion not in doctrines and dogma, saviors and sinners, but in actions and awareness and a new connection with mother earth. Ecological concerns have become a new religion for some. And more power to them! Otherwise, the question for the end of this new age is not religious but existential—will there be humans around to even practice a religion?

And there is another characteristic of Christianity in the future which can be stated with some confidence even now, because it grows from a basic human instinct which will not change even in another 2,500 years—our human need to belong to a tribe.

Postscript

Adherence to Christianity in the 21st century is likely already grounded as much in human social instincts as in spirituality. Like almost every religion, Christianity gives its adherents an identity and membership in a tribe—essential ingredients for life in a fractious time. And Christianity's most direct parent, Judaism, has long-since essentially conflated ethnicity and religion—"church" and tribe then become the same thing. There has always been a lot of terribly unfortunate "us" and "them" aspect to religious tribalism, and there will continue to be. That is not to say that strife based on religion is inevitable. It is to say, however, that before humans can be free and secure enough to be concerned for "them," they need the protective security and identity of having an "us." Religion has always played that role, and played into that phenomenon, and turning the calendar is hardly a reason to expect human nature to change.

A close friend who has been professionally involved in thousands of church services over a half-century career maintains that a major element of Christianity is the coffee/social hour after the Sunday morning service. At first blush that sounds like an attempt at stand-up comedy, but ultimately it's a difficult task to try to deny the truth of that insight. There's some evidence that the very earliest gatherings of Christians were essentially extended happy hours. The power of needing to belong to a tribe has not diminished just because our race has set foot on the moon, and religious identity is still one of the most potent tribes available to ordinary humans.

This book has ultimately been a riff on religion—what it is, what it means, what it translates to in our Christian dominated western civilization, how it affects us every day, how it changes us from what we might otherwise have been. No one seems to give it much thought on a routine basis, which I would contend is a problem—because reflected upon or not, religion is one of the most profound influences on our assumptions and subconscious thinking on a daily basis. Folks just don't stop to think how dominated they are by religious structures and dogma (and, yes, superstitions) that they had no hand in shaping, and at the same time which they don't wholly believe in intellectually either.

Christianity has simply been accepted as a given, much like most of us simply accept our birth gender or all of us have to accept our racial assignment. Some folks go through religious rites which are supposed to "Confirm" the decision made by their parents to have them Baptized shortly after birth. Others may answer an "altar call" at a revival crusade and pledge their lives to Jesus while in an emotional ecstasy. But almost no layman actually sits down and studies what Christianity is all about, gives thought to its origins or who its early leaders were, or what its customs and rites actually mean. If a modern American walks away from organized Christianity, it's likely he just got bored with church-going and became indifferent—not that he considered the matter carefully and made an informed decision.

Another problem created when a specific religion becomes a cultural norm is that most people start to forget what the religion is all about. Most Americans probably just think of Christianity in fairly simplistic terms—as the state of being 'good' or of not being 'bad.' A Christian is a person who gives money to charity, or a person who refrains from tripping little children on the sidewalk. If the guy next door is reasonably "nice," we probably just assume he's a Christian unless we know differently for some reason. Knowledge of the religion becomes perilously watered down when "everyone" goes by the title.

Whoever coined the phrase "ignorance is bliss" might well have been thinking of religion. The less one knows, the greater the conviction that one is on the side of the angels. Simply to "be" religious, or to "be a Christian," is enough evidence for lots of Americans that their opinions on matters of morality must also be the opinions of the Creator.

At university I was often part of the students who would gather at the rail station to leave campus at the end of term. Naturally a fair amount of emotion was on display as couples said good-bye to each other for a few days or a few weeks. Some of the couples (actually quite a few) were racially mixed. When I returned after one such school break, my off-campus land-lady stopped me on the way to my room. She had been scandalized while observing students saying good-bye at the rail station and had to vent her indignation about "those black guys kissing white women." Didn't I agree with her that this was just plain terrible?

Well, actually, no—I didn't think it was terrible. Her face exploded in an expression of shock and disapproval. "And *you* want to be a *minister!*" she screamed at me in disbelief. She knew I was a religion major and therefore, obviously, I should hold the same strong beliefs and preferences as did she, a nice church-going woman. How could I call myself religious when I was so obviously wrong on something she was absolutely sure was condemned by any respectable Christian group, not to mention, I'm sure, condemned in the Bible as well? Well, the trick is to interpret what Christianity and the Bible say without digging too deeply. Just stay in your bliss zone of religious zeal unburdened by knowledge (or by charity).

So the thinking is fairly simple. It must be that inter-racial romance is anti-Christian, and thus anti-Biblical, because I'm a good church-going Christian and inter-racial romance offends me. Simple. Logical. God's will, obviously.

People seem naturally resistant to the idea that their version of Christianity could be anything but dead-on accurate. Sometimes they believe that regardless of how educated and credentialed may be the person they disagree with. Sometimes they believe that even when their entire church body says otherwise.

During my childhood a leading family in our little church one Sunday disagreed with something the preacher said in his sermon. Their solution? Go off and start their own church (congregation) where they could better control the expression of religious ideas. There was no need to think about and consider what our well-educated seminary-graduate pastor had said—just a need to squelch anyone else from saying it.

Much more recently the national denomination of my childhood church decided that homosexual believers might not be the scum of the earth after all, and that they actually could be candidates for ordination and could serve as parish clergy. Again, there were members of my hometown church who knew better. It didn't matter what the denomination said. They went off and started a new parish and plugged it into a more reactionary denomination. So now there are two Lutheran churches in a little town which found it hard enough to sustain just one. But the renegades got their way. No church body was going to tell them what being a Christian in the 21st century should look like!

Ultimately the Christian version of religion as practiced in America may be the most democratic of all institutions because the individual's idea or interpretation usually stands as the final authority. People believe exactly what they want to believe. If what they choose to believe differs from the official teachings of their church, most church goers either don't realize it, or have adjusted it in their minds to a version they can live with.

I recently heard a TV interviewer talking with a defender of evangelical (fundamentalist) Christianity who said his father spanked him when he was a child. Shocked, the interviewer blurted out, "Well, that's not very Christian!" Really? Christians have done infinitely worse things than spank children, and have done them in the name of their religion. What the interviewer really was saying is "that's not very nice" but she reflexively equated niceness with Christianity, and thereby was simplifying it beyond recognition.

Yes, a Christian probably is rather nice, or at least tries to be much of the time. But does being "good" make one a Christian? Absolutely not. Christianity may impose some rules, but in the final analysis it's not about being nice or even about being good. So what is a Christian?

A Christian, for one thing, is a person who attends gatherings of people who wear the same label and repeat ancient 'creeds' which contain declarations which most likely no one in the room actually believes anymore, at least literally and in every detail. A Christian, officially at least, is a person who believes (or is supposed to believe) that another human being many centuries ago did not have a human father. He also believes that this

205

man never died, or to be technical died just temporarily. He believes that this man could raise up dead people into life again, and heal the sick without medical training. He believes that he will be saved from an ill-defined "hell" simply because he believes these things—not that he has to do very much about trying to heal the ills of the world he sees around him; he just has to "believe" in the correct religious formulae.

He believes, officially at least, that those who do not believe the same things as he believes are condemned to eternal torture and retribution. A Christian is a person who believes, or is supposed to believe, in one creator god who is composed of three distinct individual gods. A Christian is a person who believes that in community he eats the flesh of his god, and drinks the god's blood. At least a Christian is officially supposed to believe these things, and if he still attends church he has recently stood up with fellow congregants and sworn an oath to that effect—pledged that he does believe them by reciting a creed formulated centuries ago by men who had a totally different world-view.

If that's not how one wants to define oneself, maybe it's time to pay a little more attention and give some rational thought to how one interfaces with this particular cultural norm. To me it's important that if one chooses to wear a label, one should have some rational understanding of what the label actually signifies. Therefore I'd consider it a virtue for the modern Christian to stay reasonably informed on scholarship in the field—not to mention that relatively current scholarship has some very interesting variations to offer on the Biblical characters and stories we already think we know by heart.

This perspective leaves another important group on the sideline. These are the people who find the Christian story inspiring and useful to understanding some of life's grander themes, but do so without condemning science or confusing allegory or mythology with history. They can value the spiritual poetry of religion without sacrificing their intelligence or sanity. These are the folks who can mine the idea of resurrection for valuable insights, inspiration, and truth without swearing on a Bible (sorry, couldn't resist) that Jesus' physical body got up and walked around again after his death (I realize that sentence could open a whole theological can of worms). They see the beauty and value of metaphor. I merely want to be clear that this book was not a preachment against them. They have their fingers on the real pulse of justifiable religion in today's world.

As to whether Christianity in its current guise will survive Aquarius, the evidence so far at hand is not all that encouraging. If you want to place odds this far out, I'd recommend envisioning a massive change in the organizational ecclesiastical structures we currently take for granted. ⌘

Authors and Books Consulted

If you want to seriously further explore Christianity or Judaism in a contemporary scholarly perspective, a visit to the chain book store at the mall or on Main Street in most places is likely to yield mostly frustration. The "Religion" section will offer shelf after shelf of pablum devotional material—"Jesus loves Me, and Boy do I really love him back"—plus a few mega-church and TV preachers polishing their brands. The "History" section might be worth a try. But you may have better luck and a happier time if you have access to a good used book store. After that it's libraries and on-line purchases. Here are a few specific titles you could look for.

[To help a little if you want to pursue some of the ideas and themes discussed in this book, I've placed an asterisk in front of a few which I found most clear and helpful, and I've added notes at the end of some listings.]

Akyol, Mustafa "The Islamic Jesus: How the King of the Jews Became a Prophet of the Muslims" 2017 St. Martin's Press, New York

Aldred, Cyril "The Egyptians" 1984 Thames and Hudson, London [*Aldred is an art historian and noted Egyptologist and was Associate Curator of the Department of Egyptian Art at the Metropolitan Museum of Art in New York.*]

Allegro, John M. "The Mystery of the Dead Sea Scrolls Revealed" 1956 Gramercy Publishing Co., New York

Allegro, John M. "The Dead Sea Scrolls and the Christian Myth" 1984 Prometheus Books, Buffalo, NY

Allegro, John M. "The Sacred Mushroom and The Cross" 1970 Doubleday & Co., Garden City NY [*Yes, this is the mushroom book. But it's got its worthy points. We certainly can agree when the author calls Christianity one of the mystery religions and says that it had been thriving for centuries under various names before the time ascribed to Jesus. Even the venerated Church Fathers said much the same thing. But the constant emphasis on word-plays and puns, the investment of so many names with hidden meanings, is bewildering before long. For Allegro, everything in the Bible is code for something else. Some of his*] *instincts may have been on target, but he just did not stop soon enough.*] Now in print again.

Andrews, Richard & Schellenberger, Paul "The Tomb of God: The Body of Jesus and the Solution to a 2,000-year-old Mystery" 1996 Little, Brown and Company, London [*Jesus ends up buried in France—well, there is a body of folkloric legend which places him there after the crucifixion.*]

Angus, S. "The Mystery Religions" 1975 (re-issue) Dover publications, New York

Armour, Robert A. "Gods and Myths of Ancient Egypt" 1986 etc. The American University in Cairo Press, Cairo and New York [*Armour is professor emeritus of English at Virginia Commonwealth University.*]

Armstrong, Karen "A History of God" 1993 Ballantine Books, New York [*A best-seller and an admirable feat of writing.*]

Aslan, Reza "Zealot: The Life and Times of Jesus of Nazareth" 2013 Random House, New York [*This book was controversial not because of what it had to say, but merely because it existed. Aslan reaped considerable media criticism for this book because he was raised as a Muslim (how dare he then write as an expert on Jesus!), but he is also a solid scholar in the field and the book offers much of value.*]

Assmann, Jan "Moses the Egyptian: The Memory of Egypt in Western Monotheism" 1997 Harvard University Press, London [*Assmann is Professor of Egyptology at the University of Heidelberg.*]

Avis, Paul "Eros and the Sacred" 1989 SPCK London [*Avis is a member of the Church of England's Doctrine Commission, a practicing clergyman, and author.*]

Aziz, Philippe "The Mysteries of the Great Pyramid" 1977 Editions Ferni, Geneva

Baden, Joel S. "The book of Exodus: A Biography" 2019, Princeton University Press [*Baden is professor of Hebrew bible at Yale Divinity School.*]

Authors and Books Consulted

Baigent, Michael and Leigh, Richard "The Dead Sea Scrolls Deception" 1991 Summit Books, New York [*Baigent graduated from Christchurch University, New Zealand, and Leigh from Tufts University. They are coauthors, most notably, of "Holy Blood, Holy Grail." This book is a fascinating study of the politics and characters involved in deciphering the Dead Sea Scrolls.*]

Baigent, Michael "The Jesus Papers: Exposing the Greatest Cover-up in History" 2006 Harper San Francisco/Harper Collins

Bard, Elizabeth in Burstein, Dan and DeKeijzer, Arne J. (editors) "Secrets of Mary Magdalene: The Untold Story of History's Most Misunderstood Woman" 2006 CDS Books, New York

Becker, Adam H. and Reed, Annette Yoshiko, editors "The Ways that Never Parted: Jews and Christians in Late Antiquity and the Early Middle Ages" 2007 Fortress Press, Minneapolis

Beeley, Christopher A., "The Unity of Christ: Continuity and conflict in Patristic Tradition" 2012 Yale University Press, New Haven and London [*Beeley is an associate professor of Anglican Studies and Patristics at Yale Divinity School.*]

Bergsma, John "Jesus and the Dead Sea Scrolls: Revealing the Jewish Roots of Christianity" 2019 Image, Penguin Random House, New York [*Dr. Bergsma is professor of theology at the Franciscan University of Steubenville, Ohio.*]

Bible, all quotations from Revised Standard Version 1952 Thomas Nelson & Sons, Toronto, New York, Edinburgh

Bloom, Harold "Jesus and Yahweh: the Names Divine" 2005 Riverhead/Penguin, New York [*Bloom was Sterling Professor of Humanities at Yale University and always a good read.*]

Booth, Mark "The Sacred History: How Angels, Mystics and Higher Intelligence Made Our World" 2013 Atria; Simon & Schuster, New York

Booth, Mark "The Secret History of the World" 2010 The Overlook Press, New York

Borg, Marcus J. "Jesus: Uncovering the Life, Teachings, and Relevance of a Religious revolutionary" 2006 Harper Collins, New York

Borg, Marcus J., editor "Jesus at 2000" 1997 Westview Press Harper Collins

Borg, Marcus J. and Crossan, John Dominic "The First Paul: Reclaiming the Radical Visionary Behind the Church's Conservative Icon" 2009 Harper One, Harper Collins, New York

Bourgeault, Cynthia "The Meaning of Mary Magdalene: Discovering the Woman at the Heart of Christianity" 2010 Shambhala, Boston & London

Brier, Bob and Hoyt Hobbs "Ancient Egypt: Everyday Life in the Land of the Nile" 2008 Sterling, New York

Bright, John "A History of Israel" (publication date not listed) The Westminster Press, Philadelphia

Brilioth, Yngve "Eucharistic Faith and Practice: Evangelical and Catholic" 1930, republished 1961 S.P.C.K London [*Only tangentially germane to the main discussions in this book.*]

Bringas, Ernie "Going by the Book: Past and Present Tragedies of Biblical Authority" 1996 Hampton Roads, Charlottesville VA [*Bringas is a Methodist clergyman and author. Interesting perspectives. He has strong and insightful views on the way the Bible is misused and idolized within Christianity and states them in a bold way I could not quite bring myself to do in Chapter 11.*)

Brunton, Paul "A Search in Secret Egypt" 1936 republished 2015 North Atlantic Books, Berkeley [*Contains a fascinating tale of spending a night alone in the Great pyramid at Giza as well as fascinating commentary on Egyptian 'snake magic.'*]

Brunton, Paul "The Inner Reality: Jesus, Krishna, and the Way of Awakening" 2016 North Atlantic Books, Berkeley

Budge, E.A. Wallis "The Egyptian Book of the Dead" 1967 Dover Publications, New York

Authors and Books Consulted

Budge, E.A. Wallis "The Gods of The Egyptians" 1904 republished 1969 Dover Publications, New York [*Budge was Keeper of the Egyptian and Assyrian Antiquities at the British Museum, London. Probably a good place to start exploring ancient Egyptian religion.*]

Burstein, Dan and DeKeijzer, Arne J. (editors) "Secrets of Mary Magdalene: The Untold Story of History's Most Misunderstood Woman" 2006 CDS Books, New York

Butler, Alan "The Goddess, The Grail, and the Lodge: Tracing the Origins of Religion" 2004 Barnes and Noble, New York

Bűtz, Jeffery J. "The Brother of Jesus" 2005 Inner Traditions, Rochester VT [*James 'the Just' is a key figure in the formation of Christianity and yet another Biblical character we don't really know—but should definitely make the attempt to know.*]

Buzzard, Anthony F., and Hunting, Charles F. "The Doctrine of the Trinity: Christianity's Self-Inflicted Wound" 1998 International Scholars Publications, Lanham, Maryland [*Both authors are seminary graduates. Sir Anthony Buzzard holds Oxford degrees in theology and teaches at Atlanta Bible College.*]

Bynum, Caroline Walker "Jesus as Mother: Studies in the Spirituality of the High Middle Ages" 1982 University of California Press, Berkeley, Los Angeles, London [*Bynum is Professor of History at the University of Washington.*]

Cahill, Thomas "The Gifts of the Jews" 1998 Doubleday, New York

Campbell, Joseph "The Masks of God: Primitive Mythology" 1959 The Viking Press, New York [*Anything by Campbell is valuable reading.*]

Campbell, Joseph "The Masks of God: Oriental Mythology" 1962 The Viking Press, New York

Campbell, Joseph "The Hero with a Thousand Faces" 1949, second edition 1968 Princeton University Press [*A basic primer in human mythology.*]

Campbell, Joseph "Creative Mythology" 1968 Penguin Compass, London

211

Campbell, Joseph "Transformations of Myth Through Time" 1990 Harper & Row, New York

Cargill, Robert R. "The Cities that built the Bible" 2016 Harper One, Harper Collins, New York [*Cargill is an assistant professor of classics and religious studies at the University of Iowa.*]

Cargill, Robert R. "Melchizedek, King of Sodom: How Scribes Invented the Biblical Priest-King" 2019 Oxford University Press, New York [*Written for fellow scholars and so not an easy lift.*]

Carlson, Stephen C. "The Gospel Hoax: Morton Smith's Invention of Secret Mark" 2005 Baylor University Press, Waco, Texas [*Carlson holds a doctorate in religion from Duke University and is a partner in a Virginia law firm. If you want to read one of the condemnations of Morton Smith's 'Secret Mark' find, this one is a little more level headed than the others.*]

Carroll, Michael P. "The Cult of the Virgin Mary: Psychological Origins" 1986 Princeton University Press [*Carroll is Professor of Sociology at the University of Western Ontario. This book is a fascinating read if one is interested in the possible psychological underpinnings of the religious devotion paid to the Virgin Mary. It also contains carefully laid out accounts and analysis of many of the appearances the Virgin is credited with (Lourdes, etc.), and is interesting from a historical viewpoint whether one is a devotee of the Virgin or not.*]

Cooney, Kara "When Women Ruled the World: Six Queens of Egypt" 2018 National Geographic Partners. Washington DC [*Cooney is Professor of Egyptology at UCLA. Aside from offering a female-centric perspective for some important historical periods, a lot of worth-while general information on ancient Egypt is offered.*]

Coppens, Philip "The Lost Civilization Enigma" 2013 New Page Books, Pompton Plains NJ

Cox, Harvey (chapter in) "Our Religions" 1993 Harper San Francisco [*Victor S. Thomas Professor of Divinity at Harvard University, proflic author, and Baptist clergyman*]

Creighton, Scott "The Great Pyramid Hoax: The Conspiracy to Conceal the True History of Ancient Egypt" 2017 Bear & Company, Rochester, Vermont [*The Scottish author Scott Creighton is a trained engineer who has used his extensive travels to explore many of the world's sacred sites in depth, especially those of ancient Egypt.*]

Crompton, Louis "Homosexuality & Civilization" 2003 Belknap Press (Harvard University Press), Cambridge MA and London [*Crompton is Emeritus Professor of English at the University of Nebraska.*]

Daiches, David "Moses: The Man and his Vision" 1975 Praeger, New York

David, Rosalie "Handbook to Life in Ancient Egypt" 1998 Oxford University Press [*David is Keeper of Egyptology at the Manchester Museum, England, and a prolific author in the field.*]

Davis, Kenneth C. "Don't Know Much About The Bible" 1998 Eagle Brook, William Morrow, New York [*Davis is a New York Times best selling author.*]

Dennett, Daniel C. "Breaking the Spell: Religion as a Natural Phenomenon" 2006 Penguin Books, London [*Dennett is a New York Times bestselling author.*]

De Keijzer, Arne, chapter in Burstein, Dan and De Keijzer, Arne J. (editors) "Secrets of Mary Magdalene: The Untold Story of History's Most Misunderstood Woman" 2006 CDS Books, New York

Edwards, James R. "Is Jesus the only Savior?" 2005 Wm. B. Eerdmans, Grand Rapids MI [*Edwards is professor of biblical languages and literature at Whitmore College, Spokane WA.*]

Ehrman, Bart D. "How Jesus Became God: The Exaltation of a Jewish Preacher from Galilee" 2014 Harper Collins, New York [*Ehrman is a New York Times bestselling and prolific author on Christian subjects. Any of his books are worth reading although there is a lot of crossover material among them.*]

Ehrman, Bart D. "The Triumph of Christianity" 2018 Simon & Schuster, New York

Ehrman, Bart D. "The Lost Gospel of Judas Iscariot: A New Look at Betrayer and Betrayed" 2006 Oxford University Press

Ehrman, Bart D. "Forged: Writing in the Name of God—Why the Bible's Authors Are Not Who We Think They Are" 2011 Harper One, New York

Ehrman, Bart D. "Misquoting Jesus" 2005 Harper Collins, New York

Ehrman, Bart D. "Jesus Before the Gospels" 2016 Harper Collins, New York

Ehrman, Bart D. "Lost Christianities: The Battles for Scripture and the Faiths We Never Knew" 2003 Oxford University Press, New York

Eisenman, Robert "James The Brother of Jesus" 1997 Penguin Books, New York [*Another book on this largely unknown Biblical character who really needs to be understood to the extent we can.*]

Elkington, David & Jennifer "Discovering the Lead Codices: The Book of the Seven Seals and the Secret Teachings of Jesus" 2014 Watkins Publishing, London [*Although interesting if one is into the discoveries of ancient texts, it really does not contribute materially to any of the themes discussed in this book.*]

Feather, Robert "The Secret Initiation of Jesus at Qumran: The Essene Mysteries of John the Baptist" 2005 Bear & Company, Rochester, Vermont

Fideler, David "Jesus Christ Sun of God: Ancient Cosmology and Early Christian Symbolism" 1993 The Theosophical Publishing House, Wheaton, Illinois [*Fideler is a student of Hellenistic religions and an editor and author in that academic area.*]

Flem-Ath, Rand and Rose "The Murder of Moses: How an Egyptian Magician Assassinated Moses, Stole His Identity, and Hijacked the Exodus" 2019 Bear & Company, Rochester, Vermont [*A little far out on the limb, but okay if your study is in great depth.*]

Fletcher, Joann "The Story of Egypt: The Civilization that shaped the World" 2016 Pegasus Books, New York [*Dr. Fletcher is a freelance Egyptologist and author of several books on ancient Egypt.*]

Fletcher, Joann "The Search for Nefertiti" 2004 William Morrow Harper Collins, New York

Fletcher, Joann "Chronicle of a Pharaoh: The intimate life of Amenhotep III" 2000 Oxford University Press, New York

Fox, Matthew "The Coming of the Cosmic Christ" 1988 Harper & Row, San Francisco [*Fox is director of the Institute in Culture and Creation Spirituality at Holy Names College (now University), Oakland CA.*]

Frankfort, Henri "Kingship and the Gods" 1948, 1978 University of Chicago Press, Chicago & London [*Frankfort was an explorer, scholar, and director of the Warburg Institute and professor of pre-classical antiquity at the University of London.*]

Frazer, (Sir) James George "The Golden Bough: A study in Magic and Religion" 1940 The Macmillan Company, New York [*One of the classics in the field.*]

Fredriksen, Paula "Paul: The Pagans' Apostle" 2017 Yale University Press, New Haven & London [*Fredriksen is Aurelio Professor of Scripture emerita at Boston University and is a member of the Humanities Faculty of the Hebrew University in Jerusalem.*]

Fredriksen, Paula "Jesus of Nazareth: King of the Jews, a Jewish Life and the Emergence of Christianity" 1999 Alfred A. Knopf, New York

Freke, Timothy & Gandy, Peter "Jesus and the Lost Goddess" 2001 Three Rivers Press, New York [*Two Englishmen, both prolific authors. Of the 'Jesus didn't exist' books, this one is on steroids, or perhaps a magic mushroom. They see Christianity as a form of Gnosticism, and Jesus as a myth of the Exodus repeated over again (for unspecified reasons) in the setting we know. The Exodus is nothing but a myth, they write, and points to no historical aspects at all. Jesus in their view is also nothing but a myth, and has no historical moorings at all. It's an extreme version of a proposal made by others as well, but this one seems a little*]

215

undisciplined and maybe too enthusiastic—it tries to cram too many mythological ideas and stories into concepts which are ultimately a tad more direct and straight forward than credited here. Of this list, this book should probably be nearly the last read. Basically I believe it pays to be skeptical of any book which uses the word "represents" more than once or twice, as in 'X represents Y, and S represents G.']

*Friedman, Richard Elliott "The Exodus: How it Happened and Why it Matters" 2017 Harper One, New York [*Ann and Jay Davis Professor of Jewish Studies, University of Georgia, and Katzin Professor of Jewish Civilization Emeritus, University of California, San Diego. If you want to pursue the Exodus theme I'd recommend you probably should start with this book.*]

Gahlin, Lucia "Gods & Myths of Ancient Egypt" 2014 Southwater; Aness Publishing, London [*Gahlin is an Egyptologist and teacher from England.*]

Gardner, Laurence "Bloodline of the Holy Grail" 2002 Fair Winds Press, Gloucester, Massachusetts [*Gardner is a constitutional historian, lecturer and broadcaster.*]

Gardner, Laurence "Lost Secrets of the Sacred Ark: amazing revelations of the incredible power of gold" 2003 Element, HarperCollins, London [*Gardner labels himself a historian, lecturer, broadcaster, composer, author, and art conservation consultant.*]

Gibson, David and McKinley, Michael "Finding Jesus" 2015 St. Martin's Press, New York

Gillman, Neil "The Death of Death: Resurrection and Immortality in Jewish Thought" 1997, 2000 Jewish Lights Publishing, Woodstock, Vermont [*Gillman is Professor of Jewish Philosophy at The Jewish Theological Seminary of America, New York*]

Goodman, Martin "A History of Judaism" 2018 Princeton University Press, Princeton & Oxford

Gordon, J. S. "Esoteric Egypt: The Sacred Science of the Land of Khem" 2015 Bear & Company, Rochester VT

Grant, Robert M. "A Historical Introduction to the New Testament" 1963 Harper & Row, New York

Greenberg, Gary "Myths of the Bible: How Ancient Scribes Invented Biblical History" 2000 Sourcebooks, Naperville, Illinois

Greeley, Andrew M. "Myths of Religion" 1989 Warner Books, New York

Grimal, Nicolas "A History of Ancient Egypt" 1988 and 1992 Blackwell Publishers, Oxford UK and Cambridge MA USA [*Grimal is Professor of Egyptology at the Sorbonne, Paris.*]

Haag, Michael "The Quest for Mary Magdalene" 2016 Harper Collins, New York [*Haag is a prolific writer on subjects related to Christianity and this book is a good place to start if one wants to pursue Mary Magdalene further.*]

Hamilton, Edith "Mythology" 1942 Little, Brown and Company, Boston, Toronto, London

Hamilton, R. "Ancient Egypt: Kingdom of the Pharaohs" 2005 Paragon and 2006 Barnes & Noble, New York

Hancock, Graham "Fingerprints of the Gods" 1995 Three Rivers Press, New York [*Hancock is well known as an author in the areas of ancient mythology and history. Reading him will never be a waste of time.*]

Hancock, Graham "Magicians of the Gods" 2015 Thomas Dunne Books (St. Martin's Press), New York

Hancock, Graham "Supernatural: Meetings with the Ancient Teachers of Mankind" 2003 Disinformation Books, San Francisco

Hancock, Graham "America Before: The key to Earth's Lost Civilization" 2019 St. Martin's Press, New York

Harline, Craig "Sunday: A History of the First Day from Babylonia to the Super Bowl" 2007 Doubleday, New York [*This book is informative and enjoyable, but only minimally useful in studying the themes we have discussed.*]

Haskins, Susan "Mary Magdalen: Myth and Metaphor" 1993 Riverhead Books, New York

Heaton, E.W. "Everyday Life in Old Testament Times" 1956 Charles Scribner's Sons, New York [*Heaton was a Canon of Salisbury Cathedral and a graduate of Cambridge University, England*]

Helms, Randel "Gospel Fictions" 1988 Prometheus Books, Amherst, New York

Hobbs, Hoyt and Bob Brier, "Ancient Egypt: Everyday Life in the Land of the Nile" 2008 Sterling, New York

Holloway, Richard "A Little History of Religion" 2016 Yale University Press, New Haven, London [Holloway is a former Bishop of Edinburgh and a prolific writer.]

Houston, Jean "Godseed: The Journey of Christ" 1992 Quest Books, Wheaton, Illinois

Jackson, Jake (editor) "Egyptian Myths" 2018 Flame Tree Publishing, London

Jacobovivi, Simcha and Wilson, Barrie "The Lost Gospel: Decoding the Ancient Text that Reveals Jesus' Marriage to Mary the Magdalene" 2014 Pegasus Books, New York [*While I'm not sure I accept their premise, this book is well written, contains a lot of helpful material, and explains itself well. Wilson is probably responsible for the value in this material.*]

Jansen, Katherine Ludwig, in Burstein, Dan and DeKeijzer, Arne J. (editors) "Secrets of Mary Magdalene: The Untold Story of History's Most Misunderstood Woman" 2006 CDS Books, New York

Jenkins, Philip "The Many Faces of Christ: The Thousand-Year Story of the Survival and Influence of the Lost Gospels" 2015 Basic Books, New York [*Jenkins is Distinguished Professor of History and Religious Studies at Pennsylvania State University and a prolific author.*]

Jenkins, Philip "Hidden Gospels: How the Search for Jesus Lost its Way" 2001 Oxford University Press

Jennings, Theodore W., Jr. "The Man Jesus Loved: Homoerotic narratives from the New Testament" 2003 The Pilgrim Press, Cleveland [*For the most part this is a long commentary on the "disciple Jesus loved" theme from the Gospel of John. It won't leave you convinced that Jesus was "gay" but neither will it leave you convinced that there was absolutely no fire where there was a surprising amount of smoke.*]

Jeremias, Joachim "The Eucharistic Words of Jesus" 1966 Charles Scribner's Sons, New York

Johnson, Elizabeth A. "She Who Is: The Mystery of God in Feminist Theological Discourse: 1994 Crossroad, New York

Johnson, Elizabeth A. "Creation and the Cross: The Mercy of God for a Planet in Peril" 2018 Orbis Books, Maryknoll, New York

Joseph, Frank "Power Places and the Master Builders of Antiquity" 2018 Bear and Company, Rochester, Vermont

Jungmann, Joseph "The Mass of the Roman Rite" 1949, reissued in 1961 Benziger Brothers, New York etc. [*Useful only if you are really serious about the subject.*]

Kavanagh, Aidan "The Shape of Baptism: The Rite of Christian Initiation" 1978, 1991 Pueblo Book, The Liturgical Press, Collegeville, Minnesota [*The late Aidan Kavanagh, OSB, was Professor of Liturgics at Yale Divinity School.*]

King, Ursula "Christian Mystics: the Spiritual Heart of the Christian Tradition" 1998 Simon & Schuster, New York

Kelly, Lynne "The Memory Code" 2017 Pegasus Books, New York [*Dr. Kelly is an Honorary Research Associate at La Trobe University, Melbourne, Australia.*]

Kenyon, J. Douglas, editor "Secret Knowledge" 2016 Atlantis Rising [*Kenyon is editor of Atlantis Rising magazine and a number of other publications.*]

Knight, Michael Muhammad "Magic in Islam" 2016 Tarcher Perigee, Penguin Random House, New York [*Dr. Knight is a prolific writer on*

Islamic subjects. If you want to beef up your understanding of Islam, this is a good place to start.]

Knohl, Israel "The Messiah before Jesus: The Suffering Servant of the Dead Sea Scrolls" 2000 University of California Press, Berkley, Los Angeles, London [*Knohl is Chair of the Bible Department at Hebrew University.*]

*Kuhn, Alvin Boyd "A Rebirth for Christianity" 1970 & 2005 Quest Books, Wheaton, Illinois [*Kuhn was a scholar of comparative religion and an author. This book is rich in many of the themes we've explored.*]

Lamont, Peter and Steinmeyer, Jim "The Secret History of Magic: The True Story of the Deceptive Art" 2018 Tarcher Perigee Penguin Random House, New York

Lash, John Lamb "Not in His Image: Gnostic Vision, Sacred Ecology, and the Future o Belief" 2006 Chelsea Green Publishing, White River Junction, Vermont

Leeming, David Adams "The World of Myth" 1990 Oxford University Press

Leloup, Jean-Yves "The Gospel of Mary Magdalene" 2002 Inner Traditions, Rochester, Vermont [*Leloup, a Nom de Plume and the translator, is a Roman Catholic priest and scholar.*]

LePage, Victoria "Mysteries of the Bridechamber: The Initiation of Jesus and the Temple of Solomon" 2007 Inner Traditions, Rochester, Vermont [*LePage is an Australian researcher and author. Recommended.*]

Levine, Amy-Jill, and Brettler, Marc Zvi "The Bible with and without Jesus: How Jews and Christians read the same stories differently" 2020 HarperCollins, New York [*Prof. Levine teaches New Testament and Jewish studies at Vanderbilt Divinity School, and Prof. Brettler teaches Jewish studies at Duke University. Both are well established authors. I wanted to be more enthusiastic about this book than the book allowed me to be, and some of its interpretations strike me as unnecessarily tangled.*]

Authors and Books Consulted

Life Books "Jesus" 2018 Time Books, New York

Long, Jeffrey and Perry, Paul "God and the Afterlife" 2016 Harper One/ Harper Collins, New York [*Dr. Long is a nationally recognized expert on near-death experience and he and Perry have written a previous book on the subject which became a New York Times bestseller.*]

Longfellow, Ki, chapter in Burstein, Dan and DeKeijzer, Arne J. (editors) "Secrets of Mary Magdalene: The Untold Story of History's Most Misunderstood Woman" 2006 CDS Books, New York

*Maccoby, Hyam "The Myth-Maker: Paul and the Invention of Christianity" 1986 Harper & Row, New York [*This author is often very direct and plain spoken—he tells you what he thinks right upfront and in simple language.*]

MacCulloch, Diarmaid "Christianity the First Three Thousand Years" 2009 Viking

MacGregor, Neil "Living with the Gods: On beliefs and Peoples" 2018 Knopf, Borzoi Books, New York [*MacGregor is a past director of both the National Gallery and the British Museum in London.*]

Mack, Burton L. "Who Wrote the New Testament? The Making of the Christian Myth" 1995 Harper Collins, New York

Malkowski, Edward F. "Ancient Egypt 39,000 BCE: The History, Technology, and Philosophy of Civilization X" 2010 Bear & Company, Rochester VT

Marcus, Amy Dockser "The View from Nebo: How archaeology is Rewriting the Bible and Reshaping the Middle East" 2000 Little Brown and Company, Boston, New York, London

Markale, Jean "The Church of Mary Magdalene: The Sacred Feminine and the Treasure of Rennes-le-Chateau" 1989 Inner Traditions, Rochester VT [*Not as helpful in understanding Mary Magdalene's supposed role in France as I wanted it to be, but the whole Rennes-le-Chateau saga is interesting enough on its own.*]

McCannon, Tricia "Return of the Divine Sophia: Healing the Earth through the Lost Wisdom Teachings of Jesus, Isis, and Mary Magdalene" 2015 Bear & Company, Rochester VT

McGowan, Kathleen, chapter in Burstein, Dan and DeKeijzer, Arne J. (editors) "Secrets of Mary Magdalene: The Untold Story of History's Most Misunderstood Woman" 2006 CDS Books, New York

McManners, John (editor) The Oxford Illustrated History of Christianity 1990 Oxford University Press, Oxford, New York

Mendelssohn, Kurt "The Riddle of the Pyramids" 1974 Praeger, New York [Mendelssohn holds a doctorate from the University of Berlin, worked at Oxford University, and is an elected Fellow of The Royal Society.]

Mertz, Barbara "Red Land, Black Land: Daily Life in Ancient Egypt" 1966 republished 2000 William Morrow Harper Collins [Mertz earned her doctorate in Egyptology from the University of Chicago Oriental Institute and is a New York Times bestselling author. A good starting point to explore ancient Egypt in general.]

Moody, Jr., Raymond A. "Life After Life" 1975 republished 2015, Harper One, New York

Murray, Margaret A. "The Splendour that was Egypt" 1963 Sidwick & Jackson, London

Naunton, Chris "Searching for the Lost Tombs of Egypt" 2008, Thames & Hudson, New York [Dr. Naunton is an acknowledged expert on Egypt in the first millennium BCE.]

Neill, Thomas P. and Schmandt, Raymond H. "History of the Catholic Church" 1957 The Bruce Publishing Company, Milwaukee [Useful for broad perspective only; not for the particular themes of this book.]

Nigg, Walter "The Heretics: Heresy Through the Ages" 1962 Dorset Press, New York

Norwich, John Julius "The Popes: A History" 2011 Chatto & Windus, London [*Not really useful in pursuit of the themes we have discussed, but an interesting read in the field of church history.*]

Noss, John B. "Man's Religions" 1956 The Macmillan Company, New York

Nygren, Anders "Agape and Eros" 1932, republished 1953 The Westminster Press, Philadelphia [*Something of a classic in the field of modern Christian writing, but worth-while only if you are not trying to pursue further the themes of this book.*]

O'Donnell, James J. "Pagans: The End of Traditional Religion and the Rise of Christianity" 2015 Harper Collins, New York [*Reads well as history.*]

O'Grady, Selina "And Man Created God: A History of the World at the Time of Jesus" 2012 Picador St. Martin's Press, New York [*O'Grady is a producer for BBC television and radio of many history series, and an author in the areas of history and Christianity. Worth reading but a challenge at times.*]

Osman, Ahmed "The Egyptian Origins of King David and the Temple of Solomon" 2019 Bear & Company, Rochester, Vermont [*The Egyptian Ahmed Osman is an author in the areas of Christianity and ancient Egyptian religion.*]

Osman, Ahmed "Jesus in the House of the Pharaohs: The Essene revelations on the Historical Jesus" 1992 Bear & company, Rochester, Vermont [*You may well decide his conclusions are too extreme, but they certainly do raise interesting questions.*]

Osman, Ahmed "Moses and Akhenaten: The secret History of Egypt at the time of the Exodus" 1990, 2002 Bear & Company, Rochester, Vermont

Osman, Ahmed "Christianity: An Ancient Egyptian Religion" 2005 Bear & Company, Rochester, Vermont [*If you're pressed for time, just read the title which pretty much sums up the book.*]

Pagels, Elaine, Introduction to Burstein, Dan and DeKeijzer, Arne J. (editors) "Secrets of Mary Magdalene: The Untold Story of History's Most Misunderstood Woman" 2006 CDS Books, New York

Pagels, Elaine "Revelations" 2012 Penguin Books

Pagels, Elaine "Why Religion? A Personal Story" 2018 Ecco, Harper Collins, New York

Picknett, Lynn and Prince, Clive "When God had a Wife: the Fall and Rise of the Sacred Feminine in the Judeo-Christian Tradition" 2019 Bear & Company, Rochester VT [Picknett and Prince are researchers and authors in the fields of historical and religious mysteries.]

Pinch, Geraldine "Egyptian Mythology" 2002 Oxford University Press [Pinch is an Egyptologist at the Oriental Institute of Oxford University.]

Pine, Jeremy, chapter in Burstein, Dan and DeKeijzer, Arne J. (editors) "Secrets of Mary Magdalene: The Untold Story of History's Most Misunderstood Woman" 2006 CDS Books, New York

Pye-Smith, Charlie "The Other Nile" 1986 Viking, New York

Quirke, Stephen "The Cult of Ra: Sun-worship in Ancient Egypt" 2001 Thames & Hudson, New York [Quirke is curator at the Petrie Museum of Egyptian Archaeology, and Professor at University College, London. A very scholarly approach to the subject.]

Redford, Donald B. "Akhenaten: The Heretic King" 1984 Princeton University Press

Redford, Donald B. "Egypt, Canaan, and Israel in Ancient Times"1992 Princeton University Press

Reeves, Nicholas "Akhenaten: Egypt's False Prophet" 2019 Thames & Hudson, London [Reeves is a leading Egyptologist and was director of the Amarna Royal Tombs Project in Egypt as well as curator of the Egyptian collections at Eton College and the Metropolitan Museum of Art in New York City.]

Reho, James Hughes "Tantric Jesus" 2017 Destiny Books, Rochester VT [*Could easily be skipped unless you are on track to go really deeply into the question of the Jesus/Mary Magdalene relationship.*]

Rubin, Miri "Mother of god: A History of the Virgin Mary" 2009 Yale University Press, New Haven and London [*Rubin is Professor of History at Queen Mary University, London. Worthy scholarship but not an easy read. I couldn't get through a single page without being frustrated and sometimes irritated by clunky writing which kept plowing ahead at a relentless speed.*]

Sanders, E. P. "The Historical Figure of Jesus" 1993 Allen Lane, The Penguin Press, London, New York, etc.

Saul, John M., chapter in Burstein, Dan and DeKeijzer, Arne J. (editors) "Secrets of Mary Magdalene: The Untold Story of History's Most Misunderstood Woman" 2006 CDS Books, New York

Save-Soderbergh, Torgny "Pharaohs and Mortals" 1958 Barnes & Noble Books, New York

Schaberg, Jane, quoted in Burstein, Dan and DeKeijzer, Arne J. (editors) "Secrets of Mary Magdalene: The Untold Story of History's Most Misunderstood Woman" 2006 CDS Books, New York

Schaup, Susanne "Sophia: Aspects of the Divine Feminine Past & Present" 1997 Nicolas-Hays, York Beach, Maine [*Dr. Schaup is a publisher's editor and an author and lecturer.*]

Schillebeeckx, Edward "Jesus: An Experiment in Christology" 1979 Seabury Press, New York [*A BIG book, important and influential but not on your essential reading list if further pursuing the themes of this book.*]

Schonfield, Hugh "Those Incredible Christians: A New Look at the Early Church" 1968 Hutchinson & Co., London [*Dr. Schonfield is a prolific author concentrating in Biblical research and Christian origins.*]

Schulz, Regine and Seidel, Matthias "Egypt: The World of the Pharaohs" 2007 Konemann

Segal, Alan F. "Paul the Convert: The Apostolate and Apostasy of Saul the Pharisee" 1990 Yale University Press

Sigdell, Jan Erik "Reign of the Anunnaki" 2016 Bear & Company, Rochester, Vermont [*Dr. Sigdell's degrees are in engineering (electrical and medical) and he is a retired "past-life regression" therapist. The Anunnaki idea is a theme I consciously decided had no legitimate place in this book although there are people who evidently take it seriously.*]

Silverman, David P. (editor) "Ancient Egypt" 1997 Oxford University Press, New York

Shanks, Hershel (editor) "Understanding the Dead Sea Scrolls" 1992 Random House, New York [*Shanks is president of the Biblical Archaeology Society and founder and editor of the Biblical Archaeology Review and Bible Review.*]

Shanks, Hershel and Witherington, Ben "The Brother of Jesus" 2003 Harper San Francisco/Harper Collins

*Smith, Morton "Jesus the Magician: A renowned historian reveals how Jesus was viewed by the people of his time" 1978 republished 2014 Hampton Roads Press [*Dr. Smith was a Professor of History at Columbia University. If you want to explore further this would be an excellent place to start—especially if you are likely to read only one other book. This book should be in the library of anyone even vaguely interested in Christianity. I would make it required reading for all seminarians.*]

Smith, Morton "The Secret Gospel: the discovery and Interpretation of the Secret Gospel According to Mark" 1973, republished 2005 Dawn Horse Press, California

Smith, Huston "Jesus at 2000" 1997 West View Press, div. Of Harper Collins Publishers

Spong, John Shelby "Unbelievable: Why Neither Ancient Creeds Nor the Reformation Can Produce a Living Faith Today" 2018 Harper One, Harper Collins, New York [*Spong was Bishop of Newark NJ in the Episcopal Church.*]

Authors and Books Consulted

Spong, John Shelby "Born of a Woman: A Bishop Rethinks the Virgin Birth and the Treatment of Women by a Male-Dominated Church" 1992 Harper, San Francisco

Spong, John Shelby "Eternal Life: A New Vision" 2009 Harper One, Harper Collins, New York

Stone, Merlin, chapter in Burstein, Dan and DeKeijzer, Arne J. (editors) "Secrets of Mary Magdalene: The Untold Story of History's Most Misunderstood Woman" 2006 CDS Books, New York

Starbird, Margaret, in Burstein, Dan and DeKeijzer, Arne J. (editors) "Secrets of Mary Magdalene: The Untold Story of History's Most Misunderstood Woman" 2006 CDS Books, New York

Starbird, Margaret "The Woman with the Alabaster Jar: Mary Magdalen and the Holy Grail" 1993 Bear & Company, Rochester, Vermont

Strudwick, Helen "Ancient Egypt" 2006 Metro Books, New York

*Tabor, James D. "Paul and Jesus: How the Apostle Transformed Christianity" 2012 Simon & Schuster, New York [*Read anything you can find by Tabor, and especially this book.*]

Tabor, James D. and Jacobovici, Simcha "The Jesus Discovery" 2012 Simon & Schuster, New York [*Not as valuable as the above entry. Tabor is the respected scholar. Jacobovici tends to "discover" the tombs of famous Biblical characters a little too easily for my taste, and for that of many scholars as well.*]

Thompson, Thomas L. "The Messiah Myth: the Near Eastern Roots of Jesus and David" 2005 Basic Books, Pereus Books Group, New York [*Thompson teaches in the Biblical Studies program of the University of Copenhagen, Denmark, and has taught at Lawrence and Marquette Universities in Wisconsin.*]

Torjesen, Karen Jo "When Women were Priests: Women's Leadership in the Early Church & the Scandal of their Subordination in the Rise of Christianity" 1993 Harper Collins, New York [*Dr. Torjesen is the Margo L.*

Goldsmith Chair of Women's Studies and Religion at Claremont Graduate School in California.]

Torjesen, Karen Jo (in) "Jesus at 2000" 1997 West View Press, div. Of Harper Collins Publishers

Tyldesley, Joyce "Nefertiti: Egypt's Sun Queen" 1998 Viking, New York [*Dr. Tyldesley has degrees from Liverpool and Oxford Universities and is Lecturer in Egyptology at the University of Manchester, England.*]

Tyldesley, Joyce "The Pharaohs" 2009 Quercus, London

Van Dijk, Jacobus in Shaw, Ian (editor) "The Oxford History of Egypt" 2000 Oxford University Press [A professor at the Rijksuniversitat in Groningen.]

Viaud, J. contributor to "New Larousse Encyclopedia of Mythology" 1968 Crescent Books, New York

Verhoeven, Paul "Jesus of Nazareth" 2008 Seven Stories Press, New York

Walker, Williston "A History of the Christian Church" 1959 Charles Scribner's Sons, New York

Wallace-Murphy, Tim, and Hopkins, Marilyn "Rosslyn: Guardian of the Secrets of the Holy Grail" 1999 Element Books, Boston

Walzer, Michael "Exodus and Revolution" 1985 Basic Books, New York [*Walzer is Emeritus Professor of Social Science at the Institute of Advanced Study at Princeton University.*]

Watterson, Barbara "The Egyptians" 1997 Blackwell Publishers, Oxford

Wells, G.A. "Did Jesus Exist?" 1975 Elek Books, London [*Wells was Professor of German at Birkbeck College in London. Of the several 'Jesus didn't exist' books available, this one seems to be one of the most sober, scholarly, and earnest.*]

Wicherink, Jan, from Kenyon, J. Douglas, editor "Secret Knowledge" 2016 Atlantis Rising

Authors and Books Consulted

Wiles, Maurice, in McManners, John (editor) The Oxford Illustrated History of Christianity 1990 Oxford University Press, Oxford, New York

Wilkinson, Toby "The Rise and Fall of Ancient Egypt" 2010 Random House [*Wilkinson is a doctor of Egyptology and a Fellow of Clare College, Cambridge.*]

Wilkinson, Toby "Lives of the Ancient Egyptians" 2007 Thames & Hudson, London

Willis, Jim "Ancient Gods: Lost Histories, Hidden Truths, and the Conspiracy of Silence" 2017 Visible Ink Press, Canton MI

Wilson, A. N. "Jesus A Life" 1992 Fawcett, New York [*Wilson taught at New College, Oxford, for a number of years and is an author and journalist.*]

Wright, N. T. "Paul: a Biography" 2018 Harper Collins, New York [*I would not start here if wanting to pursue Paul further.*]

Wright, Robert "The Evolution of God" 2009 Back Bay Books/Little, Brown and Co., New York [*Wright has taught philosophy at Princeton University and religion at the University of Pennsylvania.*]

Wylen, Stephen M. "The Jews in the Time of Jesus" 1996 Paulist Press, Mahwah, New Jersey ⌘

Made in the USA
Middletown, DE
08 April 2022

63788988R00136